Introduction to Burkinabe Literature in English

Introduction to Burkinabe Literature in English

André Kaboré

AFRICA WORLD PRESS
Trenton | London | Cape Town | Nairobi | Addis Ababa | Asmara | Ibadan | New Delhi

AFRICA WORLD PRESS
541 West Ingham Avenue | Suite B
Trenton, New Jersey 08638

Copyright © 2022 André Kaboré
All rights reserved. No part of this publication may be reproduced, stored in a retrieval system or transmitted in any form or by any means electronic, mechanical, photocopying, recording or otherwise without the prior written permission of the publisher.

Book design: Dawid Kahts
Cover design: Ashraful Haque, Eric Kabré

Library of Congress Cataloging-in-Publication Data may be obtained from the Library of Congress.

ISBNs: 9781569027677 (HB)
       9781569027684 (PB)

Acknowledgements

I thank God for the inspiration and guidance I received throughout this project.

Many people, through their advice and suggestions, have made this research project come true. Therefore, the pleasure is mine to thank them for their kindness. First of all, I would like to show my gratitude to all my colleagues at the Department of English Studies at the University Joseph Ki-Zerbo, and elsewhere, who helped me in various ways along this research work. My sincere thanks to Professor Christopher Wise, who kindly accepted to write a preface to this book. I am no less obliged to Michel Tinguiri for proofreading this manuscript and giving me advice.

Last but not least, I cannot help showing how I am grateful to my bishops, Gabriel Sayaogo and Seraphim Rouamba, and to all the priests of the Diocese of Koupela, and elsewhere, for their continuous support of my career and my projects. May God reward you abundantly.

Foreword

We are indebted to André Kaboré for assembling the information included in this volume, on a topic that may seem surprising to some: Burkinabè literature written in English. Burkina Faso is a landlocked Sahelian country bordering Ghana, an English-speaking nation, but the postcolonial literature of Burkina Faso – a former colony of France in the days when it was called Upper Volta – is more typically written in French. Defying the will of France, Burkina Faso's president, Thomas Sankara, forged a strong alliance with Jerry Rawlings of Ghana, as well as Fidel Castro of Cuba, and urged his fellow citizens to look beyond the Francophone world as the nascent Burkinabè state underwent decolonization. The literature discussed in this volume makes an important contribution in this direction, as does Kaboré's volume.

Those who have had the good fortune to visit Burkina Faso will know that its people, including the Mossi, Fulani, Lobi, Dioula, Senufo, Gurunsi, Gurma, Tuareg, and others, are a hospitable people with a rich cultural history. Titinga Frédéric Pacéré has written elegantly of the "literature" of the talking drums among the Mossi, as well as oral literature in Burkina Faso, extending back many millennia. More recent Anglophone literature of the Burkinabè, while addressing contemporary themes and articulated in English, ultimately springs from this deeper source.

Introduction to Burkinabe Literature in English

I encourage all who read this volume to explore and learn from the Anglophone Burkinabè writing that it documents, for these authors have a great deal to teach us.

Professor Christopher Wise
Western Washington University, USA

Table of Contents

Foreword	vii
Introduction	xi
Chapter I: Burkinabe Literature in English at a Glance	1
a) Classification of Burkinabe Literature in English by Literary Genres	1
b) Classification of Burkinabe Literature in English in Chronological Order of Publication	4
Chapter II: Biographies of Anglophone Burkinabe Writers and their English Works	7
Chapter III: Notes on Some Major Works	23
a) Michel Tinguiri, *The Tribulations of a Sahelian Traveler*	23
b) Mamadou Kousse, *Reap What You Sow*	39
Chapter IV: Recurring Themes in Burkinabe Literature in English	49
a) Witchcraft in Burkinabe Literature in English: A Postcolonial Approach	52
b) Cycling and Woman's Emancipation	69
c) Feminism in Burkinabe Literature in English	92
d) Creation Myths in Burkinabe and Biblical Literatures: A Comparative Approach	114
e) Nature and Peaceful Religious Coexistence in Thiobiany's *Before the Fires I was Black*	139
Chapter V: Overview of Burkinabe Literature in French	157
Conclusion	195

Introduction

Burkinabe literature in the English language is not well known. Indeed, very little is written about Burkinabe literature in general for the English-speaking world. Ulli Beier's *Introduction to African Literature: An Anthology of Critical Writing from 'Black Orpheus'* (1967), Oladele Taiwo's *Introduction to West African Literature* (1967) and Fouad Mami's *Introduction to Contemporary African Literature: A Course Handbook* (2018), bear no critical writing on Burkinabe literature or oral tradition.

Even in the indexes to both Wilfred Cartey's *Whispers from a Continent* (1969), and David Cook's *African Literature: A Critical View* (1977), there is no mention of a Burkinabe writer, which testifies that Burkinabe literature is unknown to the English environment. Critical books on (West) African literature or writers, such as *Perspectives on African Literature* (1971) by Christopher Heywood, *African Writers on African Writing* (1973) by G. D. Killam, *New West African Literature* (1979) by Kolawole Ogunbesan, *Talking with African Writers* (1992) by Jane Wilkinson, are focused on Anglophone African writers, mostly from Nigeria, Ghana, Kenya, and South Africa. Within the selected texts for classroom use in Elizabet Gunner's *Handbook for Teaching African Literature* (1984), appear works from French-speaking writers, but none from Burkina Faso. Michael

Introduction to Burkinabe Literature in English

Parker and Roger Starkey's *Postcolonial Literatures* (1995) focus only on works by Achebe, Ngugi, Desai, and Walcott. Books that are specifically focused on African literatures in English, such as Gareth Griffith's *African Literatures in English: East and West* (2000), Stephanie Newell's *West African Literatures: Ways of Reading* (2006), Femi Abodunrin's *Black African Literature in English 1991–2001: Critical Appreciation and Reception* (2007), and Oyekan Owomoyela's *Columbia Guide to West African Literature in English Since 1945* (2008), contain no reference to any Burkinabe English-speaking writer.

Hans M. Zell's *A New Reader's Guide to African Literature* (1971) is one of the first critical manuals mentioning the literary production of Burkina Faso, then Upper Volta. It describes it briefly in one page within the framework of West African literature. Ten male authors are named: Nazi Boni, the first Burkinabe novelist; Augustin-Sondé Coulibali; Issaïe B. Coulibaly; Pierre Dabiré; Jacques Boureima Guégané; Roger Nikiéma; Kollin Noaga; Etienne Sawadogo; Frédéric Titinga Pacéré; and Daniel Zongo. All these writers wrote in French, and their works have not been translated into English. So Zell's guide is the window that opens Burkinabe literature to the English-speaking world. In this guide, below each writer's name is the mention of the bibliographical presentation of the works, and a short thematic explanation for half of them.

In addition to Zell's *New Reader's Guide to African Literature* (1971), it is in Leonard S. Klein's *African Literatures in the 20th Century: A Guide* (1988), and in Simon Gikandi's *Routledge Encyclopedia of African Literature* (2003), that English speakers can access Burkinabe literature. In the *New Reader's Guide*, Alain Ricard, in a short presentation of "Upper Volta Literature," in six paragraphs, barely within one page, gives an overall historical presentation of the country from the colonial period to the independence, through its partition between the Ivory Coast and Mali from 1932 to 1947. He introduces three Voltaic novelists to the reader, namely Nazi Boni and his novel, *Crépuscule des temps anciens* (twilight of the old times), Augustin Sondé Coulibaly and his novel, *Les dieux délinquants* (delinquent gods), and Kollin

Introduction

Noaga and his novel, *Dawa à Abidjan* (Dawa in Abidjan), as well as the playwright Pierre Dabiré and his play *Sansoa* (1970). As to the encyclopedia, it presents only eight Burkinabe writers who have written in French, namely Jacques Prosper Bazié, Nazi Boni, D. Jean-Pierre Guingané, Ansomwin Ignace Hien, Monique Ilboudo, Amadou Koné, Titinga Frédéric Pacéré, and Norbert Zongo. No mention in these encyclopedia and collections, so far mentioned, of any Anglophone Burkinabe writer, even though writers such as Malidoma Patrice Somé and Sobonfu Somé published in the early 1990s in English.

Critical works written in English on Burkinabe literature in the French language contribute to make it known near and far in English speaking territories. Three books containing a collection of essays can be mentioned: *The Desert Shore: Literatures of the Sahel* (2001), edited by Christopher Wise; *Camel Tracks: Critical Perspectives on Sahelian Literature* (2003), edited by Boyd-Buggs and Scott; and a special issue of *TydskrifLetterkunde,* "Burkina Faso: Littérature émergente et création artistique" (2007), edited by Amadou Bissiri, Salaka Sanou, and Hein Willemse. In *The Desert Shore*, the critics Christopher Wise and Albert Ouédraogo examine Pacéré's theory of talking drums, while Salaka Sanou and Michel Tinguiri analyze the writings of Patrick G. Ilboudo and Norbert Zongo. In *Camel Tracks*, Ute Fendler scrutinizes the "Political Power in the Burkinabe Novel: From Realistic to Mythic Representation"; Issaka Sawadogo throws light on "The Actor, Society, and the Theatre of Social Intervention in Burkina Faso"; and Joyce Hope Scott, one of the editors, looks at the "Theatre as Pedagogical Site in Post-Colonial Africa: Théâtre de la Fraternité of Burkina Faso," as well as a critical analysis of Monique Ilboudo's *Le Mal de Peau*. The special issue of *TydskrifLetterkunde,* in both English and in French, "Burkina Faso: Littérature émergente et création artistique" (2007) gives some critical consideration to works only written in French, such as Pacéré's writings, Guingané's drama, Rouamba's *Pouvoir de plume* and *Le Carnaval de la mort,* as well as oral texts and masks performance; but there is no examination of Burkinabe literature written in the English language.

Introduction to Burkinabe Literature in English

A tribute should be made to some former American Fulbright scholars in Burkina for their impressive contributions toward making Burkinabe literature known in the Anglophone world. Nina Tanti, the translator of *Folktales from the Moose of Burkina Faso* (2010), justifies in the preface and in these terms, the reasons why it is necessary to publish Burkinabe stories in English: "The current translation will help to introduce the English-speaking world to the very rich culture of the Moose people of Burkina Faso." Many American Fulbright scholars worked along this line. It will be difficult to list them exhaustively, with their contributions. Some will just be mentioned for illustrative purposes.

Joyce Hope Scott, the editor of *Camel Tracks*, who wrote many papers on the works of some Burkinabe writers, such as "Daughters of Yennega: *Le Mal de Peau* and Feminine Voice in the Literature of Burkina Faso," published in *Women's Studies Quarterly*, was a Fulbright professor in Burkina from 1991 to 1993. Christopher Wise, the editor of *The Desert Shore*, was also a Fulbright professor in Burkina in the mid-1990s. He translated Norbert Zongo's *le parachutage* from French, into *The Parachute Drop* (2004). He also wrote the foreword to Michel Tinguiri's debut novel, *The Tribulations of a Sahelian Traveler,* and many critical papers on the works of Burkinabe writers, and is one of the contributors to *The Routledge Encyclopedia of African Literature*.

The current work intends to fill in a gap by gathering into one work the bits and pieces which have been written about Burkinabe literature and culture, and introduces readers to Burkinabe literature written in, or translated into, English.

The following presentation of Burkinabe literature in English will start by showing Burkinabe Literature in English at a glance, then an introduction to the Anglophone Burkinabe writers and their works, or those whose works have been translated into English. This will be followed by notes on some works, for the specific benefit of secondary school pupils and university students, then thematic essays I wrote about this literature. The conclusion presents Burkinabe French literature at a glance for the Anglophone world.

CHAPTER I

Burkinabe Literature in English at a Glance

a) Classification of Burkinabe Literature in English by Literary Genres

Poetry

Batieno, Raissa. *Let the Bird Free: Book One: A Collection of Inspirational Poetry*. Self-published, 2013.

Batieno, Raissa. *Diamond Rain: A Memoire in Poetry*. Self-published, 2014.

Kaboré Cécile. *Femmes du Burkina marchons et autres poèmes*. Ouagadougou: Imprimerie Presses Africaines, 1990.

Kousse, Mamadou. *Reap What You Sow and 28 poems*. Ouagadougou: IPRESS Imprimérie, 2012.

Somdah, Marie-Ange. *Scents of Love*. Arcata: Yaniyo! Books, 2006.

Somdah, Marie-Ange. *Seeds and Deep Seasons*. Arcata, Boston and Ouagadougou: Yaniyo! Books, 1997.

Introduction to Burkinabe Literature in English

Drama

Kousse, Mamadou. *Reap What you Sow and 28 poems*. Ouagadougou: IPRESS Imprimérie, 2012.

Short Stories

Ouédraogo R. Mathieu. *A Deal is a Deal, or How Much for Your Head and Other Stories: A Reader for Burkina Faso Secondary Schools*. Ouagadougou: Imprimerie Presses Africaines, 1989.

Sawadogo, Mamadou. *The Purse and Other Stories*. Ouagadougou: 2000.

Novels

Ilboudo, Pierre Claver. *Adama*. Ouagadougou: Harmattan Burkina, 2017.

Nebié, Bali. *Secrets of the Sorcerer*. Translated by Njoaguani, Francis Chuks. Ouagadougou: Editions Poun-yaali, 2017.

Somdah, Marie-Ange. *One Wild Proposal: Where's She Going?* Arcata, Boston and Ouagadougou: Yaniyo! Books, 2020.

Somé, M. Patrice. *Of Water and the Spirit: Ritual, Magic, and Initiation in the Life of an African Shaman*. New York: Penguin Books, 1994.

Thiobiany, Prince Lamourd. *Before the Fires I was Black: A Blueprint for a Brighter Future*. Ouagadougou: Self-published, 2018.

Tinguiri, Michel. *The Tribulations of a Sahelian Traveler*. USA: Self-published, 2014.

Yaogo, Noëlie. *The Odds are Against Cycling*. Pittsburgh, PA: Dorrance Publishing, 2012.

Zongo, Nathalia. *When Everything Has Fallen*. Charleston, SC: Booksurge Publishing, 2007.

Zongo, Norbert. *The Parachute Drop*. Translated by Wise, Christopher. Trenton, NJ: Africa World Press, 2004.

Chapter 1

Zoungrana, Emmanuel. *The Ace of Spades in Disarray*. Translated by Bonkoungou, P.G. and Zaidi, S. Paris: EDILIVRE, 2014.

Orality and Folklore in General

Ouadrago, A. *Burkina Faso Art and Culture: Tradition, Ethnic group, Tribes, History, People*. Sonit Education Academy, Kindle Edition, 2016.

Sissao, Alain Joseph. *Folktales from the Moose of Burkina Faso*. Translated by Tanti, Nina. Bamenda: Langaa RPCIG, 2010.

Somé, M. Patrice. *Ritual: Power, Healing, and Community*. Swan Raven & Company, 1993.

Somé, M. Patrice. *The Healing Wisdom of Africa: Finding Life Purpose Through Nature, Ritual, and Community*. New York: TarcherPerigee, 1999.

Somé, Sobonfu E. *Falling out of Grace: Meditations on Loss, Healing, and Wisdom*. California: North Bay Books, 2003.

Somé, Sobonfu E. *Welcoming Spirit Home: Ancient African Teaching to Celebrate Children and Community*. Sacramento: Healing Wisdom Well, [1999], 2009.

Somé, Sobonfu E. *The Spirit of Intimacy: Ancient Teachings in the Ways of Relationships*. California: Berkeley Hills Books, 1997.

Zio, Luc. *Proverbs & Tales from Burkina Faso*. Kindle Edition, 2012.

Works Translated from French into English

Ilboudo, Pierre Claver. *Adama*. Ouagadougou: Harmattan Burkina, 2017.

Nebié, Bali. *Secrets of the Sorcerer*. Translated by Njoaguani, Francis Chuks. Ouagadougou: Editions Poun-yaali, 2017.

Sissao, Alain Joseph. *Folktales from the Moose of Burkina Faso*. Translated by Tanti, Nina. Bamenda: Langaa RPCIG, 2010.

Introduction to Burkinabe Literature in English

Zongo, Norbert. *The Parachute Drop*. Translated by Wise, Christopher. Trenton, NJ: Africa World Press, 2004.

Zoungrana, Emmanuel. *The Ace of Spades in Disarray*. Translated by Bonkoungou P.G. and Zaidi, S. Paris: EDILIVRE, 2014.

b) Classification of Burkinabe Literature in English in Chronological Order of Publication

More than one writer states being the first Burkinabe writer in English, or has it said in the foreword. Who is actually the first? The following classification, in chronological order, helps answer this debate on primacy.

1989: Ouédraogo R. Mathieu. *A Deal is a Deal, or How Much for Your Head and Other Stories: A Reader for Burkina Faso Secondary Schools*. Ouagadougou: Imprimerie Presses Africaines.

1990: Kaboré Cécile. *Femmes du Burkina marchons et autres poèmes*. Ouagadougou: Imprimerie Presses Africaines.

1993: Somé, M. Patrice. *Ritual: Power, Healing, and Community*. Swan Raven & Company.

1994: Somé, M. Patrice. *Of Water and the Spirit: Ritual, Magic, and Initiation in the Life of an African Shaman*. New York: Penguin Books.

1997: Somdah, Marie-Ange. *Seeds and Deep Seasons*. Arcata, Boston and Ouagadougou: Yaniyo! Books.

1997: Somé, Sobonfu E. *The Spirit of Intimacy: Ancient Teachings in the Ways of Relationships*. California: Berkeley Hills Books.

1999: Somé, M. Patrice. *The Healing Wisdom of Africa: Finding Life Purpose Through Nature, Ritual, and Community*. New York: TarcherPerigee.

1999: Somé, Sobonfu E. *Welcoming Spirit Home: Ancient African Teaching to Celebrate Children and Community*. Sacramento: Healing Wisdom Well.

2000: Sawadogo, Mamadou. *The Purse and Other Stories*. Ouagadougou: Self-published.

Chapter 1

2003: Somé, Sobonfu E. *Falling out of Grace: Meditations on Loss, Healing and Wisdom*. California: North Bay Books.
2004: Zongo, Norbert. *The Parachute Drop*. Translated by Wise, Christopher. Trenton, NJ: Africa World Press.
2006: Somdah, Marie-Ange. *Scents of Love*. Arcata: Yaniyo! Books.
2007: Zongo, Nathalia. *When Everything has Fallen*. Charleston, SC: Booksurge Publishing.
2010: Sissao, Alain Joseph. *Folktales from the Moose of Burkina Faso*. Translated by Tanti, Nina. Bamenda: Langaa RPCIG.
2012: Zio, Luc. *Proverbs & Tales from Burkina Faso*. Kindle Edition.
2012: Yaogo, Noëlie. *The Odds are against Cycling*. Pittsburgh, PA: Dorrance Publishing.
2012: Kousse, Mamadou. *Reap what you Sow and 28 poems*. Ouagadougou: IPRESS Imprimérie.
2013: Batieno, Raissa. *Let the Bird Free: Book One*: A Collection of Inspirational Poetry. Self-published.
2014: Batieno, Raissa. *Diamond Rain: A Memoire in Poetry*. Self-published.
2014: Tinguiri, Michel. *The Tribulations of a Sahelian Traveler*. USA: Self-published.
2014 : Zoungrana, Emmanuel. *The Ace of Spades in Disarray*. Translated by Bonkoungou, P.G. and Zaidi, S. Paris: EDILIVRE.
2016: Ouadrago, Amadou. *Burkina Faso Art and Culture: Tradition, Ethnic Group, Tribes, History, People*. Sonit Education Academy, Kindle Edition.
2017: Nebié, Bali. *Secrets of the Sorcerer*. Translated by Njoaguani, Francis Chuks. Ouagadougou: Editions Pounyaali.
2017: Ilboudo, Pierre Claver. *Adama*. Ouagadougou: Harmattan Burkina.
2018: Thiobiany, Prince Lamourd. *Before the Fires I was Black: A Blueprint for a Brighter Future*. Ouagadougou: Self-published.
2020: Somdah, Marie-Ange. *One Wild Proposal: Where's She Going?* Arcata, Boston and Ouagadougou: Yaniyo! Books.

CHAPTER II

Biographies of Anglophone Burkinabe Writers and their English Works

Raissa Batieno

Biography: A native of Burkina Faso, Raissa Batieno earned a Bachelor of Science in Nursing in 2010. She then went to Cleveland State University in Ohio to complete a Master of Business Administration in Operations and Systems Management. Her works bear the traces of both her African roots and the Western culture she finds herself in. Raissa Batieno loves nature, cultures, spirituality, traveling, reading, and writing.

Bibliography: Raissa Batieno wrote two collections of poems:

1) *Let the Bird Free: Book One: A Collection of Inspirational Poetry.* Self-published, 2013.
2) *Diamond Rain: A Memoire in Poetry.* Self-published, 2014.

Raissa Batieno's adventure into writing started as a therapy, suggested by her coach, to help her get through the hassle and buzzle of life. To paraphrase the title of her first collection of inspirational poems: poetry writing helps her free herself like a bird which escapes out of its cage. Her poetry revolves around life experiences made up of a cocktail of struggles, despair, and hopes, leading to losses, fears, depressions, and pains that anybody can relate to, or just imagine.

Talking about *Diamond Rain*, Batieno confesses, "I have written the experience of my life in this book. This work is the result of seven years of my inner quest and writing poetry about a life often bitter, but definitely sweet." She takes us then into the field of bibliotherapy, or poetry therapy, which provides healing through the use of literature. Batieno's writing of poems, as well as the reading of them, relieves her from the different life ailments, and keeps her open to happiness and bliss, especially thanks to her belief in God.

After reading these poems, one comes to the realization that life is meant to be beautiful – it just depends on how one interprets and relates to life experiences.

Pierre Claver Ilboudo

Biography: Pierre Claver Ilboudo is a conference interpreter. He was born on September 13, 1948, in Manga in Burkina Faso, then Upper Volta. After primary school in Manga, he went to the junior Seminary of Pabré, where he did the first half of his secondary school education before going to Lycée Philippe Zinda Kaboré, where he got his Secondary School leaving certificate. Then he went to Nigeria, where he earned a Bachelor of Arts degree from the University of Lagos. Ilboudo completed his professional studies (Conference Interpreting), earning a master's degree in Translation, and another Master in Linguistics from the Advanced School of Interpreters and Translators (ESIT) in Sorbonne Nouvelle in France. He subsequently obtained a Conference Interpreter's diploma from the Polytechnic of Central London (PCL), then a French Diploma of Higher Studies (DEA) from the University of Lille III in France, and finally, a doctorate from the University of Cergy-Pontoise in France. His thesis examines the parallel between the New French Novel and the African Novel of French expression.

Ilboudo worked at the Ministry of Foreign Affairs in Burkina Faso for three years, before moving to the Organization of African

Chapter 2

Unity (OAU). He spent two years at the OAU regional office in Lagos, and thirteen years at its headquarters in Addis Ababa, Ethiopia. In 1993, he left the OAU for the African Development Bank (ADB) in Abidjan. In 2003, due to the crisis in Côte d'Ivoire, the ADB temporarily relocated to Tunisia, where Ilboudo is currently in service.

Bibliography: Pierre-Claver Ilboudo wrote his literary works mainly in French. He translated one of his French novels, *Adama ou la force des choses,* into English as *Adama* (Ouagadougou: Harmattan Burkina, 2017), and presents it at the cover page as "one of the first Burkinabe novels written in English."

"This novel," he says on the same page, "tells the story of the main character, Adama. Adama is a man who has worked for over ten years as an accounts clerk in a small company in Ouagadougou. One fine morning, the Chief Accountant disappears with all the company's funds. Following accusations and counter-accusations, Adama is suspended from his job. He then tries his hand at several small jobs, as his financial situation worsens by the day. He discovers, to his dismay, that in present-day society there is no solidarity, no compassion, no mercy."

Cécile Kaboré

Biography: Mrs. Ouédraogo, née Cécile Kaboré, was born in 1949, in the village of Siglé, in Bulkiemdé Province in Burkina Faso. After primary school in Temnaoré, she left her native village to attend secondary school in Collège Notre Dame de Kologh-Naba in the capital city. After her university studies in CESUP, and then in France, she became a secondary school English teacher. Married, and a mother of four sons, Kaboré has been an active member of many NGOs operating in favor of women, such as Amitié Africaine, Fidélitas, Fédération des Femmes Burkinabé, and Marche Mondiale des Femmes.

Bibliography: Cécile Kaboré wrote a collection of poems, *Femmes du Burkina marchons et autres poèmes*, and had it printed through Imprimerie Presses Africaines in 1990. Half of the poems

9

Introduction to Burkinabe Literature in English

are in French, and the other in English. She shows concern for women's issues.

Mamadou Kousse

Biography: Mamadou Kousse is a Burkinabe-born musician and writer. His artist's name is Iron Bender. He is also nicknamed the Rasta Commando. Kousse was born in Daka-Tougan, in the Sourou Province in Burkina Faso. He learned English mainly through the American Cultural Centre in Abidjan (Ivory Coast), and through his artistic performances in many West African English-speaking countries. He is an "amateur" and non-professional writer. His style of writing requires more finesse, literally speaking.

Bibliography: Mamadou Kousse is the author of many music albums. Though he does not consider himself a poet and writer, his inspirations led him to produce a play and twenty-eight poems, all published in one book: *Reap What You Sow and 28 Poems* (Ouagadougou: Ipress Imprimérie, 2012). His poems appear on the website https://www.poetrysoup.com.

Bali Nébié

Biography: Bali Nébié was born on July 28, 1953, in Pouni, a small village in Burkina Faso. He is a certified biology, or earth and life science, teacher. He holds a Master of Science degree from the University of Poitiers in France, which he obtained in 1979.

Nébié was born and grew up in a village with tough traditions. From his tender age, he lived in an environment in which ghosts, spirits of the ancestors, deities, eaters of souls are everyday competitors. After his admission to secondary school, he underwent initiations in his age group.

Driven by curiosity and passionate of ancestral traditions, Nébié attempts in his fiction to probe into the mysterious world of witches and sorcerers held responsible for all the evils that befall most African communities.

Chapter 2

Bibliography: Bali Nebié wrote mainly in French. The Nigerian Francis Chuks Njoguani translated his novel, *Le Roi du Djandjo: la métamorphose des sorciers hommes-lions*, from French into English as *Secrets of the Sorcerer* (2017). The plot is about witchcraft. It introduces us, through the various steps of initiation of a neophyte called Gnama, into an unbelievable world of the brotherhood of men-lions, one of the most fearsome secret societies of sorcerers in West Africa. The initiation is when Gnama has a revelation of the secrets of the transformation of men into animals, and many other back sorcerers' supernatural powers. Sorcerers appear in this fiction as people who are likely to do evil, and who are fond of human flesh. They have supernatural powers that allow them, for example, to be changed into an animal or fly away. The novel tries to probe this belief.

Rakissouiligri Mathieu Ouédraogo

Biography: Rakissouiligri Mathieu Ouédraogo was born on December 31, 1949, in Mankoula, Burkina Faso, and died in March 2020. He attended the Catholic primary school of Temnaoré from 1956 to 1962, then the junior seminary Our Lady of Africa from 1962 to 1966, the junior seminary of Pabré in 1966, and the interseminary Saints Peter and Paul, where he earned his A-level certificate in 1969. Ouédraogo went to Centre d'Enseignement Supérieur in Ouagadougou, where he graduated in 1972. He completed his master's at the Université de Picardie in France, in 1973. From 1973 to 1977, he studied for his PhD in Science of Education, in Paris III, Sorbonne Nouvelle, in France. From 1982 to 1984, he went to the University of Nairobi in Kenya for post-graduate studies in curriculum development, then to the University of Chicago for studies in comparative education from 1985–1986. He obtained a certificate in Trends and Approaches to Teaching and Learning in 1987, at the University of Reading in the United Kingdom.

In his professional career, Ouédraogo was appointed Director of the Institut des Sciences de l'Education (INSE) from 1995 to 1996, then the Principal of Ecole Normale Supérieure de Koudougou (ENSK) from 1996 to 1998, and the Director of Formation Professionnelle Continue from 1999 to 2002. Ouédraogo became the Minister of Education from June 10, 2002 to September 5, 2005. He lectured on linguistics and curriculum development at the University Joseph Ki-Zerbo until his death in March 2020.

Bibliography: R. Mathieu Ouédraogo published many papers and coursebooks on education, and teachers' training programs in various journals and other media. He is the author of a collection of short stories – a reader for secondary school teachers in Burkina Faso: *A Deal is a Deal, or How Much for Your Head and Other Stories: A Reader for Burkina Faso Secondary Schools* (1989).

Mamadou Sawadogo

Biography: Mamadou Sawadogo was born on January 4, 1962, in Zuénoula, Republic of Côte d'Ivoire. He attended primary and secondary schools in Côte d'Ivoire, where he obtained his Advanced Level General Certificate of Education, the Baccalauréat A4, in 1983, after which he came back to Burkina Faso for higher education.

Sawadogo registered at the Department of English Studies in 1983, and came out with the Maitrise ès Lettres, option Anglais in 1988. During 1987–1988, he was in Birmingham (UK) as a French language assistant. From 1988 to 1989, he fulfilled the Service National Populaire (formerly SNP, now SND) as a teacher of English. From 1989 to 1990, he passed a test and got trained at Institut des Sciences de l'Education (INSE), at the end of which he was crowned with the Certificat d'Aptitude au Professorat de l'Enseignement secondaire (CAPES), and became a fully qualified high school teacher diploma.

Sawadogo taught for six years. After training for one academic year (1996–1997), he became a pedagogical advisor. In 2004, he was appointed at the African Union International Centre for Girls' Education (AU/CIEFFA), where he worked until 2017. He is currently working at the Direction de la Promotion de l'Education inclusive, de l'Education des Filles et du Genre (Directorate in

Chapter 2

charge of Promoting Inclusive Education, Girls' Education and Gender), under the umbrella of the Ministry of National Education, Literacy, and the Promotion of National Languages (MENAPLN).

Bibliography: Mamadou Sawadogo wrote a collection of short stories, *The Purse and Other Stories* (2000), for use especially by secondary school English classes, and is currently looking for a publisher. He also published two annals dealing with the English tests at the BEPC examination, all published in CEPRODIF:

1) *Réussir l'Anglais au BEPC, l'Epreuve écrite*. Revised 2012.
2) *Réussir l'Anglais au BEPC, l'Epreuve orale*. Revised 2012.

Alain Joseph Sissao

Biography: Alain Joseph Sissao was born in Bobo-Dioulasso, in Burkina Faso. He is a researcher at the Institute for Social Sciences at the National Scientific Research Center in Ouagadougou. The scope of his research includes both the Burkinabe oral and written literatures, and many aspects of Burkinabè culture.

Bibliography: Alain Joseph Sissao listened to Burkinabe tales in Moore language, then transcribed them into the written form in Moore, before translating them into French. Nina Tanti translated the French version into English as *Folktales from the Moose of Burkina Faso* (2010), taking caution to retain the oral quality of the language, including the frequent repetitions, colloquialisms, proverbs, jokes, and songs.

As can be read on the back cover page: "The folktale is the most appropriate form for teaching young children to express themselves, to structure their thoughts, and to reason. The tales portraying familiar animals will be reserved for the group of youngest children. The legendary gluttony and foolishness of Mba-Katré, the hyena, in contrast with the cunning and finesse of Mba-Soâmba, the hare, will interest, above all, children from ten to twelve years of age. The stories describing the origin of things, the reason for various social taboos, the legitimacy of social functions and structures, as well as character flaws ..., are reserved as a priority for adolescents."

Marie-Ange Somdah

Biography: Born on October 19, 1959, in Burkina Faso, Marie-Ange Somdah grew up in a family of eight children. His secondary school education took place in the junior seminary of Nasso, in Bobo-Dioulasso, and at Lycée Newton, in Ouagadougou. At an early age, he developed a passion for reading, which gave him writing skills.

Somdah then attended the University Joseph Ki-Zerbo of Ouagadougou, in Burkina Faso, and the University of Franche-Comté in France, where he helped run *Couleur Locale*, a local magazine in which he published his early works.

Somdah published his first book, *Demain sera beau*, shortly before the defence of his PhD thesis in French, African, and comparative literatures at the University de Franche-Comté. He received further training at Boston University and Harvard University Extension School (USA), and taught in many universities in the USA and in Africa. He has been honored on several occasions for his activities in international development, with the Teachers for Africa Award (TFA) in 1998 and in 2008. Somdah was indeed involved in developmental and educational programs in Africa through NGOs. His volunteering works in Benin and Djibouti stand as examples.

A bilingual (French and English) poet and novelist, critic, translator, and consultant based in Boston for a long time, Marie-Ange Somdah currently resides in Burkina Faso to share his rich experience and work on the implementation of new training programs for young generations. He teaches at the Aube Nouvelle University (New Dawn University), in the Anglophone Studies Department, in the Communication for Development (C4D) Department, and for the MBA program. Somdah is passionate about reading, music, cinema, photography, cooking, travel, and sports.

Chapter 2

Bibliography: Marie-Ange Somdah is a bilingual writer using both French and English as medium for his research and numerous published fiction works. His creative works include:

1) *One Wild Proposal: Where's She Going?* (2020)
2) *The Dream of Little Awa.* Boston, Ouagadougou: Yaniyo! Books, 2013.
3) *Le Rêve de la petite Awa.* Paris: EDILIVRE, 2013.
4) *Pen & Dreams from My Students.* Boston, Ouagadougou: Yaniyo! Books, 2013.
5) *Te amo.* Boston, Ouagadougou: Yaniyo! Books, 2013.
6) *Scents of Love.* Boston, Ouagadougou: Yaniyo! Books, 2006.
7) *Saisons d'amour.* Boston, Ouagadougou: Yaniyo! Books, 2006.
8) *Libertés, chocolat & cie.* Paris: Le Manuscrit, 2005.
9) *Images de vie.* Paris: Le Manuscrit, 2005.
10) *Un long fleuve.* Paris: Le Manuscrit, 2005.
11) *Hôtel la Désirade & autres récits.* Le Manuscrit, 2005.
12) *Un Soleil de Plomb.* Paris: L'Harmattan, 2003.
13) *Rêves de Savane.* Boston, Ouagadougou: Yaniyo! Books, 2002.
14) *Seeds & Deep Seasons.* New York: Mellen Press, 2009.
15) *Campus Blues.* Paris: Nouvelles du Sud, 1998.
16) *Le Nombril de la terre.* Paris: L'Harmattan, 1994.
17) *Adjoa, l'Aurore.* Besançon: Couleur Locale, 1992.
18) *Demain sera beau.* Paris: Silex, 1989.

Upcoming Books

1) *New Seasons*
2) *Aurore, perles et lueurs*
3) *The Rain & Her Luggage*

Somdah has run various creative workshops to help the younger generation sharpen their writing skills. An example is the 2010 publication, *Pen & Dreams from My Students*, a collection of poetry works from three of his students, meant for triggering emulation among his pupils at the University of Djibouti.

Maldoma Patrice Somé

Biography: Malidoma Patrice Somé was born in Dano (Burkina Faso) in 1956. His father is Elie, a farmer and miner. His mother is Colette Somé, a farmer and homemaker.

Somé studied at the University of Ouagadougou, where he obtained a BA in sociology, literature, and linguistics in 1981, and an MA in world literature in 1982. In 1983, he got a DEA in political science at Sorbonne, University of Paris, then a PhD there. At Brandéis University, he earned an MA in 1984, and a PhD in literature in 1990.

Somé married Elisabeth Sobonfu on June 26, 1989, and later divorced. He was a Literature and French lecturer at the University of Michigan from 1990 to 1993, and a visiting lecturer at Stanford University from 1992 to 1993. He currently lives on the West Coast of the United States, where he writes books and teaches workshops on West African spirituality.

Bibliography: Malidoma Patrice Somé wrote: *Ritual: Power, Healing, and Community* (1993); *Of Water and Spirit: Ritual, Magic, and Initiation in the Life of an African Shaman* (1994), which is a fictional autobiography; and *The Healing Wisdom of Africa* (1999). He is the author of several articles on spirituality. His self-expressed goal in life is to convey his knowledge of the spiritual life of his people to the rest of the world.

Sobonfu E. Somé

Biography: Sobonfu E. Somé is a woman from the Dagara tribe in the southwestern region in Burkina Faso. Her name, Sobonfu, means *keeper of ritual*. She was married to Malidoma Patrice Somé in an arranged marriage. The couple moved to London, and later to the United States. Then they divorced. She died in January 2017.

Bibliography: Like her husband, Sobonfu E. Somé is a writer who specialized in topics of spirituality, looking at relationships and intimacy through the lens of African spirituality and teachings. She founded the organization Wisdom Spring to teach African spirituality to westerners, and to provide drinking water to villages in Burkina Faso. Her books include:

1) *The Spirit of Intimacy: Ancient Teachings in the Ways of Relationships*. California: Berkeley Hills Books, 1997.
2) *Welcoming Spirit Home: Ancient African Teaching to Celebrate Children and Community*. Sacramento, CA: Healing Wisdom Well, [1999], 2009.
3) *Falling out of Grace: Meditations on Loss, Healing, and Wisdom*. California: North Bay Books, 2003.
4) *Women's Wisdom from the Heart of Africa*. Louisville, KY: Sounds True, 2004.

Prince Lamourd Thiobiany

Biography: Prince Lamourd Thiobiany, the pen name of Lamourdia Thiombiano, was born in the town of Fada N'Gourma, in the Eastern part of Burkina Faso. Initiated and brought up in the African community within the Gulmu Kingdom, he gives credit to that community for his determination, resilience, and love for learning. He is currently a senior high level official of the Ministry of Agriculture.

Preservation of the cultural identity of this community is at the center of his call upon the new generations of Africans living anywhere in the world. As a Burkinabe diplomat, Thiobiany had the opportunity to travel around the world and visit many countries, immersing himself in multicultural environments, the experiences of which he uses in his works.

Bibliography: Prince Lamourd Thiobiany wrote: *Principles for Excellent African Leadership,* and *Before the Fires I was Black: A Blueprint for a Brighter Future* (2018). In the latter, he shows himself as a master storyteller under the character of Yaldia, who spends sixteen evenings telling, with emotion, the amazing story of Africans and their descendants, to his children.

Michel Tinguiri

Biography: Michel Tinguiri was born and raised in Kiembara, a village in the northwestern region of Burkina Faso. He attended primary school there, and completed part of his high school education in Tougan and in Bobo-Dioulasso. After his A-level, he went to the University Joseph Ki-Zerbo for his graduate studies in Anglophone African literature and translation.

Tinguiri holds a master's degree in Translation Studies, and a master's certificate in Anglophone African Literature. After teaching introductory courses in the Translation department at the University of Ouagadougou, he undertook linguistic studies at Syracuse University in New York State. He holds a PhD in cultural anthropology from American University in Washington, DC, and is a lecturer at Montgomery College in Maryland, USA. He also teaches French and Culture at the Foreign Service Institute (Department of State).

Michel Tinguiri is married, and is the father of two daughters. His main pastime activities include reading African novels, ethnographies, cultural anthropological books, watching soccer games and documentaries, drawing, painting, and writing.

Bibliography: Michel Tinguiri is the author of two fictional works: a novel and a collection of poems. The first, *The Tribulations of a Sahelian Traveler* (2014), is in English. And the second, *La Parole muette et les échos de la justice* (2017), is in French. In both works, he shows interests in the sociocultural and political realities of his native country, Burkina Faso.

Noëlie Yaogo

Biography: Noëlie Yaogo was born on December 21, 1973, in Manga, in the Zoundweogo Province, in Burkina Faso. She holds a master's degree in English. She was a secondary school English teacher and lived in her home country for thirty-eight years before going abroad.

Yaogo taught English at Lycée Provincial of Boromo until October 2005. From there, she was appointed to Lycée Technique

Chapter 2

Amilcar Cabral of Ouagadougou, then, for health reasons, to another school in Tampouy District in Ouagadougou, the Capital of Burkina Faso. Her interests include reading, music, and of course, cycling.

Bibliography: Noëlie Yaogo published her first novel in French, *Les Plaisirs du Mal...Les Plaisirs du Mâle*, which was printed and released in 2007 without being edited. This work focuses on women and their issues to help them thrive despite all obstacles.

In *The Odds Are Against Cycling* (2012), which she claims to be the "first English-written [book] to be published in this French-speaking country of Burkina Faso," Yaogo uses cycling to fight in favor of women. While some people, to make life pleasurable and worth living, use a pet or a child to pass their time with, and to find a constant in their lives in a changing world full of poverty and uncertainty, Noëlie Yaogo, under the protagonist Nebnoma Elisa, uses the bicycle as her constant.

In this novel, Yaogo portrays the integration of young people in poverty-stricken Burkina Faso. Life is difficult, and people, especially women, struggle to find jobs and defeat established gender roles. Through it all, there is one thing on which Nebnoma Elisa can rely: her bicycle.

Noëlie Yaogo herself summarizes the novel as follows:

Nebnoma Elisa, the bicycle fanatic of Newbuilt land, displays her own story to this troublesome period of life, on a bike. As a matter of fact, news about Elisa, in many respects, appears as messy as her wandering handlebars, seeing that her life aim is more directed by the same wheel. From her native countryside to the correct town, easily handed down to a campaign manager, we follow her transitions as a skilful biker, strong and stout, to fit odd requirements as an odd-job man. Elisa's story starts on the road and ends by the road through an unexpected declining velocity. With different acceptations of the word "odd," she makes her own account of all road expenses, while yearning for both biking and breading. Truly passionate in the first, Elisa gives clear indications that the odds are against cycling on roads, and hereby in youthful life. (ix)

The Odds Are Against Cycling is a story of triumph against mounting odds, and ultimately, a love letter to a bicycle that was much more than a means of transportation. It was instead an instrument of improving quality of life through challenging times and events.

Luc Zio

Biography: Luc Zio is a scientist. He has an in-depth knowledge of six-sigma statistical principles using control charts. He is experienced using Machine learning algorithms as well as statistical methods to solve business problems.

Bibliography: Luc Zio wrote *Tales and Proverbs of Burkina Faso*, a collection of enlightening proverbs and tales from Burkina Faso, in whose traditional society wisdom and informal education are acquired when elders pass on to the youth stories and proverbs, with the purpose of equipping and preparing them for many life situations. Tales and proverbs are often used to educate, warn, and prepare the youth for real-life events that they may face in the future.

Nathalia Zongo

Biography: Nathalia Zongo was born in Burkina Faso. She is the daughter of Etienne Zongo, a former aide-de-camp of President Thomas Sankara. After the assassination of President Sankara, Nathalia Zongo's father became a refugee and was missing from her life for seven years.

At twenty-one, she went to the USA for studies, where she attended Brookhaven College in Dallas, Texas. The publication of her autobiographical novel is the culmination of her lifelong dream.

Chapter 2

Bibliography: Nathalia Zongo wrote *When Everything Has Fallen*, an autobiographical account of the events following the 1987 coup d'état which led to the killing of Captain Thomas Sankara and his Comrades. It is a deeply personal memoir of these events, and the family's struggles to pick up the pieces in the following years. It gives a detailed account of military raids on the Zongo family household as soldiers searched relentlessly for Lieutenant Zongo, and tells of his exile in Ghana, where he lived for seven years, away from his family. The book is the author's stirring memoir about helping her mother keep her family together during this tumultuous time in Burkinabe history.

Norbert Zongo

Biography: Norbert Zongo (July 31, 1949–December 13, 1998) was also known under the pen name of Henri Sebgo, or HS. After the completion of his secondary school studies, Zongo pursued legal studies at Université d'Abidjan, in Côte d'Ivoire, and journalism at the Université du Benin in Togo. The latter university expelled him, and he was imprisoned in Burkina Faso after the publication of his political novel *Le Parachutage*. He later finished his education in journalism at the Université de Yaoundé in Cameroon.

Zongo became a Burkinabé journalist, and the manager of the newspaper *L'Indépendant*. He was assassinated after his newspaper began investigating the murder of a driver who had worked for the brother of the Burkinabe president Blaise Compaoré.

Bibliography: Norbert Zongo wrote his first novel, *Le Parachutage,* later translated into English by Christopher Wise as *The Parachute Drop* (2004). Critics analyze it as being a thinly disguised political critique of Gnassingbé Eyadema, the then Togo president. The preface of the novel, in 1988, mentions Norbert Zongo being arrested and beaten for writing it. He followed this novel with *Rougebeinga,* a novel with a colonial setting, and which was also a political satire of leadership.

Emmanuel Zoungrana

Biography: Emmanuel Zoungrana was born in Bigtogo, a village of Burkina Faso, in December 1981. From 1993 to 2000, he attended the national military school of Kadiogo (PMK) for his secondary school education, obtaining his leaving certificate in 2000. Then he joined the Officers Cadets School of Togo and graduated as second lieutenant in 2003.

After taking part in several Rangers trainings in Morroco, France, and Kpewa centers, in 2005, Zoungrana obtained the Commando highest level qualification – the Train of the Trainer Certificate. Since January 2011, Emmanuel Zoungrana has been captain of the parachute infantry.

Bibliography: Emmanuel Zoungrana wrote *L'As de pique en débandade,* which has been translated into English as *The Ace of Spades in Disarray* (2014), by Philipe G. Bonkoungou, who produced the first draft of the translation, and Saeb Zaidi, who edited it with the author's assistance. The following synopsis of the novel can be read on the back cover page:

> *In Ivene, a country in Black Africa, the society was haunted by its own mores. Those who wanted to uphold the cruel rituals outrightly rejected the proponents of change. Plunged in its tragedy, adventures, drama, and disarray, the Nation, upset and undecided, faced its social disintegration. For a long time, this society sought, perhaps way beyond what was necessary, the required scheme of evolution. In this social backdrop appeared Azi Josué Marien, a man with accurate sense of smell, whose behaviour and achievement dazzled everyone in the city. Spectacular as this city boy may be, the man perhaps didn't realise it, and the humanitarian role he played should have driven the country through success. Indeed, the moment when the Ivene society could read his mind, too late perhaps, things and people around the Ace of Spades had already turned the other way. It is in this context that the escalation went beyond control.*

CHAPTER III

Notes on Some Major Works

a) Michel Tinguiri, *The Tribulations of a Sahelian Traveler*

Plot Overview

The Tribulations of a Sahelian Traveler is about N'Djilékou and his family. It starts with aunt Pèlo's narrative on the socio-economic impacts on the lives of villagers in regard to cotton farming, road and dam building. Her story underlines how this farming and building leads to the loss of many lives, lands, and properties.

It is against this somber background that N'Djilékou, the protagonist, decides to leave his native village, Tiala, despite some oppositions from members of his family, for better opportunities in a neighboring village, Lafidougou. On his journey there with his wife, Banko, and daughter, Banambonon, N'Djilékou meets Samba, a shepherd of Lafidougou. The latter welcomes them and enquires about the news of Tiala.

Finally, the Sahelian travelers get hospitality in the chief's compound. The community celebrates their arrival, amid sounds of tom-toms, shouts, handclaps, and food sharing. The griot gives

Introduction to Burkinabe Literature in English

a welcoming speech on the behalf of Wendé, the chief. Then, N'Djilékou takes the floor to thank the people of Lafidougou for their hospitality. He settles in Lafidougou, works hard, and becomes prosperous.

After a seven years' stay in Lafidougou, Banambonon, NDjilékou's daughter, finds a suitor, Gorko, Samba's cousin, from the village of Sanfodougou. The marriage takes place after the formalities around the bride price have been fulfilled. The new couple has their first baby, Abdu, the year after their wedding.

In his side, N'Djilékou and his wife have two boys, Gontran and Pèret. They live in harmony within the society. They are able to organize *Kudjèma* – that is, to gather people to help them till their farm in the rhythm of tom-toms and handclaps. They get a good harvest that year, which leads N'Djilékou to build two barns to keep his harvest.

But one day, N'Djilékou goes to his farm and dies there. His body is carried to Tiala for burial, according to tradition. After N'Djilékou's death, Touko and his wife, Bèrè, and their son, Saaga, plunder N'Djilékou's heritage to the detriment of Banko and her children. Banko remarries with Djibo.

As for Gontan and Pèret, after staying first at their Uncle Touko's house, they move in with their sister Banambonon because of ill-treatment. They stay with her for a year and a half, and eventually go back to Tiala, dismissed by their brother-in-law, but this time to live with their mother in her new husband's compound. There, they work hard and have a good harvest. They even become petty traders.

Then Gontan gets married to Sè and has a boy named Tchiri. Gontan decides to move to another country, Felikro, for better opportunities. In his journey, he makes acquaintance with Salif, who has been living in Felikro for years. He proposes to take Gontran as a worker in his coffee and cocoa plantations.

After the hassle and tussles on the road with corrupted police and custom officers, Gontran finally arrives in Morikro, their destination in Felikro. He is welcomed by his friends, Lamouni and Sibiri, who help him to settle in Morikro and teach him farming techniques. He later writes a letter, with the help of Sibiri as the

Chapter 3

scribe, to his family back home. His mother, wife, and brother are overjoyed when they receive the letter, and decide to celebrate the good news.

Later, Gontan decides to learn how to read and write. He even enrolls in the primary school exam and passes it. He now writes his letters by himself. He travels to Yakro, the capital of Felikro, for shopping. In his journey, he makes acquaintance with Samori the philosopher, who tells him of a military coup in Ganda-Gulo, his native country. The coup is led by General Zana.

The novel ends with Gontan meditating on the philosopher's reflection on African politics and leadership: "Toxic and radioactive leadership cannot save Africa."

Summary of Chapters

Chapter 1 - The Chiefs' Whims: Cotton, the Road, and the Dam

This opening chapter introduces Aunt Pèlo, an old woman. She is sitting under a baobab tree in front of her house, spinning cotton. She tells her grandson Kô how she learned to be a cotton weaver from her cousin N'Djilékou. While describing N'Djilékou, she shows how he and the whole population suffered from the *lansara*'s (white people) imposition of cotton farming, but also during the building of the road to the capital, Mogodougou, and the dam in Markadougou, to connect the country Ganda-Gulo to Bamanandougou. Young people are recruited by force for these activities, through the chief who cooperates with the *lansara*.

A year after the building of the dam, N'Djilékou moved from the village of Tiala to Lafidougou for better opportunities.

Chapter 2 - Memories: Fragmentation and Tribulations

From Aunt Pèlo's memory in the first chapter, follows Yiri N'Djilékou's in the second chapter. He remembers Tobri's life and death, and the fulfilment of Gonku's prophecy about the two major droughts. Tobiri is the symbol of power and unity for the extended Yiri family members. His death brings about the fragmentation of the family. Many famines and other disasters fall on the country, and the local and national authorities embezzle charity money for themselves, letting people suffer and die. That's why N'Djilékou decides to move to Lafidougou.

Chapter 3 – The Voice

This chapter is an interior monologue that reveals what is going on in N'Djilékou's mind while weighing the pros and cons of his decision to leave Tiala for Lafidougou. His inner voice reminds him of the hardships he witnessed in the past, through cotton cultivation and the building of the road and the dam, and advises him to decide to go to the unknown for better opportunities.

Chapter 4 – Departing: Exploring New Possibilities

N'Djilékou, known as a *den-horon* – that is, an honest and honorable child – decides to leave his village and go to Lafidougou for better opportunities. His cousin, Pengo, is against this decision. The old man Zèrè, however, advises him to go, and gives him his blessings.

On their journey to Lafidougou, N'Djilékou and family meet Samba, a shepherd of Lafidougou. He welcomes them and enquires about the news of Tiala. Then they are given hospitality in the chief's compound.

Chapter 5 – The Arrival: Celebrating Togetherness

The community of Lafidougou gets ready to celebrate the arrival of N'Djilékou and his family. Old Papa Moussa tells stories to children. With tom-toms, shouts, and handclaps, people express their joy while welcoming the newly arrived in the village. At that occasion, there is plenty of food for all. One of the notables, the griot, delivers a welcoming speech on the behalf of Wendé, the chief. The griot hands the floor to N'Djilékou, who thanks the people of Lafidougou for their hospitality.

Also, Samba discusses, with his wife, Fatima, suffering and the meaning of life. They agree that it is better to see the world as it is rather than wanting it to be as one wants. The narrator then

Chapter 3

reflects on how the love for money destroys everything: "Money has no humanity, even though it is made by humans!" He gives the example of Tinga's wife, Louti, who died of malaria because people refused to help Tinga, who was penniless.

Chapter 6 – Banambonon's Marriage

After settling in Lafidougou for seven years, Banambonon finds a suitor – Gorko, Samba's cousin – from the village of Sanfodougou. Gorko has to bring a hen, or *kolo-mundo*, during the harvest feast. This is followed by *djo-djiyan*, which consists in mobilizing one's relatives and friends to work on the in-laws' farm. Then they pay the *taguma-paa*, or formalities price.

Eventually, the marriage takes place, which is a source of joy for everybody. The following year, Banambonon has her first baby, Abdu, named after his paternal great-great-grandfather. A celebration around his birth is organized.

Chapter 7 – Your Farm is Our Farm

N'Djilékou, his wife, and their two boys, Gontan and Pèret, are living peacefully in Lafidougou. They live in harmony within the society. They organize *Kudjèma*, the gathering of people to till one's land, as part of their farming practice. People farm to the rhythm of tom-toms and handclaps, and then are given food and drinks. That year, the harvest was good. N'Djilékou builds two barns to keep his harvest.

Chapter 8 – It Came Like Lightening from the Sky

One night, N'Djilékou has a nightmare. A boa wants to kill him. A couple months later, a real boa came to his bedroom in daylight. With the help of his neighbors, he kills it. Then one day, he goes to his farm and dies there. Tired of waiting for him, his wife Banko goes to the farm and finds him dead. She returns to the village to bring the sad news to the chief, who sends messengers to Tiala to inform N'Djilékou's relatives, and also sends messengers to his daughter, Banambonon.

N'Djilékou's body is carried to Tiala for burial. Everything is carried out according to tradition. Everybody is worried, except Touko, the deceased's brother. He is busy collecting N'Djilékou's belongings and properties.

Chapter 9 – The Orphan Wipes His Own Tears

Touko and his wife, Bèrè, and their son Saaga, plunder N'Djilékou's heritage to the detriment of Banko and her children, for drinking *dolo* and having fun.

After years of suffering, Banko decides to remarry with Djibo. Gontan and Pèret first remain at Touko's house. Ill-treated there, they move to live with their sister, Banambonon, for a year and a half, until her husband asks them to leave his house. They go to Tiala to live with their mother and her new husband, Djibo. There, they receive a warm welcome and thoughtful advice to help them fare well in life.

Chapter 10 – Coming of Age and Being Self-Reliant

Gontan and Pèret work hard and have a good harvest. They also get involved in small trade in the village, selling fish and kola nut. Gontan gets married to Sè and has a boy named Tchiri. He plans to move to Felikro for better opportunities.

Chapter 11 – On the Road

Pèret, Banko, and Sè accompany Gontan to the bus station before his journey to Felikro, and say goodbye to him. On the bus, Gontan makes acquaintance with Salif, who has been living in Felikro for years. He proposes to take Gontan as a worker in his coffee and cocoa plantations.

On the road, all travelers go through different hassles, and witness corruption from the police and custom officers. Once in Morikro, Lamouni and Sibiri, Gontan's friends and countrymen, introduce him to life in Morikro.

Chapter 12 – News from Felikro

Lamouni and Sibiri teach Gontan farming techniques. Weeks later, with the help of Sibiri, he sends a letter to his family back

Chapter 3

home to inform his mother, wife, and brother of how he is faring in Morikro. The people of Tiala are overfilled with joy when they receive the letter, and decide to celebrate the good news.

Later on, Gontan decides to attend school to learn to read and write. He enrolls in the primary school exam and passes it. He is now able to write letters on his own to the village.

Chapter 13: The Man Who Called Himself "Philosopher"

One day, Gontan decides to travel to Yakro, the capital of Felikro. During the journey to Felikro, he makes acquaintance with Samori the philosopher, who tells him of a military coup in Ganda-Gulo, led by General Zana. Once he arrives in Yakro, Gontan is shocked seeing the poverty of the suburb of Yama.

Salif's brother, Moussa, meets him at the bus station and takes him to the market to do his shopping. Salif keeps thinking on the philosopher's reflection on African politics and leadership: "Toxic and radioactive leadership cannot save Africa."

List of Characters

Aunt Pèlo: N'Djilékou's cousin, Kô's grandmother
Kô: Pèlo's grandson
N'Djilékou: Pélo's cousin, Banko's husband
Banko: N'Djilékou's wife
Sèguè: local guard
Logo: N'Djilékou's uncle
Gonku: a diviner
Tobri: member of the Yiri family
Pengo: N'Djilékou's cousin
Zèrè: a patriarch
Banambonon: N'Djilékou's daughter
Saa: Banambonon's favorite friend
Samba: the herder
Wênde: the chief
Fatima: Samba's wife
Tinga: a poor man of Tiala, wife died of malaria
Louti: Tinga's wife

Banlè: Tinga's uncle
Gorko: Samba's cousin, Banambonon's husband
Gontan and Pèret: N'Djilékou's boys
Kanama: a flutist
Doro: the *tiéla,* or workers' manager.
Lamouni and Djikouma: workers
Manlè: Dji's brother, Gnessa's son
Dji: Manlè's brother
Tialo: traditional beer bar owner
Touko: N'Djilékou's brother
Bèrè: Touko's wife
Saaga: Touko's son
Djibo: Banko's new husband
Larba: Djibo's friend
Nado: Gontan's aunt
Sè: Gontan's wife
Tchiri: Gontan's boy
Gouli: one of Gontan's friends
Koro: a prosperous man who lives in Felikro
Salif: cocoa and coffee farm owner
Sibiri: worker on Salif's farm
Lamouni: worker on Salif's farm
Alima: Salif's junior wife
Marcel: a local youth leader with xenophobic attitude
President Mori: Ganda-Gulo's president.
General Zana: military man who led the coup
Samori: philosopher

Analysis of Major Characters
N'Djilékou

Protagonist. His name means *self-control,* and he is always true to his name, with a calm and poised demeanor, according to Pèlo, his cousin. The narrator says he is "a smart and courageous gentleman who had been raised by a family that believed in truth, dignity, and self-respect, and the respect of others."

When N'Djilékou was about seven years old, he stood tall

Chapter 3

from his childhood playmates through his skills and smartness. Many admired him – men, women, and children. Adults used to call him "my son" (p. 43). He is a *den-horon* – that is, an honest and honorable youth.

He marries Banko, and together they beget three children: Banambonon, Gontan, and Pèret. N'Djilékou is one of the first farmers who tries to grow cotton. He lived under the *lansara,* or white man's rule, and is one of the survivors of the quarry collapse. He witnessed the major droughts following the building of the road and the dam, and decides to move to Lafidougou to explore new opportunities. N'Djilékou dies there on his own farm.

Banko

She is a good wife for N'Djilékou, and is the mother to Banambonon, Gontan, and Pèret. Banko's goodness appears, for example, when she forgives a woman who verbally abused her because Banambonon beat her daughter. Banko does not reject her, but welcomes the woman into her home and gives her food and drink.

Banko discovers her husband dead on his farm, and goes back to inform everybody. She mourns his death. Later, she remarries with Touko, and later welcomes two more sons.

Banambonon

Daughter of N'Djilékou and Banko. Shy, active, and creative. She was eleven years when her parents left for Lafidougou. She once beat her neighbor's child, and the child's mother insulted Banambonon's parents.

Banambonon suffers a great deal from the death of her father. She welcomes her two brothers, running away from their Uncle Touko's house, and gives them hospitality for almost two years.

Samba

A herder and hard worker who enjoys cracking jokes. He used to say that his success depends on himself, self-reliance, and on the contribution and blessing of God and other people. Samba usually brings game to his wife, Fatima, at the end of the day, after running across the bush, after his cattle. He enjoys bathing with warm water.

Fatima

Samba's wife. She is a great woman, with culinary and social skills. She often gives good advice to her husband. Fatima is not "a foul-mouthed person who would spend the day cursing around and treading on others. She [is] instead a person of principle, kind and reserved. She always [prefers] actions to words" (p. 77). It is the reason why her husband, Samba, always loves and cherishes her. She lives in a beautiful and quiet mud-built house.

Gorko

Samba's cousin. Gorko is from Sanfodougou. He is caring, reliable, and responsible. He marries Banambonon, and they beget a little boy, Abdu.

After providing hospitality to Gontan and Pèret for a year and a half, Gorko gives them food and clothes, and begs them to leave his house – for he married their sister, not them. The narrator says that by this time, "he had become too obnoxious, with no regard to his wife's opinion" (p. 124).

Gontan and Pèret

Gontan was eleven years old, and Pèret was nine when their father died. They go through all kinds of ordeals following their father's death. Ill-treated by their Uncle Touko, they find refuge in their brother-in-law's house and stay there for almost two years, and then move to their mother's second husband's house. They work hard there, on their own farms, as well as on their mother's.

Gontan and Pèret are said to have grown up quickly, and became more mature than expected. They get a good harvest and build a huge barn for it. They build their own house and get involved in a small trade in the village. They become rich, and Gontan buys two bicycles: one for his stepfather, and one for himself. Even Touko, their wicked uncle, used to ask them for

Chapter 3

assistance. Gontan marries Sè and has a boy, Tchiri. Believing that Felikro can be a "source of more prosperity and happiness for him" (p. 151), Gontan leaves his beloved behind and goes there. He frequently sends his family letters to give them news. He tells them that he passed his primary school exam and can now read and write.

Touko

N'Djilékou's older brother. The narrator describes him as "a man with a stony heart, a self-centred person whose only concern was to drink traditional beer and be merry. He had no compassion at all for Banko and her children" (p. 122). Touko sells everything belonging to his deceased brother to fund his partying and merrymaking with his wife, Bèrè, and son, Saaga.

Djibo

Banko's new husband. His father comes from Sampara. Unable to withstand the colonizers, his father flees to Tiala. Djibo becomes rich through hard work. He welcomes his wife's two children from her previous marriage, after consulting his father, who does not object. Djibo is kind and responsible. She takes care of Banko when she gets "guinea worm."

Themes, Motifs, and Symbols
Land

Dispossession of land is a major issue. People fight for lands. N'Djilékou and his uncle Logo go to court over a land issue. The chief tries the case and decides to keep the land for himself and turns what used to be "the only fertile land left for N'Djilékou," into a cotton farm (p. 19).

People complain of lands being taken to farm cotton, to build roads and dams. Aunt Pèlo's narrative explains the successive disappointment of people in the progressive taking of lands for different reasons: "First, it was about cultivation of cotton, and then we lost our lands, and our young people. Then the road came,

33

and again, we lost our lands and our young people. Then the dam; another thing forced upon us. We didn't ask for it. The building of Markadougou's dam took away our lands, some of our young people too; and even worse, seven villages were wiped out by the waters of Joliba" (p. 22).

People and the spirits of their ancestors are willing to fight to free the land (24). "According to tradition, one does not just give land to anybody, because land is sacred and belongs to the ancestors. Anybody acting against traditional land management and distribution rules was severely punished" (p. 132). The population sees the droughts and famines following the building of the dam and the road as punishments from the gods. These disasters are the fulfillment of the diviner's prophecy following the taking over of the lands for the different undertakings.

Oppression

People are forced not only to work on the chief's cotton fields, but also to provide cotton to help the white people wage war in Europe (p. 16). Speaking on behalf of the population, the narrator says he cannot understand why people "should be forced to grow cotton to fight a war so far away" (p. 16).

People are forced to work under the scorching sun, digging the laterite quarry to build a road to the city Mogodougou. The narrator says, "When someone was recruited by force to go work on the road, family members would cry as if the person were dead. And indeed, the road took many lives" (p. 19).

Love and Marriage

Some customs around marriage rites are explained. For example: "As required by his tradition, you don't approve a marriage request immediately when someone requests your daughter for marriage. Also, you don't refuse bluntly if someone asks your daughter for marriage. There were various forms of marriage in his society: love-based marriage; arranged marriage, also called *lusi*, which literally means *receiving a woman*; and leviracy" (p. 87).

Chapter 3

Colonization

The period of hardships in colonial times is often recalled in conversations. "Long ago, the White men came in our land with cannons and shot people who refused to submit to their will" (p. 135). The example of Sampara's refusal to submit is given. Its young people got organized to face the white men and fight for their freedom and beliefs. But their war weapons were not even comparable to the white man's. They were armed with clubs, machetes, spears, and arrows. The white man with guns, or "fire sticks," which kills hundreds of people (p. 135). When it became impossible to resist their enemies, the people ran away, abandoning everything.

Unity

The narrator lays emphasis on the lack of unity. Unity is important for any endeavor. Traditionally speaking, "construction of a house was always done collectively. It was a sign of solidarity in the community. "Everybody needs everybody to make progress in this life," they said. And the people understood and set up a social system that guides and enables them to fight and resist unforeseen forces and evils of the dark" (p. 144–5).

There is a call for African unity: "Africans need to unite; African youth need to wake up. But unfortunately, most promising African leaders, especially some young leaders, started to create associations to praise the corrupt leaders. They praise in their songs and speeches such corrupt leaders as the new Messiah, as monuments of African leadership. Some young African artists became modern-day griots" (p. 194–5).

Disunity is the cause of problems in Africa. What hinders African development is not so much foreign bodies than people born and bred in Africa: "Real evil comes from inside, not from outside. As the popular saying goes, 'A house divided against itself cannot stand'" (p. 196).

Corruption

The corruption of African leaders and civil servants is underlined. Of police and custom officers, it is said: "Corruption became part of their habit and daily behaviour and discourse. Every traveller to Felikro knew that and was psychologically and morally prepared to abide by their rules. The local authorities and the respective governments did not care about what was happening at their borders as long as their power was not threatened. To avoid trouble, people became cynical and even encouraged the police and customs officers to misbehave" (p. 156).

Disillusionment

One of the current themes of postcolonial literature is unmistakenly that of disillusionment. It is underlined in this novel in many instances. "You see," the old man said, "during the days of the white man's rule, we used to pay taxes and we were forced to work for free. We thought that with the white man leaving our homeland and giving power to our own brothers, we would live in peace and happiness. That did not happen at all. Our own brothers turned against us and started looting and cheating us" (158).

Samori the philosopher also points out to Gontan, after reading out about the military coup, that "independence became a nightmare for all of us. We fought for it, and now our own brothers turned to looting our wealth. Instead of building our young nations, they were busy transferring funds to bank accounts in Switzerland" (p. 192).

Symbolic Setting

Ganda-Gulo represents Burkina Faso. Its capital, Mogodougou, is a close adaptation of Ouagadougou, the capital of Burkina Faso. Bamanandougou, Sanandougou, Lafidougou, by their endings, sound like Koudougou, Beregadougou, and other places in Burkina. Felikro referring to Ivory Coast, a neigboring country of Burkina Faso, and its capital, Yakro, reminds one of Yamoussokro, the political capital of Ivory Coast.

President Mori may refer to President Maurice Yaméogo,

Chapter 3

Burkina Faso's first president when it became independent. The incident surrounding President Mori's stepping down from power in the novel resembles President Maurice, who flies for honeymooning in Monaco after asking his citizens to make sacrifices because there is no money in the treasury. This incident is hinted at in the novel in Samori's talk to Gontan: "When the great famine hit Ganda-Gulo, President Mori, Ganda-Gulo's President himself, came here to ask for support from his close friend, our President.... Subsequent news revealed that instead, he took the money and celebrated his second wedding on a remote island while his people were perishing. Civil servants and trade unionists went on strike to denounce his misbehaviour and oppressive laws. Through a decree, President Mori had drastically reduced their already meagre salaries by twenty-five percent. He had called the measure patriotism, and those who opposed his decision were labelled as terrorists, traitors, and scums plotting to undermine his own success as the Messiah" (p. 193).

The novel can be seen as a fictional representation of historical reality.

Questions for Discussion

What do you think of the characterization in the novel? Does the author resort to more narrative or demonstrative techniques? In other words, is the writer more concerned with telling the story than showing it through characters' actions?

What criticism does the author make of the introduction of cotton cultivation? Considering that the novel opens with it as something of greatest importance, can it be said that the author is for or against it? Are the bad effects of cotton growing clearly expressed?

The writer tried to use the narrative within a narrative technique, typical of African storytelling techniques. (It is also found in Conrad's *Heart of Darkness*). How far is he successful in the use of this technique? Are the following chapters the unfolding of the story of N'Djilékou, told by the old woman, aunt Pèlo, to her grandchild, Kô? Because the story is brought back to memory again in the second and third chapters, does that make the first chapter an epilogue? What effect would it have to the story if Aunt Pèlo and Kô appeared only at the beginning and end of the narrative?

Do you find the story in the novel realistic? Are representations of some characters true to life? Where did Banko stay years and years after her husband's death, before remarrying Djibo? Was leviracy applied, and why not? For a year and a half, she did not inquire about them. Does this sound realistic? Yet, when the two boys come back to their mother, she tells them that she lost weight because of their absence. Can it be true, or is it a sign of hypocrisy? Imagine an alternate ending to the story, where the widow moves with her children to her new husband's house.

***

Chapter 3

b) Mamadou Kousse, *Reap What You Sow*
Plot Overview

Reap What You Sow is a forty-three-act play. It tells the story of the misbehavior of Amoussa, who has been spoiled by his mother, Ginamousso. His father, Old Gazaadji, tries in many ways to bring up Amoussa, but he always faces the opposition of his wife, who thinks he is too hard on the young lad. The couple continues to quarrel because of him.

One day, Amoussa steals his father's money through a well-planned strategy, and disappears to spend it in the big town of Tchibiri. Once there, he realizes that the people are more wicked than he is. A notorious street bandit called "Do and Go" steals everything from him and takes off. Amoussa is now penniless in an unknown environment. He can't go back because severe punishment awaits him. Yet he has no means to live in town. He is hopeless.

A man finds Amoussa in this state and decides to play the good Samaritan. The man comes to his rescue and asks his friend, Mr. Ousman, a wealthy businessman, to take care of him. Amoussa tells them that his name is Jack, and that he is a neglected orphan haunted by the witches of his village. Mr. Ousman and his wife, Edith, believe Jack and decide to take care of him. They welcome him to their house, and later employ him as a storekeeper.

Amoussa, who now passes as Jack, falls in love with a teenager, Veronica. Her mother is dead, and she lives with her father. Jack lies to her and says Mr. Ousman is his uncle. He takes items from the shops and gives them to her as presents. He invites her home when Mr. Ousman and his wife are away, where they talk and finally make love together. Four weeks later, she comes back to tell him that she is pregnant. Then Veronica and her father, Mr. Olivia, go to see Jack's supposed uncle to sort things out. It is then that the unveiling of Amoussa's lies begins. Mr. Ousman learns that Amoussa tells everybody that he is his uncle, and decides to stop helping the boy.

Mr. Olivia brings the news of his daughter's pregnancy to the village, especially to his deceased wife's sister, who happens to be Amoussa's mother. Yet Amoussa and Veronica don't know that they are cousins. Neither does Mr. Olivia know that Amoussa is Ginamousso's child. Hearing what happened to her niece, Ginamousso vies to punish the boy that got her niece pregnant, saying: "I swear the person that did that to my daughter shall see red pepper. I shall squeeze him like a sponge and polish him like a shoe, and he shall regret what he has done and shall never forget it till he is in the grave" (p. 58). Mr. Olivia gives her the bus fare and returns to Tchibiri to await her arrival.

Mr. Olivia goes to meet Ginamousso at the bus station and brings her home. Ginamousso and Veronica meet for the first time. Mr. Ousman and Edith attend the family to solve the problem. Ginamousso tells them that they have to look after Veronica until she gives birth. She then asks to see the man responsible for her pregnancy. Mr. Ousman and Edith go back home and come back the following day with Amoussa. Upon seeing his mother, Ginamousso, Amoussa starts trembling and tries to run away, but Mr. Ousman prevents him. Ginamousso falls unconscious. They pour water on her and she recovers. Mr. Olivia, Mr. Ousman, and Edith do not understand what is going on because Amoussa, "Jack," has told them he is an orphan. They eventually come to realize that Amoussa is not without parents and that his name is not Jack.

Weeks later, Veronica becomes sick and is taken to hospital, where the doctor discovers that she has taken tablets to abort the baby. Mr. Olivia reports this to the police, since it is Amoussa who forced her to take the abortive drugs. Ginamousso should now reap what she has sown in Amoussa.

Amoussa runs away to his village, Banganni, to escape the police, who are looking for him. There, he meets his father, and a policeman comes in and arrests him. Mr. Olivia encourages his daughter to tell the truth once in court. Ginamousso wants her son released. Amoussa is tried and sentenced to two years imprisonment with hard labor.

Chapter 3

Characters Analysis
Old Gazaadji

Amoussa's father and Ginamousso's husband. In the Samo language, *Gazaadji* means a *warmonger*, or a *troublesome fellow*. He calls himself "the great warrior of Banganni" (p. 2). Gazaadji is a farmer living in the village of Banganni. How can one no make friends in the village of Banganni, which is far from the main town, Tchibiri. He is his father's second-born child, and his father is supposed to have been the first black man to slap a white man in the village. Gazaadji is a second-generation citizen of the postcolonization period. He claims to be "the warrior who killed seven white soldiers with a single arrow in the Hitlar war" (p. 21).

Mr. Olivia calls him by his nicknames: "the war-monger, Red Pepper, Venomous Viper that never sleeps, red ant that kills the great elephant of the black forest" (p. 55).

Gazaadji is fun of *dolo* and cola nut. He uses a foul language, and is a miser, according to Amoussa. Gazaadji does not tell lies, and does not allow people to laugh at his family.

Ginamousso

Lerfourouna's daughter, Gazaadji's wife, and Amoussa's mother. In the Samo language, *Ginamousso* means a *short-tempered woman*, and *Lerfourouna* means *hypocrite* or a *sharp-tongued person*. She has given birth to three children, two of which are dead (22), leaving Amoussa.

Her husband refers to her as "madam Hitlar" (p. 2), and calls her foolish. She always defends her son, Amoussa, telling her husband that a child should play while his responsible father works to take care of him. Amoussa is an angel in her eyes. She says: "My life and my soul is my son" (10).

Ginamousso was in conflict with her younger sister, Mr. Olivia's wife. Ginamousso and her relatives accused her of being a prostitute or harlot.

Ginamousso faints when she recognizes her son as the author of her niece's pregnancy, and sobs when her son is sentenced to prison.

Amoussa

His parents are Old Gazaadji and Ginamousso. He has been given this name because he was born on Thursday. In the Samo language, *Amoussa* means a *boy born on Thursday*. When Amoussa is sixteen years old, his father finds him to be disrespectful, lazy, dishonest, and a thief. He refuses to follow his father to the farm for work. He is caught red-handed stealing Boussouyan's meat. Amoussa frequents the market for drinking, and comes home late at night. He tells lies to his parents and adoptive parents. He lies that his uncle appeared to him in a dream and asked him to perform a sacrifice.

Amoussa steals his father's money and heads to the town of Tchibiri, where he finds the freedom he was longing look for. He tells Mr. Ousman that his name is Jack, and that he is an orphan. He lies to Veronica by telling her that Mr. Ousman is his uncle. Under Mr. Ousman's care, Amoussa makes love with Veronica and she becomes pregnant. When he discovers that Veronica is his cousin, he forces her to take abortive tablets. Amoussa is arrested and sentenced to two years imprisonment for that.

Boussouyan

In the Samo language, *Boussouyan* means *sickness is finished*. Boussouyan is the hunter's wife. She is said to be barren. She stands in contrast to Old Gazaadji's family, which has three children. There is enmity between the two families because of Amoussa's misbehavior. They always insult each other.

Boussouyan catches Amoussa red-handed, stealing her meat. She informs his parents, but his mother denies it. Boussouyan witnesses Amoussa's arrest by the policemen and laughs at the boys' father. She is present at his trial, and was happy with the court's decision.

Boussouyan is an advocate for justice, for mending things before they become rotten, for straightening the plant when it is still green, before it becomes dry. She wants Ginamousso to scold Amoussa and make him behave, but Ginamousso closes her eyes to her child's misbehavior, and that's why he turns out to be a

Chapter 3

bandit. The forewarned is twice guilty. That's why Boussouyan shows no sympathy to Ginamousso when Amoussa is arrested and sentenced to prison.

A Man Nicknamed "Tiger"

Amoussa's savior. He finds Amoussa crying and takes him out of a dangerous place.

Tiger presents himself as "an old fish in the sea," – that is, somebody who is used to life in the city. He smokes, and says he is a Roman Catholic priest (p. 26). He may be a chaplain to street children and drug addicts because knows this environment well. This may explain why he was in that dangerous place when he found Amoussa.

Tiger is Mr. Ousman's friend. He asks Mr. Ousman to take the so-called orphan, Jack, into his custody.

Mr. Ousman

Nickname is "Smanoto." He is Tiger's friend, Edith's husband, and Amoussa's boss. He introduces himself to Amoussa as "a simple man," but a man who is "good and bad at the same time" (25).

Mr. Ousman is a businessman. He warns Amoussa to respect customers and not to make friends, and also not to give out credits (p. 28). How can one not make friends? It can be said that he reaps what he sows through this piece of advice, as Amoussa turns out to be unfriendly to him through his misbehavior. Amoussa makes friends with nobody, not even with Mr. Ousman, even though this is not what he meant or expected through his advice.

Edith

Mr. Ousman's wife. She loves her husband. She is a secretary to the American ambassador.

Edith is apparently childless. She accepts her husband's proposal to welcome Jack home as an orphan. She lies, trying to please Ginamousso, by telling her that she argued with her husband on the subject of the world turning around the sun (p. 66).

Sometimes she pleads, asking her husband not to sack Amoussa. At other times, she wants him dismissed because he is a liar.

Mr. Olivia

Veronica's father and Massana's husband. Building contractor. A man of peace, respect, and love (p. 50). He has brought up his daughter by himself, since her mother died two weeks after her birth.

Mr. Olivia can handle the problem of his daughter's pregnancy, but because he wants to respect tradition, he goes to see her aunt. He is about telling lies, but wants justice to be done.

Mr. Olivia is vengeful. As Ginamousso made him suffer when his wife was still alive, he is adamant to avenge himself by bringing her son's case to court and have him sentenced to prison.

Veronica

Mr. Olivia's only daughter, "the only valuable thing [he has] in the world" (p. 50), and Amoussa's girlfriend. A nice young girl, gentle, and respectful. She does not know her mother because she died a week after she was born.

Veronica receives her first gift from Amoussa, apart from her father's gifts. She is educated, yet is fooled by an uneducated Amoussa.

Do and Go

The nickname of a one-eyed bandit who has been to prison many times. He was wearing a red shirt and wielding a knife when he attacked Amoussa. He robs Amoussa's bag with all the money inside. Do and Go dies tragically, and the news of his death starts to spread on the day of Amoussa's trial.

Setting

The setting is significant in its symbolism and diversity. Set in a postcolonization period, the story opens in the village of Banganni. In the Samo language, *Banganni* means *gone are the days of good*

Chapter 3

doing. This name foretells what will happen. Banganni is near the river Mounsouso, or *water is sweet*, which is about 555 kilometers from the town of Tchibiri, the second largest town in Africa. The diversity of settings, village, and town, is also a premonition of conflict caused by rural exodus.

Themes
Drinking

Drinking is presented as one of the causes that lead Amoussa to go astray. He drinks a lot and can no longer control himself. As Old Gazaadji says: "Drinking is sweet, but too much is bad and dangerous" (p. 10).

Amoussa becomes a drunkard, yet the playwright does not associate any of Amoussa's misdeeds with drinking, including stealing the meat of the hunter's wife, or robbing his father of money, or even his sex affair with Veronica. In the stage directions in Act 27, when Amoussa goes home with Veronica, it is said that "Amoussa sat down comfortably, serving Veronica with a bottle of minerals, music blowing." There is no mention of drinking alcohol, or any alcohol-induced attitude in Amoussa, until having sex with Veronica, as they stay together from 8:15 a.m. to 10:00 p.m., which is unrealistic.

Thievery

Amoussa and the bandit Do and Go are all involved in thievery. So thieves are found in villages as well as in towns. Ginamousso says that Old Gazaadji's brother, Magaayie, was shot dead for stealing a goat in the village of Sambola (p. 18). For her, Amoussa's thievery stems from his father's side. The difference is that in towns, bandits can kill people if they dare resist. Small thieves in villages become gangsters in town.

Village vs. City

The story is built around rural exodus. Young people like Amoussa are lured into the town as a dreamland. They are unaware of the difference that exists between villages and towns. Yet, as Mr.

Introduction to Burkinabe Literature in English

Ousman says: "Town is town, and village is village" (p. 47). In a village, everybody knows each other, unlike in a town. The morals differ as well.

Mr. Olivia tells Ginamousso that what can be done in the village, in terms of punishment, cannot be done in town, for in town "pregnancy is not a problem at all" (p. 63). All this underlines the change of things in postcolonial Africa (p. 61).

Characters have different appreciations of the village. The man Tiger says that "people in the village are very sympathetic and kind" (p. 23). Veronica thinks that "in the village one can easily learn the past history of his ancestors and have a good African education and not imported ones" (41). Amoussa hates the village. He says that villages are "full of witches and demons and ghosts and ants and mosquitoes and devils" (p. 41).

Hypocrisy

Hypocrisy is the main theme of this drama. Characters can be classified in two categories: the liars and the truthtellers. Amoussa is involved in telling lies. He lies that his father is killed spiritually, through witchcraft. His mother, too.

The man Tiger, a Roman Catholic priest, points out this hypocrisy of African people: "This is the black continent with black people who shout Jesus…Jesus…Mohammed…Mohammed, and later in the night transform themselves to seek for the blood and souls of their brothers and sisters" (23).

Mr. Ousman thinks that Amoussa is shedding hypocritical tears (p. 51). Ginamousso is hypocritical in mourning her sister's death (p. 57), while everybody knows that when she was still alive, they did not love each other. Mr. Olivia, Ginamousso's sister's husband, rightly reminds her of her hypocrisy: "Massana was sick for months and you, Ginamousso, did not ever mind to come and see her even for a single day. Oh God! I tried to convince you in vain, and your old husband supported you.… But see! You are now shouting because her daughter that you don't even know, is pregnant.… Oh, this world can never change. How can I understand all this hypocrisy? How and how and how?" (p. 59).

Chapter 3

Love and Prostitution

Veronica tells Amoussa that "love is something like a vehicle; it takes you sometimes to where you don't want to go, and sometimes forces you to do what you don't want to do" (p. 36). There are many couples in the play. They often talk about love. What is at stake is the sincerity of that love. Old Gazaadji marries Ginamousso, knowing that she was not a virgin, as she pretended.

Prostitution is also presented as contagious, transmitted from mother to daughter. Boussouyan says to Old Gazaadji, following Amoussa's arrest by policemen: "Your wife is a prostitute, her sister Massana a prostitute, yourself a lazy coward..." (p. 79).

Prostitution exists in towns and villages. Old Gazaadji reminds Ginamousso that her "sister was said to be the queen and champion of all the prostitutes in the great town of Tchibiri... I know your history, prostitutes and liars" (p. 17). He also later reminds Ginamousso not to boast as if he married her when she was a virgin, because many villagers slept with her before she became his wife (p. 58). Gazaadji himself boasts of the time when beautiful girls surrounded him in the evenings, and he would choose one for the night (p. 9).

Questions for Discussion

1) What do you think of the mastery of the English grammar throughout the play? Does it reflect the characters' language, or are there some mistakes from the writer?
2) What do you think of the playwright's use of language for characterization? Is he successful? Why, and why not?
3) What do you think of the author's choice of words and phrases, such as "fowl excrement..." Do you find it rude?
4) What do you think of the structure of the play? Would a division of the play into three acts be better? For example: Act One – from Act 1 to 8; Act Two – from Act 9 to 31; Act Three – from Acts 32 to 43.

CHAPTER IV

Recurring Themes in Burkinabe Literature in English

Five thematic concerns will be examined. Some of them have already been the subject of papers I published in different journals. They include:

1) Witchcraft
2) Cycling and woman's emancipation
3) Feminism
4) Comparing creation myths in Burkinabe and biblical literatures
5) Ecocritical reading of Thiobiany's *Before the Fires I Was Black*.

The theme of witchcraft appears in Burkinabe Literature in English. My analysis will highlight the fact that that Burkinabe writers show concern for witchcraft because they are not satisfied with how it has been handled by colonial white people who have dismissed its existence, and so Burkinabe writers have decided to give proofs of the reality of witchcraft's existence, even though the efficiency of its mystical powers remains debatable.

The works under consideration include Malidoma Patrice Somé's *Of Water and the Spirit: Ritual, Magic, and Initiation in the Life of an African Shaman* (1994), Noëlie Yaogo's *The Odds Are Against Cycling* (2012), Mamadou Kousse's *Reap What You Sow and 28 poems* (2012), Michel Tinguiri's *The Tribulations of a Sahelian Traveler* (2014), Emmanuel Zoungrana's *The Ace of Spades in Disarray* (2014), and Bali Nebié's *Secrets of the Sorcerer* (2017).

As to the theme of cycling and woman's emancipation, it

Introduction to Burkinabe Literature in English

concerns mainly Pierre Claver Ilboudo's *Adama* (2017), and Noëlie Yaogo's *The Odds Are Against Cycling* (2012). The consideration of cycling and emancipation comes from the fact that throughout world history there has been a cause and effect relationship between women's cycling and feminism. The American women's rights activists, Susan Brownell Anthony (1820–1906) and Elizabeth Cady Stanton (1815–1902), for example, contended that the bicycle has contributed more toward women's emancipation than anything else in the world. It is also a fact, from the 2010 statistics, that Burkina Faso is the only non-European country where 84 percent of households own a bicycle. This paper examines the contribution of cycling in women's emancipation in Burkina Faso, "the country of the two wheels." Through an analysis of two literary works written by Burkinabe authors, from a feminist perspective, namely Pierre Claver Ilboudo's *Adama* (2017) and Noëlie Yaogo's *The Odds Are Against Cycling* (2012), it appears that the bicycle is a hard-work training tool which predisposes women cyclists to taking on roles previously reserved for men in society. The bicycle helps housebound women, like the ones in *Adama*, escape from the house and join the women in Yaogo's novel who are committed to cycling against the odds for a better future.

Concerning feminism in Burkinabe English Literature, a survey of Burkinabe literature written in English shows variations in literary portrayal of men and women. The images of women promulgated by Burkinabe literature in English are mostly traditional ones and cannot be a representation that mobilizes social constructivism in modern times, as few educated women would be ready to play the role patriarchy assigns to women. A comparative approach shows that two out of three selected writers advocate women's situation as natural, part of Burkinabe age-long tradition. Only one writer, Noëlie Yaogo, tries to fight against traditional beliefs and customs that are contrary to women's empowerment. She shows that the roles traditionally assigned to women, as well as the women-related mores, are socially constructed. An analysis of the representation of women in these literary works shows that the novels of Michel Tinguiri and Bali

Nebié have a patriarchal agenda, while Noëlie Yaogo's, despite the author's claim of a feminist agenda, is actually ideologically conflicted.

The fourth thematic concern is the presence of proverbs, maxims, and myths in Burkinabe literature. The myths about nature and creation in Ouédraogo's collection reveal some similarities and differences with the biblical ones. They are embedded in Moose culture and traditions while responding to colonialism. The myths in Ouédraogo's work enact a postcolonial ethic of encounter that foregrounds and challenges colonial strategies of cultural annihilation.

Finally, nature and religious coexistence are at the heart of Thiobiany's *Before the Fires I was Black*. Reacting to colonialism and its aftermaths, and opposing any ideology that intends to destroy the cultural biodiversity for a globalized culture, Prince Lamourd Thiobiany's novel ecologically examines the ways in which African traditions and values can survive in an increasingly globalized world, and be strategically essential to further development. Resorting to the metaphors of "tree" for African traditional culture, and "fires" for aggressive foreign invaders, the author blames colonizers for "othering" and firing away African culture and age-long traditions, and looting its natural resources, regardless of the existing taboos. The rehabilitation of African traditional religion, care of Mother Nature, and inculturation are therefore the ways and means the author strongly puts forward in favor of a peaceful coexistence between the different religions in Burkina Faso.

a) Witchcraft in Burkinabe Literature in English: A Postcolonial Approach[1]

Introduction

Colonial officials did not believe in witchcraft. They considered it as a manifestation and tangible proof of the backwardness of the African continent, and of European intellectual, technological, and moral superiority over Africans (Vasconi 2017, p. 83). They saw it as a fear-instilling superstition. As Vasconi explains: "With bizarre beliefs and alleged abhorrent and awful practices, witchcraft provided the opportunity to confirm the European vision of Africans as primitive people dominated by superstition and fear of evil" (p. 83).

Africans, on the other hand, believe in witchcraft. In the prologue to the *Secrets of the Sorcerer* (2017), Bali Nebié says that one of the things African intellectuals have in common is the "belief in witchcraft" (p. 6). And unsurprisingly, the theme of witchcraft and sorcery abound in Burkinabe fictions written in English. For example, in his poem "Axaxagabazuehi the Greatest Witch of the Forest," Mamadou Kousse synthetises the "powers of the darkness, called witchcraft" (2012, p. 36). In *The Odds Are against Cycling* (2012), Noëlie Yaogo also expresses her convictions in witchcraft by mentioning witches among the exceptions of people who do not give her applause when she is on her bike (p. 11). As to Michel Tinguiri, in his novel *The Tribulations of a Sahelian Traveler* (2014), he has N'Djilékou, the main character, recall a story about the belief in witchcraft (pp. 45, 46). Likewise, Emmanuel Zoungrana, in *The Ace of Spades in Disarray* (2014), tells the story of an old lady, Lorane, who is a witch because, after saving a baby when executioners came to kidnap his parents, she later sacrificed it for personal objectives (p. 83).

Bali Nebié's novel shows the fraud involved in witchcraft and sorcery, while in Malidoma Patrice Somé's fictional autobiography, *Of Water and the Spirit* (1994), the African shaman has a different outlook on such supernatural things.

Chapter 4

Why so much concern for such a retrograde theme in an ever-modernised world? A probable hypothesis is that these writers are not satisfied with how this theme has so far been handled by foreign anthropologists (Somé 1994, p. 12) and want to voice their own views and convictions on witchcraft. In this regard, it is convenient to resort to a postcolonial approach in the examination of their works, as this criticism has as a subject matter of which the analysis is "literature produced by cultures that developed in response to colonial domination" (Tyson 1999, p. 365).

Postcolonial criticism draws attention to issues of cultural difference in literary texts, and so contributes "to further undermine the universalist claims once made on behalf of literature by liberal humanist critics" (Barry 2009, p. 185) based on a single supposedly universal standard, regardless of social, cultural, and regional differences. In fact, one of the characteristics of postcolonial criticism is the awareness of representations of the non-European – witchcraft in this case – as exotic or immoral 'other.' By using this theory, I intend to show that postcolonial Burkinabe writers, namely Bali Nebié and Malidoma Patrice Somé, recreate, in their fictions, their own perceptions of witchcraft, and want these to be considered worldwide. This theory will also help me to point out the description of African witchcraft that these writers offer from the inside, and also to lay stress on their triple cross-cultural identities (Burkinabe, French, and English), which are aspects of postcolonial criticism.

Of the different Burkinabe fictions written in English, Nebié's *Secrets of the Sorcerer* (2017), and Somé's *Of Water and the Spirit* (1994), and some of Koussé's poems, deal mainly with the theme of witchcraft in the domain of religion and ritual. The other works mention this theme sparsely. My analysis will be focused on these main works, and the others will be referred to whenever appropriate. In the analytical interpretation, I shall highlight three aspects. First, how Burkinabe postcolonial writers show the various operations involved in witchcraft. Second, how they describe African witchcraft as the opposite of Western or modern values. And finally, their opinions on it as fraud or reality.

Description of Witchcraft

Some of the methods used by sorcerers and fortune-tellers, as spelled out mainly in the *Secrets of the Sorcerer* (2017, pp. 13–16), include using mice, cowries, calabash, potion, and corpses. Sometimes the fortune-teller is referred to as the "man with the mice." He has a bag containing a mixture of sand and dirt. When somebody goes to consult him, he empties his bag on the floor and uses that person's finger to spread it out smoothly. Then both of them go out and shut the door to allow the mice to come and express themselves in the sand, and so help discern the concerns brought by the guest. After some time, both fortune-teller and guest open the door and enter the hut to verify the predictions of the magical mice through the "footprints" they left behind. The fortune-teller then deciphers the coded literature in footprints of the enigmatic and erudite mice to his illiterate guest.

Other fortune-tellers use cowries. They have a bag of cowries, and when a guest comes in to consult them, after listening to the person, the fortune-teller takes their cowries and throws them on the floor. Then they interpret the positions of the cowries and read the message to the guest. For example, tired of waiting for the fulfilment of the predictions of the mice, Gnama, the protagonist in the Nebié's novel, went to consult a witchdoctor who uses cowries. But after six months of no fulfilment of the expectations, he concluded that this fortune-teller was a fraud, and decided to look for another one (Nebié 2017, pp. 17–20).

Later on, as a sorcerer, Gnama himself was using a calabash. "Leaning over his calabash, Gnama was interpreting the vision being sent to him by a fluid" (Nebié 2017, p. 37). He balanced the calabash mystically several times, and then consulted it and translated the message to his guest.

In addition, Gnama also used the truth potion, usually for settling disputes unsatisfactorily resolved in the law courts. The technique involves placing a small calabash on the floor and inviting the plaintiffs to come forward and openly swear the following oath: "If I am guilty, let the fetish point me out. And if I deny my guilt, then let it put an end to my life!" (Nebié 2017, pp. 51–52). The priest, after performing some rites, and guided by his

Chapter 4

fetish, points out the culprit. If this one denies his guilt, then he is submitted to drinking the truth potion. After drinking it, the culprit enters into trance and admits he is guilty. The potion can lead him into a deep coma or to death.

Finally, there is the use of the corpse of the person whose death people want to inquire about the cause. In villages, every death is believed to have a mystical cause. Therefore, a sudden death needs explanation. The deceased's corpse is used to find out the culprit. "The corpse [is] tied to a special stretcher. Two people then [carry] the stretcher, and driven by the force of the spirit of the victim, they [point] out the killer" (Nebié 2017, p. 101).

Once the problem is identified through any of these methods– that is, once a culprit who has caused the death is designated– the witch or fortune-teller shows how to get rid of that person so that the guest can prosper. For, in addition to explaining the causes of some deaths and predicting one's future, witchcraft is resorted to for advancement in social life (particularly with people with huge ambitions), for protection, and for passing exams. It is a money-earning business for witches and sorcerers. In Nebié's novel, Claude offers Gnama, the sorcerer, five hundred thousand francs for promising to make him a Member of Parliament (MP) (Nebié 2017, p. 43).

It is also said that the sorcerer has power to watch people's academic careers (Nebié 2017, pp. 47, 48). Malidoma Patrice Somé, the author of *Water and the Spirit* (1994), says he owes the success of his academic career to the power of the talisman he received at the end of his initiation, and that it still continues to help him as a shaman "to speak in big assembly halls" (p. 5). He describes his talisman as "an oval-shaped pouch stuffed with a stone from the underworld and some other secret objects collected in the wild" (Somé 1994, p. 4). In Nebié's novel, the main character, Gnama, has been given, at his initiation, three talismans– "pouches made of white cotton cloth" (Nebié 2017, p. 167). One of them contains the seven cowries he gave for his initiation, a tuft of his wife Atia's hair, and her fingernails. It represents the two lives he sacrificed for his initiation. Another one contains small pieces of plant and animal organs. The third one contains a yellowish

55

powder that is poison. Gnama is instructed to use these talismans in the service of good or evil. It is, therefore, relevant to recall here Somé's assertion, talking about the talismans as dangerous powerful objects, that "depending on the actions of its bearer, such objects have the power to help, but also to hurt" (Somé 1994, p. 4). Gnama is warned that if ever the fraud in his practice is discovered, he has to take the poison to kill himself to avoid dishonor (Nebié 2017, p. 168).

Other talismans are used as charms to harm individuals, or to call mishaps upon them, or to brighten one's own future. In her novel, *The Odds Are Against Cycling* (2012), Noëlie Yaogo refers to such practices as "making douah." She tells the story of a red-veiled man advising a lady who fails to get a husband to "just make douah composed of a white cock, a red cloth, and a black hen; with four notes. Leave them all to an old man… And you'll be relieved" (Yaogo 2012, p. 138). In this way, she is going to get a husband mysteriously.

In the *Secrets of the Sorcerer*, Gnama follows similar advice unsuccessfully when desperately looking for a job in Abidjan (Nebié 2017, pp. 17–21). But when he becomes a sorcerer, he does not hesitate to use charms to fight against his guests' enemies. For example, he tries to frighten Robert, his guest Claude's rival, first by throwing a dead cat into his compound, then by placing a charm composed of the tail of an animal with black, white, and red ropes around it in front of his office for him to tread on. And finally, by putting a charm, *lambwa*, made with cowries stuck on it, on the body of a dead pup inside a circle surrounded by ashes inside his house in the village (Nebié 2017, p. 57). All these are meant to bring him bad omens. But as Robert does not believe in witchcraft, such things do not have effect on him.

Through these descriptions of the workings of witchcraft, these writers try to affirm and re-establish the reality of the phenomenon of witchcraft, which has been downplayed by foreign anthropologists (Go 2014, p. 15). They assert its existence both in the colonial past, as well as in the present day. They present it as part of Burkinabe culture – nay, African culture. They further highlight it as properly Burkinabe or African by drawing a

Chapter 4

parallelism and contrast to Western or modern values for a better understanding of it.

African Witchcraft as the Opposite of Western, or Modern, Values

In most Burkinabe fiction written in or translated into English, African witchcraft and the Western world are presented as antinomies, incompatible entities. In the *Secrets of the Sorcerer* (2017), Gnama the sorcerer says that "the only item made by the Nasara that he was obliged to accept, was the telephone" (Nebié 2017, p. 30). Gnama prefers, for example, sleeping in a traditional hut to a modern breeze-block house, and sleeping on the bare floor to using a bed, because these things connote the Nasara and his legacy. Interestingly, one of the characters in the same novel, Robert, who opposes Gnama's authority, is nicknamed "the Nasara, meaning the White Man" (Nebié 2017, p. 58) because he does not believe in witchcraft, which he actually calls "village stories." So witchcraft and the modern world are laid out in contrast as two worlds apart.

Witchcraft is also presented as being at the crossroad of antinomies, or as being the opposite of modern values. For example, witchcraft appears, in Somé and Nebié's descriptions of it, strongly associated with darkness, dirt, village, tradition, blind faith, and decadence, as opposed to light, cleanness, city, modernity, reason, and progress. Witchcraft is thus presented as going against the values of modernity, or the West.

Most Burkinabe fiction in English testifies that witchcraft goes hand-in-hand with darkness. Witchcraft operates well at night and in the bush. Such an atmosphere and scenery installs fear in people. One likely environment appears in N'Djilékou's account on belief in witchcraft, in Michel Tinguiri's *The Tribulations of a Sahelian Traveler* (2014):

> *It was said that the night is full of mysteries; that sacred trees moved and went to chat with their friends. Spirits wandered and played during the night. Stones, insects, everything spoke.... His ancestors used to say that when you violate Mother Nature's laws, the gods and spirits react in a*

harsh way.... *When asked why, the answer was always, "it's tradition, it's n'yé-yiranè," meaning that they 'were born and found it'* (pp. 45–46).

People believe that "at night, bad spirits roamed the country, and they were likely to harm night time party-goers" (Tinguiri 2014, p. 62). Witchcraft works in darkness. Hence, Kousse calls it the powers of darkness, and explains how it works in these lines:

> *Old am I, with wrinkled body; you see*
> *But pity, am the prettiest in the darkness.*
> *I have fried human heads*
> *And chewed children's bones.*
> *In the darkness, I perform wonders*
> *In the deep darkness, I control souls*
> *Am Axaxagabazuehi*
> *The greatest witch of the forest* (2012, p. 36).

The repetition of the word *darkness*, and the use of antinomies *wrinkled* and *pretty*, *odious activities* and *wonders*, powerfully conveys and lays emphasis on the deep obscurity in which witchcraft operates. The poet further says that Axaxagabazuehi has a pot of human blood in her kitchen, and at night invokes her forces in order to invisibly float in the air to capture any human soul to satisfy her desires.

In the *Secrets of the Sorcerer* (2014), Gnama, the main character, recounts how initiation into the Djadjo witchcraft requires the sacrifice of one's beloved person in order to acquire powers. At Gnama's initiation, Old San said to him: "The Djadjo demands the life of your wife and that of your child that she is carrying, as condition for your initiation!" (Nebié 2017, p. 117). He also said that at his own initiation, he had to sacrifice his first son (Nebié 2017, p. 137). Axaxagabazuehi, too, killed all her children to become famous (Kousse 2012, p. 37). Gnama submitted to this ritual also. Disguised as a man-lion, Gnama killed his pregnant beloved wife, Atia, at night and removed her liver and heart following the odious and ignominious rite of initiation. At the ritual meal, "the newly initiated member had the heart all to himself, and the liver was shared amongst the others.... They ate the flesh raw" (Nebié 2017, p. 133). These are works of darkness. Anybody that is able to do such ignominies for any purpose is then called a witch. It is the case of an old lady, Lorane, in *The Ace of Spades in Disarray* (2014), who is called a witch, because after saving a baby when executioners came to kidnap his parents, she later sacrifices it for personal objectives. Likewise, in *The Odds Are Against Cycling*, Noëlie Yaogo calls witches *excisors* (female-genital mutilators), as well as those who do not give her applause when she is on her bike (Yaogo 2012, p. 11). A witch is then synonymous to a bloody wrongdoer, a killer.

In the world of light and reason, such practices, namely of the kind described by Gnama, are nothing but manslaughter, cannibalism, and Satanism. It is no wonder witches and sorcerers are reluctant to enter the light, lest their activities be revealed and ended.

Anglophone Burkinabe writers' portrayal of witchcraft also links it to dirt, ugliness, and backwardness. For example, it is said in Nebié's novel that the old man, in charge of initiating people into witchcraft, "wore only a cache-sexe, a traditional G-string" (p. 98), and that "Gnama almost never took a bath because the spirits of the Djadjo required him not to. He was filthy and stank" (p. 29).

Nakedness is required for candidates going through initiation in Somé's fictional autobiography. The candidates have to take off their shirts and shorts, even Malidoma Patrice Somé himself. He sees nakedness as appropriate, being the "expression of one's relationship with the spirit of nature. To be naked is to be open-hearted" (Somé 1994, p. 193).

It follows that as there is hardly a place for such primitiveness in the modern world, it cannot be a commonplace practice in modern cities and towns. It is then understandable that witchcraft is usually seen by its unbelievers as "mere village stories" (Nebié 2017, p. 61), because it is practiced mainly in villages and bushes. Interestingly, Rouzgani, one of the old man's children, though familiar with the fetish of the Djadjo because he was born and bred in that village, says that once he "discovered the city, these village stories no longer interest [him]" (Nebié 2017, p. 82).

Witchcraft is mainly circumscribed to villages, bushes, and forests. Believers in it who are city dwellers must travel to villages to practice it. That's why on Fridays, the day of Djadjo, long convoys of public transport buses full of government officials, politicians, traders, and students arrive in Layou, looking for miraculous solutions to their problems (Nebié 2017, p. 27). Gnama was believed to be endowed with supernatural powers that enabled him to find solutions to life issues. Yet he could not find a solution to his own predicament when his fraudulent machinations were revealed in daylight.

Witchcraft as Fraud or Reality

The question of whether witchcraft is true or false divides the Anglophone Burkinabe writers under study. As if to mimic the colonizers' thoughts, some writers point to the fraudulent nature of witchcraft, while others show it as mere reality. But at this stage, it is relevant to distinguish between the existence of the phenomenon and its effectiveness. The descriptions of the macabre practices in the initiation into witchcraft, in all works under study, are alike and can be expressions of reality of the existence of witchcraft, because anything is possible with sinful human beings, even horrible things such as human sacrifice. Since witchcraft is characterized by secrecy, its members having pledged to commit suicide to protect it if need be, it is difficult to know it from inside out. Even people who, like Somé Malidoma Patrice, say they experience it, refuse to reveal its secrets. Therefore, the effectiveness of the powers involved in witchcraft is a matter of debate in the works under study.

Secrecy surrounds witchcraft in both Nebié's and Somé's works. In Nebié's novel, Tagadougou, the place where the initiation into witchcraft or sorcery operates, is insulated from foreign nations, like the village of Ilunjinle in Soyinka's *Lion and the Jewel* (1962). Foreign religions failed to settle down there. It is said that a Christian, whom the white man established there by force, had been chased away by the inhabitants and had to flee the village to save his life. As a result, there is "neither chapel nor mosque in Tagadougou" (Nebié 2017, p. 101). Initiatives undertaken by members of foreign religious groups to settle down

Chapter 4

in Tagadougou met a stony wall in the laws of the community, which require that "any foreigner wishing to settle down in the community must be sponsored by an indigene. None ever got a sponsor" (Nebié 2017, p. 101). Foreigners and their religions are thus feared because they can destroy witchcraft by revealing its fraudulent nature. A glaring example is the victory of the colonizers against the native witches and sorcerers, thus showing that the so-called witches' "powers of invulnerability in war, supposedly untouchable by gunshot and capable of making [themselves] invisible to the eyes of the enemy," were nothing but illusions, a pure scam (Nebié 2017, p. 157). Learning from that, it is better to avoid any other warfare of that kind by keeping foreigners away. Hence, in Gnama's village, and Tagadougou alike, the customary authorities do not welcome foreign religions (Nebié 2017, p. 160).

A similar secrecy and insulation from the Western, or modern, world surrounds the traditional initiation of the Dagara people, as narrated by Malidoma Patrice Somé in *Of Water and the Spirit* (1994). Talking about his first night at the initiation camp, he confides that "the council of initiation is very secretive" (Somé 1994, p. 192). This secrecy finds an echo in the *Secrets of the Sorcerer,* where the old man in charge of Gnama's initiation, Old San, teaches him that "every human organisation must have a secret nucleus of leaders," that "every community [is] led by secret societies called by different names" (Nebié 2017, p. 138). Somé's Dagara society, and the society of men-lions in Tagadougou, are all but different names of the same secret societies. It is no wonder that, like Somé refuses to reveal the secrets of the initiation, Gnama finds himself, at the end of the novel, "unable to break the fundamental law of the brotherhood of the men-lions concerning the secret of their existence" (Nebié 2017, p. 185).

Besides, Somé's experience prior to his initiation is much like Gnama's. He writes, "That night, I could not sleep. Each time I closed my eyes, I saw ghosts all over the place. I lived the whole night in the country of ghosts" (Somé 1994, p. 192). Likewise, Gnama lay down but stayed awake all night during his initiation process (Nebié 2017, p. 120). The description of the grotto and the "narrow alley that had the shape of the letter Z" that led to "a clearing of about 10 square metres, lit by two torches" (Nebié 2017, p. 127) is also closely similar to Somé's narration of his journey into the Underworld in Chapter 23, and his descriptions of the Portal, the Light Hole, and the Pool from Chapters 19 to 21.

In addition, both Gnama and Somé try to convince their adherents, or readership, of the truth of their practice. The narrator unveils Gnama's practice as fraud, and so does an in-depth analysis of Somé's work. In fact, Somé's narrative, though it is catalogued as a biography in the Library of Congress, is more fiction than an autobiography. My personal investigations reveal that Jesuits never ran a seminary in Burkina Faso, and the seminary he actually attended is a Diocesan seminary run by mostly local Diocesan priests. His alleged kidnapping at the age of four is hardly believable. As the Kirkus review of the book reveals, there is no evidence that Somé has really lived the harsh village life that he praises, nor does he "address the crucial question of whether and how traditional ways can flourish in anything but the tribal context" ("Of Water and the Spirit: Kirkus Review" 2017). Somé's alleged biography rather shows him to be more of a foreigner than a native, because in his narrative, he says that he remembers very little of his first four years of his life in his home village. It is only during the brief time of his initiation that he was in real contact with the Dagara culture. Yet he had no knowledge of the Dagara language to talk with his family members. Because of the language impediment, he could not even understand the initiation. So what he describes is rather his own coinage based on the little he understood of the initiation, and so holds no true value. Initiation in the Dagara tribe is not shamanism. It involves making boys know their roles as men within the tribe. It does not turn boys into ceremonial leaders. These reasons reveal a fraud that Somé, the first-person narrator, like Gnama in Nebié's novel, claims to be the truth.

Another similarity lies in the fact that the two characters from both works are being called "strangers" by the people whose group they want to enter through initiation. Maawa, one of Gnama's wives, always calls him "stranger." Alienated from the culture, Gnama asks her why she calls him "stranger" instead of using his

Chapter 4

first name. She then explains that she calls him that because he comes from another village. Otherwise, traditionally speaking, he would have been called "friend of my brother" (Nébié 2017, p. 106). Patrice Somé, too, is called "Malidoma," roughly meaning, "Be friends with the stranger/enemy" (Somé 1994, p. 1). Contrary to Somé's explanation, this name actually means his exclusion from the Dagara community. How can a friend of one's enemy be a friend? By giving this name to Somé, the elders cautiously and politely keep him away, maintaining him at the margins of their society. He then tries to give a positive interpretation of the name in a way that suits him. He thus makes the most of the marginal position in which the Dagara elders put him by interpreting their decision as a mission to constitute himself into a bridge with other societies. Both Gnama and the first-person narrator, Malidoma Patrice Somé, are hybrid men, alienated from the communities they want to be initiated into.

These similarities between the two books lead to the conclusion that their authors try to describe witchcraft and related practices that are alien to the Western, or modern, world. Yet they look at witchcraft from different perspectives, though both received modern education. Bali Nébié, as a modern intellectual, dismisses the efficiency of the mystical powers attributed to witchcraft, and denounces it as fraud. Whereas Somé, who is a shaman, shares his elders' conviction that the "West is as endangered as the indigenous cultures it has decimated in the name of colonialism" (p. 1), and that the duty is his, as "a man of two worlds, trying to be at home in both of them" (p. 3), to save the West by serving as a bridge that strikes some kind of balance. He is trying to show the importance of what "territorial colonialism," then "neo-colonialism," (pp. 4, 5) tried to suppress. He is aware of European representations of his Dagara initiation as an exotic or immoral "other," and so wants to rehabilitate it by presenting it in his own way, conscious himself of his own identity as hybrid.

If the practices involved in witchcraft, and described by these writers, hold the truth as to the reality of the powers of witchcraft, it is a matter of debate. Somé tries to convince anybody of its truth, while the whole novel of Nebié is built to present it as a fraud.

In Nebié's novel, all the characters, except two, do not believe in witchcraft. Those two are Robert and Jo-the-Lefty, or Jo-the-Expeditious. Robert is nicknamed the "Nasara" – that is, the white man – because he behaves and believes like white people. Unlike his wife, he does not believe in witchcraft (Nebié 2017, p. 58). As for Jo-the-Lefty, son of a commander in Toum, he is a gendarme who grew up in Layou. He disbelieves such stories, considering charlatans and other fetish priests as simply criminal disguised swindlers. "He scoffed at his colleagues who, nearly all, wore black rings on their fingers that they believed protected them against bullets and other evil spells" (Nebié 2017, p. 176). At the end of the novel, the combination of Robert and Jo's actions brings witchcraft in Layou to a sudden and unexpected deadly end with the arrest and trial of Gnama and his associates, and their confession that "the Djadjo was nothing but deceit" (Nebié 2017, p. 184). Yet they did not break the secret of the existence of their society, which is already made manifest to the reader through the narration.

The narrator in Nebié's novel highlights the paradoxical attitude of some characters, namely those who are educated and yet still believe in what is irrational and unreasonable. Claude, for example, is a trained computer engineer. The narrator says that "even the most ardent believers in superstition wondered how [Claude] was able to combine…the rational par excellence with the irrational" (Nebié 2017, p. 33). Claude himself says that he is a white man when he is on a computer, but becomes an African again once out of his administrative office (Nebié 2017, p. 33, 34). So witchcraft is looked at from the point of view of Africans who now share foreign ideas. For Gnama, the uneducated sorcerer, receiving the white man's education goes against believing in witchcraft. The narrator lets the reader know Gnama's inner thoughts, through an interior monologue, after receiving money from Claude, a highly educated man:

> *How can educated people, people who went to school for about twenty years, people who have travelled, even to the country of the Nasara, how can they allow themselves to be*

Chapter 4

manipulated by a person like me who have never been to school? They believe all the nonsense that I tell them. How strange this life!... I really do wonder what they teach them for so many years in the Nasara's school, yet they want us to believe the Nasara is a super wizard. (Nebié 2017, p. 55, 56)

Gnama simply bemoans African elites' naivety. He also sees modern technology as another kind of witchcraft which was believed to be superior.

This syncretism of beliefs also points to African people's hybrid identity. A possible motivation behind it is fear exerted by witches upon individuals, or by one's family members who strongly believe in it. Gnama, in Nebié's novel, came to learn from his experience that sorcerers endowed with powers to fly, or to metamorphose into a human being or tree, is nothing but "pure fiction aimed at conditioning the people" (p. 138), keeping them in a state of fear. It means that sorcery exists, but the mystical powers given to it are subject to debates. Gnama shows that witches and spirits that haunt villagers at night are but men in disguise. One has to be strong enough, like Robert, to go against the popular flow and his own family's pressure. Somé and Koussé, on the other hand, show that witchcraft is endowed with true mystical powers.

Another motivation that can explain this hybridity is the realization that moral standards in the modern world are in decadence. It is specifically the case of Malidoma Patrice Somé, whose book *Of Water and Spirit* is synthetically "the story of [his] initiation into two different and highly contradictory cultures" (Somé 1994, p. 2). He is completely hybrid. His initiation into the African tradition comes second. He undertook this additional initiation when he realized that a looming crisis awaits Western culture. He writes:

At this time in history, Western civilization is suffering from a great sickness of the soul. The West's progressive turning away from functioning spiritual values; its total disregard for the environment and the protection of natural resources; the violence of inner cities with their problems of poverty, drugs, and crime; ...and growing intolerance toward people of colour and the values of other cultures – all of these trends, if unchecked, will eventually bring about a terrible self-destruction (p. 1).

The instability of Western culture and probable future chaos, with the overwhelming homosexual agenda vehemently criticized by Africans, leads Somé to revisit and reconsider his ancestral tradition, whose moral standards have so far remained healthy and sound, especially when viewed from inside. He is in the West to tell them about his people, and in this way help them avoid self-destruction. He decides to tell the story himself because he regrets that, so far, such stories have been told by ethnographers, sociologists, and foreign anthropologists or native anthropologists who have been "foreignized" (Somé 1994, p. 12). He wants to offer an authentic and genuine account of Dagara tradition to the reader.

One assumes from this comment, that he does not consider himself a "foreignized" native writer, but he offers no arguments why he is not one. Having been initiated first in the white man's culture through schooling, then later living and working in the West, he is at least a "been-to," or to use Adichie's concept, an "Americanah" (Kaboré 2016, p. 13) – a twice "foreignized" native Burkinabe English writer. He is twice alienated because he was first acquainted with the French culture before embracing the English world order, even though his initiation into his native Dagara tradition happens in-between the two foreign ones. Yet he starts writing his account after completing all three initiations, which makes his narrative far removed from reality than that of a simple "foreignized" native anthropologist.

Conclusion

Though a postcolonial approach is used in an attempt to obtain a unique and authentic Burkinabe description of witchcraft that differ from colonial ones, a final analysis shows that it is difficult to get to the gist of the phenomenon of witchcraft fundamentally. First, because of the hybridity of the authors who describe it. The postcolonial writers who try to give an authentic description of it, namely Somé, Tinguiri, Koussé, Yaogo, and Nebié, are hybrid and would be considered by witches and sorcerers and their adherents,

Chapter 4

as "foreignized" people who are taken by the white man's cause and manipulated by him to perpetuate his colonial criticism, because they have been educated into the white man's system. Yet if this allegation were true, such criticism would still remain relevant to our debate because it is part of what postcolonial criticism calls "mimicry," – that is, "the always slightly alien and distorted way in which the colonized, either out of choice or under duress, will repeat the colonizer's ways and discourse" (Bertens 2014, p. 182). This mimicry constitutes a mirror that slightly but effectively distorts the colonizer's image and identity when he sees himself in this mirror (Bertens 2014, p. 182), and so plays an important role in the colonized people's fight against the colonizer in an attempt to free themselves.

Second, another difficulty pertains to the secret nature of the phenomenon. The nature of witchcraft is to remain unknown to the uninitiated. The initiated have to keep secret what they have received for fear of being killed by their peers. Yet the different descriptions of the gruesome aspects involved in its initiation process coalesce to show it as another version of Satanism, which also feeds on evil and is well-known in Western history.

Works Cited List

Barry, P. *Beginning Theory: An Introduction to Literary and Cultural Theory*. Manchester: Manchester University Press, 2009.

Bertens, H. *Literary Theory: The Basics*. Third edition. London and New York: Routledge, 2014.

Go, I. *Poétique et Esthétique Magiques*. Ouagadougou: Harmattan Burkina, 2014.

Kaboré, A. "Migration in African Literature: A Case Study of Adichie's Works." *Revue du CAMES: Littérature, langue et linguistique*, no. 4 (2016), pp. 1–17.

Kousse, M. *Reap What You Sow and 28 poems*. Ouagadougou: IPRESS Imprimérie, 2012.

Nebié, B. *Secrets of the Sorcerer*. Translated by Njoaguani, Francis

Chuks. Ouagadougou: Editions Poun-yaali, 2017.

Of Water and the Spirit: Kirkus Review. September 3, 2017. https://www.kirkusreviews.com/book-reviews/malidoma-patrice-some/of-water-and-the-spirit/.

Somé, M. P. *Of Water and the Spirit: Ritual, Magic, and Initiation in the Life of an African Shaman.* New York: Penguin Books, 1994.

Tinguiri, M. *The Tribulations of a Sahelian Traveler.* USA: Self-published, 2014.

Tyson, L. *Critical Theory Today: A User-Friendly Guide.* New York and London: Garland, 1999.

Vasconi, E. "Medecine and British Colonial Rule: Anthropological Analysis of Colonial Documents in the Gold Coast." Mariano Pavanello, editor. *Perspectives on African Witchcraft.* pp. 81–103. Oxon: Routledge, 2017.

Yaogo, N. *The Odds are against Cycling.* Pittsburgh, PA: Dorrance Publishing, 2012.

Zoungrana, E. *The Ace of Spades in Disarray.* Translated by Bonkoungou P.G. and Zaidi, S. Paris: EDILIVRE, 2014.

Chapter 4

b) Cycling and Woman's Emancipation[2]

Introduction

In Pierre-Claver Ilboudo's novel of desperation, *Adama* (2017), now translated from French into English, the fall of the main character, Adama, from the top of the middle class down to the bottom of the lower class, is visually conveyed through the different means of transportation he successively uses in his life. First, a motorbike. Then a loaned bicycle. And finally, his feet. The narrator presents him reduced to the level of women, who, in this novel, have nothing but their feet as means of transport. Hence, they mainly stay at home. Thus, transportation informs us about social class. It also shows the possession of some means of transportation as incentive to development, helping one ascend the social strata. The two wheels, for example, helped Adama rise from rags to riches before falling down.

Women's underprivileged fate in this novel is linked to their lack of motorbikes or bicycles. There is hope, in this predominantly male-focused narrative, that the possession of such a vehicle could empower housebound women to development. This is what Noëlie Yaogo also contends in her novel of an evocative title, *The Odds Are Against Cycling* (2012), as if responding to Ilboudo's work. She invites women to cycle against the odds, symbolizing the patriarchal tradition, which used to present it as a taboo.

She herself used to cycle, and fictionalized her experience into her novel. In this fiction, she uses cycling as a metaphor for women's emancipation. Like her, many Burkinabe girls and women stop being housebound and use bicycles as means for development. Does this account for the fact that the participation of Sub-Saharan women in the active population of their countries is globally higher than in other parts of the world (Otokoré and Kamelgarn 2016)? If so, can we argue that women's plight is linked to the means of transportation they use under the weight of patriarchal tradition, as presented in Ilboudo's novel, so much so that cycling appears as an incentive to women's development, as Yaogo highlights in her novel?

Introduction to Burkinabe Literature in English

Using a feminist approach, and through a critical analysis of female characters in the two novels, this paper intends to show that women's high or low level of emancipation can be seen in the means of transportation they use, especially bicycles. In other words, the objective is to highlight the importance of cycling as a tool for women's emancipation, and to show to what extent feminism in Burkina Faso can be equated with Burkinabe women's cycling activities. I shall start by giving facts and figures about cycling in Burkina Faso, before analyzing the two kinds of feminism found in the two novels, interpreted through the means of transportation women use in each.

Facts and Figures of Cycling in Burkina Faso

A colleague lecturer in sociology at the University Abdou Moumini in Niger, where bike availability in households is around 20 percent (see map in appendix), was once positively delighted in Ouagadougou at the sight of so many female students using bicycles to go to University Ouaga 1 Professor Joseph Ki-Zerbo, because at his university in Niger, girls' parents used to drive them to their place of education, or they would use public buses. He could not help praising Burkinabe girls for biking, thus enduring hardship. Such facts may explain Safia Otokoré and Daniel Kamelgarn's assertion, talking about women's emancipation, that the participation of women in the active population of Sub-Saharan Africa is higher than in other parts of the world (Otokoré and Kamelgarn 2016).

In fact, in Burkina Faso, the homeland of bicycles in Africa, the bicycle has played an important role in the population's development. It gradually replaced horses and donkeys and became part and parcel of Burkinabe culture. Burkina Faso registration statistics show that two wheels outnumber cars by 10 percent annually (Coulibaly 2016). By 2016, there was an estimation of less than 300,000 four-wheel vehicles, compared to 1.5 million two-wheels (Coulibaly 2016), with bicycles outnumbering mopeds.

One foreign observer, namely the Organization Vélos pour le Faso, published on its website, its astonishment at the realization

Chapter 4

that the bicycle is the most used means of transport in Burkina Faso. In fact, statistics show that despite the dire rivalry with mopeds, the bicycle is by far the most used method of transportation. Pupils and students use it to travel to school. Men and women traders employ it for carrying goods to the marketplace. Farmers use it to ride to their farms, to carry wood and water.

The INSD statistics show that in 2003, 79.7 percent of households owned a bicycle, 23.0 percent used mopeds, and 2.3 percent possessed cars. Two years later, the number of household bicycle owners increased to 82.4 percent, before falling down to 82 percent in 2007. In the same periods, the percentage of mopeds and cars owners in the country was 30.0 percent and 3.1 percent in 2005, then 32.0 percent and 2.8 percent in 2007 (INSD 2016, 58). Practically every household owns at least one bicycle – it is no wonder that the nation is nicknamed "capitale des deux roues" (country of the two wheels).

The immense percentage of bicycles in the country is such that any Burkina Faso visitor quickly notices it on arrival. It inspires singers and fiction writers thematically. In the near past, the first thing Burkinabe migrants to Ivory Coast did when they came back home to Burkina was to buy a brand-new bicycle. Bride and bridegroom even went to their church wedding on bicycle.

In the Burkinabe writer Michel Tinguiri's début novel, *The Tribulations of a Sahelian Traveler* (2014), the bicycle is presented as a sign of prosperity in rural areas through the example of the orphan Gontan buying two bicycles – one for his stepfather, and one for himself (145) – in order to show off his new social status, and to use this means of transportation for his job, and thus become richer.

Furthermore, a paper based on surveys from 150 countries, between 1989 and 2012, corroborates the above Burkinabe State statistics on the prevalence of bicycles in the country. It reveals that four out of ten households on the planet own a bike – that is around 42 percent of households (Oke 2015). The researchers further state that bicycle ownership is most common in developed countries such as Denmark and the Netherlands, where around four-fifths of households have at least one bike. Yet they underline that in

West, Central, and North African countries specifically, bicycles are more uncommon, with less than a fifth of households owning one. But most interestingly, the study reveals the astonishing truth that a West-African country, Burkina Faso, is the only non-European country in the top tier, with 84 percent of households owning a bicycle in 2010. According to lead author of this study, Jimi Oke, an American civil engineer, this is due to the country's investment in cycling infrastructure, such as separated bike lanes, road lighting for cyclists at intersections, and a "positive attitude" toward cycling among the population.

It is interesting to investigate the extent to which this "positive attitude" regarding cycling influences women's emancipation in the country. This paper focuses on the positive attitude of cycling by examining the fictional representation of the phenomenon in two novels by two Burkinabe writers Pierre-Claver Ilboudo and Noëlie Yaogo.

Housebound Feminism in *Adama*

The novel *Adama* (2017) tells the story of the main character, who gives his name to the title. Fired from his job as an accounts clerk at a small company, Adama uses his motorbike to roam about, looking for jobs. He tries his hand at many jobs, including helping a politician, Moumouni, for an election campaign, but is not rewarded at the end, as promised. As his financial situation worsens, Adama sells his motorbike at the buyer's price. Finally, employed as a shop attendant, he benefits from his boss's bicycle during weekdays, but not on weekends. Unfortunately, the novel ends as it began – that is, with the sad news that this bicycle has been stolen: "The bike he had parked ten minutes ago in front of the workshop had disappeared. When he realized that the bicycle and the clothing material were gone, he really felt lost" (Ilboudo p. 5). Adama is now reduced to walking, as is his expectant wife, and all women in this novel.

Women are indeed presented in *Adama* as not owning a bike, entirely dependent on their husbands for livelihood, and seeing marriage as an achievement. They are described through the lenses of patriarchal tradition, which deems female bike-riding

Chapter 4

indecent. They appear in the whole novel as stock characters, living under men's shadows. Women are housebound, and as in patriarchal societies, the woman is expected to "be a 'traditional' mother and stay home" (Adichie, *Dear Ijeawele* p. 8). They do household chores such as cooking, cleaning the house, and taking care of children.

The Nigerian feminist Chimamanda Ngozi Adichie fights against such "genderization" of some jobs because "women are [not] born with a cooking gene" (*We Should*, p. 35), and rather invites women to take advantage of the same opportunities men have.

In the whole novel of *Adama*, only four characters out of fifteen are women, of which only one is named, the other being referred to as X's wife. Hence, woman's existence is strongly dependent on man. Without man she is almost nothing. For instance, describing Nobila's compound, the narrator mentions his two wives as if they were his property, without naming them, and informs the reader that they live in a far corner of the compound, while their ten children play loudly outside (Ilboudo 33). Likewise, the wife of Moumouni (the teacher and politician who used Adama for his political campaign) features as an appendix or a decorative addendum. She is not even named. Yet one's name is important for one's existence. She is first mentioned during a political meeting, where the narrator makes her presence felt, describing her busy serving drinks to her husband's party members (Ilboudo 95). A second time, during the announcement of the poll results, the narrator refers to her again as "the teacher's wife," who in vain talked of supper to people engrossed in political matters (Ilboudo 100). Thus, the focus is on men rather than on women.

In fact, the first five chapters of the novel are only about the male main character, Adama. Talking about his family, the narrator underlines that, after being a bachelor, "he had got himself a wife, and the wife had given him two children" (22). The man is thus getting a wife, as he gets property or a tool, whose role partly consists to beget children, not for herself, but for the man. Woman is, therefore, square-boxed by her husband, children, and the four walls of the house, being defined in reference to them. Only in

Chapter 6 does the narrator mention the name of Adama's wife, Azara, describing her unsurprisingly as housebound, "sitting on a mat in the sitting-room, their last-born sleeping next to her" (Ilboudo 24). She is said to be a tall woman who has grown plump. She used to help her mother sell vegetables. Her activities, then and now, are briefly presented in the following terms:

> *Azara went long distances on foot every day to buy wholesale at the municipal garden and from various gardeners. Adama bought fruit and vegetables that she retailed. Now, she had less work to do. She cooked, knitted, took care of the children and visited a neighbouring house to gossip with the wife of a bicycle mechanic* (Ilboudo 27).

There is a contrast between the activities Azara used to do prior to her marriage, and those she did after it. She stopped working to earn her living after her marriage, thus following the patriarchal conception that in families, the husband is the provider, and that "motherhood and work are mutually exclusive" (Adichie, *Dear Ijeawele* p. 9). Azara is confined to household activities, which require no means of transport. She is then a pedestrian. Tired from walking long distances, she stays at home while her husband uses his motorbike to go anywhere he wants and to work for the upkeep of his family. He used to have an old Belfo bicycle which helped him work hard to afford his new means of transportation, a sign of social advancement.

Throughout the novel, the author uses the different means of transportation – bicycle, motorbike, and car – to classify people. At the bottom of the ladder are the cyclists, followed by those riding motorbikes, and crowned by the rich people who can afford cars. Adama is in the middle class, as he owns a motorbike – "the symbol of his belonging to a certain class," as he proudly acknowledges (Ilboudo 41). The narrator's own experience also leads him to make the following observation of a social phenomenon, which testifies to social stratification from one's means of transportation, including the use of mere feet:

> *In today's society, you are classified according to your means of transport. Pedestrians do not count. You therefore have at the bottom of the ladder, those who pedal. In the intermediate*

Chapter 4

rung are those with motorbikes. And at the top, those who parade in cars. Adama had fought hard to climb from the bottom of the ladder to the intermediate category (Ilboudo 41).

Following this classification, women are not even at the bottom, but rather underground. They simply "do not count," as they are pedestrians. A case in point is that of Azara, who used to go long distances every day on foot to buy groceries. Strangely enough, her husband, who is in the middle class like the two merchants Salim and Nobila, does not share his means of transportation with her, nor does he buy her a bicycle, which would have contributed to move her at least to the bottom class. One reason may be that the old West African patriarchal prohibitions of women from climbing trees (Oneyoka, p. 94) was extended to mounting bikes.

Even though Azara insisted that he buy her a knitting machine so that she could work from home, and so "contribute more meaningfully in catering for [their] needs" (Ilboudo 24), he did not listen to her. The phrase, "more meaningfully," means that housebound wives contribute meaningfully to the upkeep of their families. They live a specific type of feminism. Yet Adama does not give heed to that feminist suggestion, and goes on trying to take care of his family alone, following the patriarchal tradition of man as provider for his wife and children.

However, even though he successfully manages to hold on to his motorbike when he is penniless, refusing to fall down from the social ladder, he eventually has to sell it at a cheap price to take care of his mother-in-law, his two children, and expecting wife. He is thus shamefully reduced to the state of those who do not count, walking to do precarious jobs, before finally getting his boss's bicycle for use during weekdays only.

Moumouni the politician, on the other hand, goes from rags to riches. The visual portrayal, toward the end of the novel, of the destitute Adama leaving his motorbike to run to the car transporting the MP Moumouni (Ilboudo 107), well conveys the dichotomy between Moumouni's quick ascension to the top of the ladder without resorting to hard work – which the use of the bicycle symbolizes – and Adama's descent into the hell bottom.

Adama falls because he sold his breadwinning two wheels, and also because Moumouni keeps postponing the fulfillment of his political promises to Adama, who used all he has earned through hard work to help Moumouni become a car owner.

Adama's failure to successfully run his family and business without his wife's help shows the limits of housebound feminism, where most often women's contribution is reduced to begetting children and taking care of the family. The revelation of shortcomings of this type of feminism obviously calls for another one.

Adama finally realizes that he did a mistake by not listening to his wife. At the end of the novel, in his dire poverty and misery, having become a pedestrian, he expects anything from his wife except giving him children, as this dialogue between husband and wife reveals:

> *There was silence. Adama wondered whether his wife or somebody in the neighbourhood saw him loitering over there in the fields. Finally, she said:*
>
> *"I hope that your new job will be well paid, because I am expecting."*
>
> *Adama's heart skipped a beat.*
>
> *"You are expecting what?" asked Adama, flabbergasted.*
>
> *"A child, of course! What else do you want me to be expecting?" asked Azara.*
>
> *"Oh yes, okay," Adama quickly said, as he painfully swallowed his saliva.* (Ilboudo 130)

In his difficult moments, Adama, who is reduced to doing the mean job of selling unsurveyed land, and whose last-born child is only a year old, is expecting anything from his wife but a pregnancy. Yet his wife's calm and worriless reply to his "expecting what?" comment, shows that he forgot that he has assigned her the role of the ever-expectant mother. His wife's answer and question remind him of this painful reality.

The following day, he started having a headache just thinking

Chapter 4

over this puzzle. He stops believing the tradition that teaches that any child is invariably God-given and should be welcomed with gratitude. Rather, he considers this pregnancy as a misfortune similar to his previous misfortunes, including the loss of his means of transportation. From this lesson of life, one may think that in the future, Adama would encourage his wife toward emancipation by buying her a sewing machine or a bicycle as a tool for a more meaningful contribution toward catering to their family needs.

Thus, a critical analysis of *Adama* from a feminist perspective reveals that affording means of transportation for women, and removing the patriarchal obstacles out of their way, can help women work alongside their male counterparts, for the welfare of families and the development of nations. It is at this stage where Ilboudo's novel *Adama* shows the limits and weaknesses of patriarchal tradition, that Yaogo's novel comes to the rescue with its urge for women to cycle hard against patriarchal odds in order to reach a full-fledged emancipation.

Emancipation through Cycling

Patriarchy did not always favor the emancipation of women, with the prescription of gender roles. The feminist critic Adichie complains that in childhood, "baby girls are given less room and more rules, and baby boys more room and fewer rules" (*Dear Ijeawele*, p. 19). Among the many rules prescribed to females is the interdiction of climbing trees and riding donkeys and horses in the past, and recently, bicycles. Before her, the feminist Simone de Beauvoir, explained, in her phenomenology of the body, that in childhood, the young girl's body is experienced in a different way from that of the young boy. He is encouraged to climb trees and play rough games. She is encouraged to treat her whole person as a doll, "a passive object…an inert given object" (306), and learns the need to please others. Women thus live their bodies as objects for other people's gaze.

Historians testify that, in the past, women cyclists, when they started riding, caused much outrage and consternation to other men and women (Vivanco, p. 32–34). Female cycling was seen as immoral, with the particular concern that the act of straddling the bicycle might cause sexual arousal, and clothing adopted for cycling was viewed as immodest and unfeminine (Vivanco, p. 32–34). So cycling was perceived at the beginning, as unseemly for women. One can then understand that cycling is, for women, an enterprise that involves going against the odds on the road of emancipation.

Indeed, throughout world history, there has been a cause-and-effect relationship between women's cycling and feminism. Writing about the contribution of cycling to women's emancipation in Yemen, Jessica Abrahams situates the appearance of the bicycle in the first half of the nineteenth century, and its development into modern form, which happened together with the first wave of feminism, by the 1880s. The bicycle helped housebound women, like the ones in *Adama*, escape from the house. From her own experience as a cyclist, Jessica Abrahams further shows that cycling assists her growth as a feminist, helping her find freedom from the snares of patriarchy.

The American social reformer and women's rights activist, Susan Brownell Anthony (1820–1906), who played a key role in the women's suffrage movement, stated in 1896, that the bicycle has contributed more toward women's emancipation than anything else in the world (Vivanco, p. 32–34). Elizabeth Cady Stanton (1815–1902), an American suffragist, social activist, and leading figure of the early Women's Rights Movement, also wrote that the bicycle was a tool which gave courage to women to take on roles previously reserved to men in society (Vivanco, p. 32–34). Yaogo also believes that the bicycle is able to create such liberation for Burkinabe women, considering the place it holds in Burkinabe culture.

In the Moore language in Burkina Faso, *weefo* means *bicycle* and *horse*. To differentiate, one would have to use a determiner by adding the material with which it is made. For example, *iron*, hence *kut-weefo* for *bicycle*. Or add the maker or owner – *nasaar weefo* or *wed-moaaga*, literally meaning *bicycle of the white man,* or *bicycle of the Moaaga*.

Traditionally, in Burkina Faso, rarely does a woman ride a horse or donkey by herself. She usually sits on the back of the animal, with her legs on the same side, and a man guides the animal and looks after her as a child, as in the illustrations below, drawn by Kabré Eric.

Similarly, with the arrival of the "iron" horse, a transposition is made: the man, always in front, rides the bicycle, and the woman sits on the luggage rack, her legs on the same side, as in Kabré Eric's drawing above. In both ways of transport, the man does the hard job, providing all comfort to the woman, who is treated childlike. The situation is similar to that of Adama providing alone for his family, in Ilboudo's novel.

Yet people's attitudes toward cycling have evolved through the years. As Noëlie Yaogo observes in her novel, women in patriarchal societies in the past were "wrongly not allowed to cycle because of the so-called frailness of their female constitution" (Yaogo, p. 11). She does not believe in this reason, arguing that a compared examination of both men and women would reveal unbelievable results. Yet she shares her experience as to how parts of the woman's physical constitution, namely her sexual organs, including the breasts, can be uncomfortable while cycling when they are not well-taken-care of. In other words, women have to specially dress their bodices in order to cycle at ease. For example, they should secure their breasts by any means, for a better cycling performance. Talking from her experience as a woman cyclist, Yaogo says that her "breasts are often annoying because they are either hanging on or loading [her] down. But for the cycling, [she] succeeds in adapting them within the brassiere" (Yaogo, p. 25).

Introduction to Burkinabe Literature in English

Considerations related to sexual organs explain and help one understand the traditional taboos against women's cycling in patriarchal societies. For example, women have to stretch their legs wide to ride bikes, thus running the risk of exposing their private parts to the public (even if covered by underwear), which would be shameful.

Shame is extremely important in Moaaga tradition, so much so that some people prefer committing suicide to facing shame (Badini, p. 114). One should hide one's private parts to avoid being ashamed. That is why in this tradition, as well as in other African traditions (Fondation Reine Hangbe), women are supposed to keep their legs together while sitting on the floor (as in the illustration above), on horseback, or being carried on bicycle. While men, as they wear trousers, may cross their legs and open their thighs when sitting on the floor for eating (as in the illustration above). This woman's position is supposed to hide her *yandé*, or shame, her nudity (Badini, p. 144). or to help her avoid being offensive to the beholder (Oneyocha, p. 94). If a woman's genitals are seen, even if covered by underwear, this is shameful. Therefore, in the different body positions in her everyday life, a woman should mind her genitals, lest they be exposed to onlookers, thus debasing herself.

In other cultures, especially in Yemen, this woman's sitting position is meant to protect her vagina from injury, the act of straddling the bicycle being perceived as likely to cause sexual arousal through pedaling (Jessica Abrahams). But with time, all these apprehensions proved unfounded. "The bike hurried

Chapter 4

disillusionment and other awakenings," (Yaogo, p. 11) enabling people to grow in wisdom.

In her novel, Noëlie Yaogo shows, from her experience, how cycling can bring about a revolution in women's lives. She used to cycle in Ouagadougou, the capital of the two wheels, where "the streets are always jammed with people, lined up on both sides…full of public bicycle trailers and other traffic are bothering cyclists" (Yaogo, p. 69). She extols cycling, interjecting, "Hallowed be cycling! Hallowed be lady-cyclers" (Yaogo, p. 96). She underlines two incentives in favor of cycling. One is that "bicycles are environmentally friendly" (Yaogo, p. 11). The other is related to economy and finances. Yaogo strongly argues that "the bicycle is a marvel of fuel efficiency…. Traveling by bicycle is indeed far more economical than traveling by horse, motorcycle, or car, and even more economical than walking or running" (11), in terms of energy used in comparison to distance covered.

The importance of cycling in woman's emancipation is that it brings to woman's mind, that nothing good can be achieved without suffering. Noëlie Yaogo confides that the lesson she learns from cycling is that, "if you achieve something without a struggle, it's not going to be satisfying" (Yaogo, p. 11). Women should not be content begetting children and living like children at their husbands' expenses, like Azara in Ilboudo's *Adama*. They should work hard alongside their husbands so they can help each other in life. One way of learning how to face a hard life is by using the bicycle. Hence, Yaogo concludes that "Biking is struggling, and it will still be emancipating women," and be "the foundation of women's freedom" (Yaogo, p. 11).

The second obstacle toward woman's cycling is that it requires a specific adapted short dress instead of traditional long ones. Noëlie Yaogo praises the fact that, "With the right new turn of mind in history, some long heavy-dressed women, and others with tight bone corsets, had been liberated from these outdated things in society, thanks to the bicycle. These women still applaud the bicycle. Social virtue, freedom, and self-reliance always take profit" (Yaogo, p. 11).

She praises the fact that thanks to cycling, women can wear

clothes that they would not normally wear, out of respect for patriarchal tradition. Tradition requires that women put on, not mini-skirts, but long dresses. Yet such long skirts are not suitable for cycling, but rather mid-length skirts are. So cycling gives women the opportunity to reduce the length of their attire. Noëlie Yaogo herself prefers mid-length dresses while cycling. She finds traditional dresses so encumbering and disgusting that she never uses them. She rather prefers her "jean-cut trousers, always black and comfortable to work" (Yaogo, p. 25).

Moaaga patriarchal tradition even provided room for this adaptation, as the following three proverbs attest. *Zând-zând yaa kurg koèèga* means *For a quick run, you need short trousers*. It is permitted to shorten one's trousers to meet the purpose of running quickly. Likewise for cycling. Another Moaaga proverb also says, *Yel-be-rat kurg kôn loog a rumd ye*. That is, *the trousers of an ill-intentioned person does not go lower than his knees*. The reason is that if ever his/her mischief is discovered and people run after him, he may run away easily without his clothes preventing him. This underlines the existence and use of shorts for specific purposes, especially for moving fast. Last, another Moaaga proverb: *Waaf yeelame ti ned kam fâa zomb a sên kôn lui – The snake says that anybody should ride by sitting in a way that prevents him from falling down*, advises anybody to adopt any attitude or decision that suits him best. Therefore, cyclists may use any suitable dress for specific purposes.

However, these aforementioned provisions mostly apply to men. The *kurg* (trousers) in the proverbs is traditionally a man's dress. Feminist activists like Yaogo are working hard to allow women cyclists to wear trousers, or at least avail of the same provisions of using a suitable dress for the specific purpose of cycling.

Yet vigilance should be taken so that cycling dresses should not give way to immoral exhibitionism. Feminism should not get rid of moral decency. Hence, Yaogo vehemently criticizes women's provoking dresses, even outside of the woman's cycling debate. The following description of the indecent dressing of a

Chapter 4

pretty teenager is telling:

> *She was believed to be recently 18 because of the scant clothes she had put on. In her "see-through," that's to say, her type of transparent blouse, she was softly passing.... Without any brassiere, her pear-shaped breast could then be easily seen through the blouse; a bosom in fashion. The hem of her blouse was so short that her entire abdomen was displayed to any onlooker. Furthermore, her attractive coloured skirt was even pushed so low that her pubic hair was somewhat obvious to closed eyes. Worse still, this skirt was so short that anytime she took a step, any observer could see her panties with no effort.* (Yaogo, p. 60)

Yaogo condemns such ways of dressing. The person is not cycling, but walking, being thus part of those who do not count, according to the social ladder given in Ilboudo's *Adama*. The immoral way she is dressed while walking means that she is far from being eligible to cycling against the odds. In other words, she stands in dire need of emancipation in her present social status of a pedestrian before moving to the next stage of cycling to become a real feminist. Such girls have a long way to travel on the road to feminism.

The third reason why patriarchal tradition was against woman's cycling is that it transforms women to become man-like through the clothes they use. It brings about unisex or transgendered clothing. The narrator in *The Odds Are Against Cycling* reports how women characters "with manly clothes and behavings, purposeful speed and acrobatics, [are] nipping in and out within the traffic" (Yaogo, p. 64). Women adopt manly garments and manners. Cycling thus contributes to merge, for better or for worse, the outward differences between men and women, making them appear equal in the way they are dressed, and thus advocating for equality of man and woman in everyday life.

Cycling is thus a training exercise in the road to women's emancipation against the odds – that is, presumably, traditional patriarchal taboos. One of the objectives of feminism is the entering of anything that has so far been reserved for men, such as cycling, manly clothes (trousers), sitting positions, jobs, and so forth. In Iran, where women are not allowed to ride bikes –

women in Marivan were arrested for riding a motorbike in 2017 – some women resort to cycling or biking as a means of protest. For example, Iranian-born Yazarloo decided to ride a BMW F650GS across the world to challenge the unwritten law which creates gender stereotypes in Iran. With the support of her husband, she strongly believes that the success of her ride will "stand in solidarity with the women of Iran, West Asia, and India – proving to the world that women are also capable of very significant achievements" (Tripathi, p. 1). She is confident that her ride will help break stereotypes, overcome fears, and inspire women to deal with obstacles they confront in their day-to-day lives. Biking appears then, in her experience, as well as in that of Noëlie Yaogo, as a powerful instrument that can help bring about social changes in favor of women's emancipation. From their experiences, they invite and strongly urge women to cycle in order to become man-like or equal to man.

Since Burkinabe women started invading the field of cycling, things started to change in Burkinabe families and the society at large. Otokoré and Kamelgarn's assertion that the participation of Sub-Saharan women in the active population of their countries is globally higher than in other parts of the world comes certainly as a result of women's emancipation through cycling (Otokoré and Kamelgarn 2016). Thus, thanks to cycling against the odds, what used to be taboo, like biking and wearing manly clothes, is now a generally accepted shameless practice. Girls ride horses and donkeys, sitting like boys. They mount bikes shamelessly like boys. They have become active in the economy, and not only housebound consumers. The bicycle has thus freed Burkinabe women from the heavy constraints of traditions and customs, showing that whenever a woman decides to cycle against the odds, she becomes more emancipated, and the whole society benefits from her hard work.

Cycling further opens the way for women to play many roles traditionally considered man's in Burkinabe culture. Yaogo gives the following examples: "Women in leadership staff! Female ministers expected in charge of economic portfolios! Yes! Your interests to be more reflected in economic decision-making!"

(Yaogo, p. 111), and the reaching of the "UN target of 30 percent female representation in positions of power...both political and economic decision-making posts" (Yaogo, p. 112). Yaogo's novel thus presents cycling as a modest means. But once really undertaken by women, it can lead to fruitful emancipation, and to the realization of major feminist dreams and projects.

Conclusion

Even though both *Adama* and *The Odds Are Against Cycling*, are from Burkinabe writers who draw their inspirations from a fundamentally patriarchal culture, they share some obvious differences. The narrative in Ilboudo's *Adama* is chauvinistically masculine, focused on man, with the main character being male and overshadowing the few female characters. On the other hand, Yaogo's *The Odds Are Against Cycling* is feminine and feminist-oriented, drawn from the author's own cycling experience.

Both describe Burkinabe cultural, political, and economic realities. Means of transportation is used in the first to highlight social stratification, showing politicians ascending from nothing to the top without using a bicycle on the way, but at the expense of the middlemen, who use bicycles to earn their living, but whom politicians send to rock bottom. Cycling especially is used in the second novel as a metaphor for struggling, which is necessary for women's emancipation, and for their ascension from low to upper class. So a feminist approach to the two novels shows that these fictional works come to each other's rescue and coalesce to call for a balance in the training of boys and girls, husbands and wives, to strive to work together to ensure the wellbeing of families, of the nation – nay, the whole world. Or to paraphrase the feminist Nigerian writer Chimamanda Ngozi Adichie's leitmotif and the title of her essay, *We Should All Be Feminists*, for the development of humanity.

Works Cited List

Abrahams, J. "Freewheeling to Equality: How Cycling Helped Women on the Road to Rights," https://www.theguardian.com/lifeandstyle/womens-blog/2015/jun/18/freewheeling-equality-cycling-women-rights-yemen-bicycle-liberation. Accessed March 3, 2018.

Association vélo pour le Faso, "Le vélo au Burkina Faso – le Moyen de déplacement," http://velospourlefaso.org/index.php?option=com_content&view=article&id=204. Accessed March 3, 2018.

Badini, A. *Naître et grandir chez les Moosé traditionnels*. Paris-Ouagadougou: SEPIA, 1994.

Coulibaly, N. "à-ouagadougou-etes-quatre-deux-roues," http://www.jeuneafrique.com/328724/societe/a-ouagadougou-etes-quatre-deux-roues. Accessed March 3, 2018.

De Beauvoir, S. *The Second Sex*. London: Jonathan Cape, 1953.

Eco-business, "World Bicycle Ownership Going Downhill," February 18, 2016, http://www.eco-business.com/news/world-bicycle-ownership-going-downhill. Accessed March 3, 2018.

Fondation Reine Hangbe, "Rapport de Formation des formatrices, Hôtel Excellence, 23 au 27 février, Lomé, Togo," www.fondationreinehangbe.org/docs/ecole-filles-lome.pdf. Accessed March 3, 2018.

Goffinet, L. "au-moins-580-millions-de-velos-dans-le-monde," January 7, 2016, https://www.gracq.org/actualites-du-velo/au-moins-580-millions-de-velos-dans-le-monde. Accessed March 3, 2018.

Lompo, G. J. "Le vélo, le cheval moderne des Burkinabè," February 28, 2015, http://lenfantdupays.mondoblog.org/2015/02/28/le-velo-le-cheval-moderne-des-burkinabe/. Accessed March 3, 2018.

Oke, O. J., et al., "Tracking Global Bicycle Ownership Patterns," *Journal of Transport and Health*, vol. 2, issue 4 (December 2015), pp. 490–501.

Oneyocha, I. M. "Formation of Character in Traditional Nigerian Moral Education." T. Okere editor. *Identity and Change: Nigerian Philosophical Studies, I*. Washington: Paideia

Publishers, 1996, pp. 89–116.

Otokoré, S. and Kamelgarn, D. "Journée internationale des femmes: les 4 + 1 priorités des Africaines," *Le point Afrique*, March 8, 2016, http://afrique.lepoint.fr/economie/journee-internationale-des-femmes-les-4-1-priorites-des-africaines-08-03-2016-2023986_2258.php. Accessed March 3, 2018.

Tiéné, R. "Le vélo a encore de beaux jours au Faso," December 6, 2017, http://www.dw.com/fr/le-v%C3%A9lo-a-encore-de-beaux-jours-au-faso/a-39206997. Accessed March 3, 2018.

Tinguiri, M. *The Tribulations of a Sahelian Traveler*. USA: Self-published, 2014.

Tripathi, S. "Her Way on the Highway," *The Hindu Metro Plus Travel*. May 3, 2018. p. 1.

Vivanco, L.A. Reconsidering the Bicycle: An Anthropological Perspective on a New (Old) Thing. London: Routledge, 2013.

Yaogo, N. *The Odds Are Against Cycling*. Pittsburgh, PA: Dorrance Publishing, 2012.

Appendixes

Appendix 1: Bike availability worldwide.

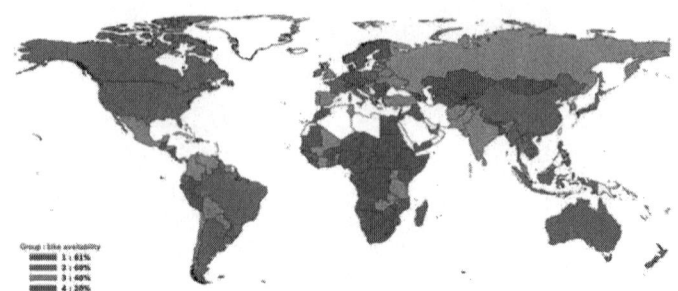

Source: Oke, et al. (2015)

Chapter 4

Appendix 2: Percentage of the possession of goods in households by Burkinabe regions in 2003, 2005, 2007.

		Bicyclette	Mobylette	Voiture	Radio	Téléviseur	Lit ou matelas	Réfrigérateur
	2003	89,9	20,3	0,7	68,7	7,7	65,2	1,3
Boucle du Mouhoun	2005	88,6	22,7	1,0	70,1	9,4	26,3	0,9
	2007	90,6	35,0	1,2	69,9	16,5	35,4	2,1
	2003	90,8	41,0	1,1	77,2	5,1	55,2	2,3
Cascades	2005	93,0	53,8	1,0	88,9	8,5	74,4	2,7
	2007	86,9	50,2	2,5	76,9	13,7	68,8	2,5
	2003	73,4	54,2	12,2	87,9	39,7	88,5	19,7
Centre	2005	76,0	62,8	14,4	87,4	53,3	87,7	24,8
	2007	71,6	62,1	13,1	83,5	53,6	83,6	24.0
	2003	82,8	11;9	1,2	57,6	6,8	47,8	2,8
Centre-Est	2005	84,7	14,4	3,2	61,0	8,8	20,4	5,0
	2007	81,4	14,1	1,6	62,4	9,2	35,2	3,4
	2003	84,9	14.7	0,8	66,0	4.2	40.2	1,31
Centre-Nord	2005	65,6	13,0	1,1	43,8	3,8	30,5	1,7
	2007	86,6	21,1	0,9	63,5	6,8	34,1	1,4

	2003	80,0	22,0	1,5	69,9	5,2	49,8	2,5
Centre-Ouest	2005	87,7	32,4	2,2	71,2	12,4	42,3	2,9
	2007	80,7	34,4	1,1	65,3	12,7	31,3	3,2
	2003	78,7	6,9	0,2	57,8	1,3	26,1	0,0
Centre-Sud	2005	88,5	12,8	0,7	56,6	1,9	28,9	0,5
	2007	86,6	18,1	0,7	68,0	6,8	38,1	1,2
	2003	86,7	11,7	0,9	52,4	3,1	67,4	1,7
Est	2005	93,6	19,9	1,5	54,0	5,1	15,2	1,6
	2007	91,2	21,3	0,6	66,3	6,2	38,7	2,3
	2003	74,6	39,6	3,4	84,7	18,9	78,3	7,3
Hauts-Bassins	2005	78,8	46,3	3,0	77,8	20,5	70,8	5,5
	2007	81,9	42,6	3,7	78,3	28,1	66,4	7,5
	2003	80,1	19,6	0,3	72,8	5,8	61,4	1,3
Nord	2005	90,0	30,2	2,0	74,1	8,8	75,1	2,8
	2007	84,9	32,4	1,4	73,7	13,0	38,1	2,8
	2003	86,5	19,0	0,7	68.7	2.0	60,8	1,2
Plateau Central	2005	96,8	30,7	1,5	71,1	5,0	58,4	2,9

	2007	90,9	28,5	0,5	69,9	9,1	37,8	1,6
	2003	60,2	7,7	0,4	45,8	1,4	53,3	0,7
Sahel	2005	60,5	17,9	0,4	40,7	1,9	10,3	0,4
	2007	60,3	20,8	0,8	57,2	3,5	40,4	1,7
	2003	73,9	9,3	0,7	48,0	24	34,5	0,5
Sud-Ouest	2005	79,8	13,2	0,0	53,6	4,5	24,6	0,7
	2007	79,6	11,9	0,7	55,3	5,5	29,8	1,5
	2003	79,7	23,0	2,3	67,7	10,0	59,6	4,2
Burkina	2005	82,4	30,0	3,1	66,3	13,6	45,1	5,0
Faso	2007	82,0	32,4	2,8	69,5	16,9	46,2	5,4

Source : INSD, Enquête burkinabé sur les conditions de vie des ménages 2003 et enquête annuelle sur les conditions de vie des ménages (EA – QUIBB) 2005 et 2007.

c) Feminism in Burkinabe Literature in English[3]

Introduction

In most Burkinabe tribes, in both urban and rural areas, men and women are traditionally assigned different tasks according to patriarchal ideology. In rural areas for instance, both man and woman do farm work, but an activity involving blood shedding, such as "hunting and butchering is always a male activity," while culinary activities and "the collection of firewood and water is seen...as female tasks" (Ouadrago 2016, "Responsibilities and Statuses"). In addition, husband and wife have different statuses in society according to patriarchal ideology. The husband is supposed to be the head of the family, and should solely provide for it (Adichie 2017, p. 8). To be a wife and mother stands first and foremost in the woman's role in Burkinabe society. As Ouadrago (2016) underlines in his description of Burkinabe cultures and traditions, a woman in her thirties who is still unmarried or childless is severely stigmatized socially, and the married but childless woman is likely to be repudiated (Ouadrago 2016, "The Relative Status of Women and Men").

The narrator in Noëlie Yaogo's novel *Les Plaisirs du Mal... Les plaisirs du Mâle* (2007), says: "According to villagers' culture and mentality, it is very awful for one to look at a childless couple" (p. 6), and makes the point that the aim of marriage is nothing but childbearing. The importance given to childbearing may explain the high average fertility rate of 6.2 children per woman of reproductive age in rural areas (CIA 2016, "People and History"). Arranged marriages and levirate marriage are still practiced in the countryside.

The Burkinabe society is, thus, patriarchally organized. How do Burkinabe writers relate to this patriarchal ideology? Do they reinforce it or undermine it? In other words, are Burkinabe writers advocating Burkinabe women's social situation as a natural part of Burkinabe age-long tradition, and content themselves with reproducing these roles in their works to perpetuate it? Or are they trying to fight against it by questioning the authority behind

Chapter 4

it and showing that the roles assigned to women may be socially constructed?

Since French is the official language of Burkina Faso, Burkinabe literature in French is well-known, especially with Salaka Sanou's publication of his *Littérature Burkinabè: l'histoire, les hommes, les oeuvres* (2000), which unfortunately makes no mention of Burkinabè literature in English, most of which appeared recently. The choice falls on this literature because it is unknown and extremely limited in number – therefore, a manageable scope for a study.

The focus will mainly be on three novels which represent the three main stands on patriarchal ideology. Through a comparative study of these representative novels, this paper strives to present a feminist analysis of Burkinabé literature in English. In fact, focusing on the three works while referring now and then to the others, and using feminism as a critical approach, specifically Simone de Beauvoir and Irigaray's body-related feminist theory, Hélène Cixious's *"écriture féminine"* and Chimamanda Ngozi Adichie's feminist viewpoints, I want to examine the representation of women in their literary works, and specifically show that the novels of Michel Tinguiri and Bali Nebié have a patriarchal agenda, while Noëlie Yaogo's, despite the author's claim of a feminist agenda, is actually ideologically conflicted.

Since representation of men and women in literature generally provides the role models which show to people of each sex what constitutes acceptable and legitimate manners pertaining to males and females, the paper also aims at showing the degree to which traditional representations of women cannot be a representation that mobilizes social constructivism in modern times, and so the examination of the patriarchal ideology behind the portrayal of women characters in these three novels of Burkinabe literature in English therefore constitutes ways of challenging these portrayals of women as "other," or as part of "tradition," and thus draw women's attention to the literary "stars" that they might aspire to imitate.

Representation of Women in Tinguiri's Novel

Feminism has drawn attention to the destructive role of patriarchy in equating femininity with submission, encouraging women to let themselves be taken care of by men, and to view marriage as the guarantee of happiness, and the proper reward for a good young woman (Tyson 1999, pp. 87–88; Adichie 2017, p. 31). Observing that the African world still largely values a woman's marital and maternal roles more than anything else – to the extent that at baptism ceremonies, some guests already wish the baby girl a good husband – the Nigerian feminist critic and novelist Adichie (2017), in her feminist manifesto in fifteen suggestions, advises her friend to be a feminist in these terms:

> *Do not define yourself solely by motherhood. Be a full person.* (pp. 7, 8)
> *Reject the idea that motherhood and work are mutually exclusive.* (p. 9)
> *Question the idea of marriage as a prize to women.* (p. 15)
> *Never speak of marriage as an achievement.* (p. 30)

Like the Igbo culture, Burkinabe society is mostly patriarchally organized. Most Burkinabe literary writings in English bear witness to the presence of this patriarchal ideology. In many works, the representation of women is similar to nineteenth century English fiction in the sense that the focus of most female characters is on marriage. The preoccupation is to find a marriage partner who will look after them and make them happy.

In Tinguiri's novel, for instance, female characters number nine, and all of them, are or have been married. For example, no sooner than we are told that Banambonon, the protagonist's daughter, is an eleven-year-old youngster, the narrator shifts to talking about her marriage seven years later (Tinguiri 2014, p. 85). This passage from her childhood directly to her marital life is so swift, without a tangible transition, that it takes the reader by surprise. Marriage is thus presented as the target of all female characters, following patriarchal ideology. The decision of this girl's mother, Banko, to remarry following the difficulties that

Chapter 4

arise after her husband's death, further shows the extent to which a woman's happiness is tied to marriage, under the supposed care of a husband. Such an idyllic presentation shows the female readership of this novel what any woman's aspiration should be. In addition, in Tinguiri's novel, in all cases, the reader is told that all female characters beget children as soon as they get married. Marriage and begetting children are inseparable. For example, the narrator says that after her marriage, "a year later, Banambonon was blessed with her first child" (Tinguiri 2014, p. 91). Then later, he informs the reader that Banambonon's brother "Gontan married Sè and had a handsome little baby boy called Tchiri" (Tinguiri 2014, p. 145). Earlier, the reader was told that her father, N'Djilékou, "married Banko and they had three beautiful children" (Tinguiri 2014, p. 14). As it can be noticed, the schema *married + children* is a repetitive pattern in these examples and throughout the whole novel. The plot of this novel implies that marriage to the right person is a guarantee of happiness, and the proper reward for a right-minded girl. The death of Banko's husband signals the end of her happiness, and her remarriage the opening of another era of happiness.

Begetting children is also presented as a key to woman's self-realization. In this sense, it is understandable that, describing the traditional marriage procedure, the narrator lays emphasis on rituals related to reproduction. For example, *mèwara* is a ritual intended "to keep away bad luck and evils from undermining the woman's reproductive capacity" (Tinguiri 2014, p. 89). The reader is informed that any sexual intercourse without this tradition being accomplished can sterilize the woman.

Furthermore, in Tinguiri's novel, as well as in Somé's, emphasis is put on women's roles as the persons in charge of cooking, fetching wood and water. Somé's narrative shows his mother carrying him on her back to go to the farm, or to fetch wood and carry it home on her head for cooking (Somé 1994, pp. 14–15). Likewise, in *The Tribulations of the Sahelian Traveller*, female characters like Banambonon are described fetching water (Tinguiri 2014, p. 85). Her mother's neck is said to have been shortened from carrying bundles of wood and basins of water

Introduction to Burkinabe Literature in English

on her head (Tinguiri 2014, pp. 126, 131). Alima offers water to her husband's guests for their needs (Tinguiri 2014, p. 168). And Fatima and Nado are praised for being good cooks (Tinguiri 2014, pp. 72, 134).

Yet, once a woman becomes a widow, all of her late husband's possessions pass on to one of her brothers-in-law. For example, when Banko's husband dies, she and all her children, and all that the family possessed, are taken by her brother-in-law, Touko, who is married to Bèrè. The narrator describes Touko and the ill-treatment of the widow in these terms:

> Touko, N'Djilékou's senior brother, was a man with a stony heart, a self-centered person whose only concern was to drink traditional beer and be merry. He had no compassion at all for Banko and her children. Touko had collected the entire heritage and had sold everything. Touko...plundered the heritage to the detriment of Banko and her children (Tinguiri 2014, p. 122).

After enduring such ordeals for some years, the widow, Banko, finally made up her mind to remarry, leaving her children with their uncle, as tradition requires. Tired from suffering in their uncle's house, the children will later go to their married sister's house, where they receive hospitality for some time, and finally had to go back to live with their mother and her new husband.

It can be noticed from these examples that the writer describes women who live and do things the way they are traditionally laid down. There is no attempt at challenging women's situation as socially constructed and unnatural. The novel has a patriarchal agenda, in feminist perspectives. It does not criticize the gynophobia or loathing of women as sexual and reproductive people. Femininity is equated with submission, tolerance of familial abuse, and marriage as reward for "right" conduct.

To a limited extent, the author of this novel could be seen as an African feminist of the first generation who just fought for more equality between men and women without strongly challenging traditional roles of women. I say, to a limited extent, because even these early African "feminists" would not tolerate his unquestioning of the widows' plight, being disinherited of

Chapter 4

their late husbands' wealth, even though merely exposing the state of facts – the negative patriarchal power structures and actors – may draw people's attention to fighting against it.

Yet, to a certain extent, one can see an attempt from the part of the writer at women's empowerment through the character of Aunt Pèlo. She is the only woman who is apparently not taken care of. She is said to have children and grandchildren, and spends every day spinning cotton to meet their needs. Nothing is said about her husband. None of her children are mentioned. Only one grandson is referred to by name – Kô.

Aunt Pèlo appears to be self-reliant. She provides clothing for the whole family (Tinguiri 2014, p. 12). Through her, the reader can perceive the writer trying to empower women, encouraging them to stop depending on men, and work to take care of themselves and their families. If not, they will die poor and in silence, like Louti, a wretched woman (Tinguiri 2014, p. 84).

Unfortunately, such an interpretation falls short of stronger arguments when the narrator gives the information that what Aunt Pèlo does – taking care of her grandchildren and spinning cotton – is what is traditionally expected of women when they grow old (Tinguiri 2014, p. 12). It can be considered as a positive aspect of patriarchal ideology that is worth keeping. So all being considered, the novelist, Michel Tinguiri, is at best, an anthropologist who describes Burkinabe traditional customs for foreigners' attention without taking a position or challenging them as socially constructed. Yet the comparative approach shows us that his stake on the matter is milder than some of his peer writers whose works appear masculinized, as opposed to the strongly feminist "*écriture féminine.*"

Secrets of the Sorcerer as "écriture masculine"

"Teach her that the idea of 'gender roles' is absolute nonsense. Do not ever tell her that she should or should not do something because she is a girl" (Adichie 2017, p. 14). This is the third suggestion the feminist writer Adichie is giving to a friend of hers. This idea of gender roles, against which feminists are fighting, is strongly expressed in Bali Nebié's *Secrets of the Sorcerer* (2017).

Similar to Tinguiri's novel, female characters in Nebié's novel are happy playing the roles traditionally assigned to them. The narrator describes women busy fetching water for household use, and serving as stewards dedicated to offering welcome water to the house guests for drinking, as well as having a shower at morning and evening (Nebié, pp. 96–98). Polygyny is accepted therein as normal.

The following description of Gnama, the protagonist of the novel, and his two wives, Atia and Maawa, gives the reader a glimpse of how a polygamous household operates, and the traditional roles women play in it in a patriarchal society.

> *Both women [Atia and Maawa] tolerated each other as much as two co-wives could.... Maawa was breast feeding, and so, no longer had access to Gnama's hut at night. She demanded that whenever it was her "turn to cook," Atia should not be allowed access into Gnama's hut. She was hoping that this would somehow delay a possible pregnancy for her rival. In polygamous homes...the one who had the kitchen turn of the day was expected to share the man's bed for the night.* (Nebié 2017, p. 114)

The two women share the same man. Each is happy having a man and children. They even have a competition as to who will have more children than the other, and each one tries to find strategies to prevent the other from becoming pregnant. So they both look at marriage and giving birth to children as a woman's self-fulfillment. They are good women because they are submissive and follow the patriarchal ideology.

The descriptions of these women, as engrossed in following patriarchal and cultural expectations, are only meant either to meet the curiosity of foreign readership or to elevate them. The writer is more preoccupied with men – the tradition holders – than with women. Throughout the novel, women just appear as stereotypes. They are used as appendages to men. Thus, one can understand that Gnama's filthiness does not prevent him from having a real harem of women – a hundred of them (Nebié 2017, p. 29) – who give him so many children who can't even recognize him as their father because they see him so seldomly (Nebié 2017, p. 76).

Women are objectified, heavily dependent on men to such a

Chapter 4

point that they give themselves to anybody who is rich, regardless of how smelly he is. They stubbornly assume the role patriarchy has assigned for them. Patriarchy, thus, plays a destructive role, as Tyson observes, in her explanation of feminism, because it "equates femininity with submission, encouraging women to tolerate familial abuse, wait patiently to be rescued by a man, and view marriage as the only desirable reward for 'right' conduct" (p. 87).

In Tinguiri's novel, all the villagers, men and women alike, are uneducated, except Kô, who went as far as the fifth grade, and Gontan, who decided to enroll in adult evening classes. But in Nebié's novel, characterization reveals that women are discriminated against regarding education and employment. The patriarchal concept of femininity at play in this novel is similar to that described by Tyson in her description of feminism, in which she points out its link to weakness, timidity, and modesty – everything that contributes to disempower women in the real world – with injunctions such as "it is unfeminine to be successful in business, it is unfeminine to be very intelligent, it is unfeminine to earn a big salary, it is unfeminine to have strong opinions, or to assert one's rights" (Tyson 1999, p. 87). As a matter of fact, none of the women in this fiction novel is a civil servant, a politician, or a leader of the village. All government people, educated and influential people in this patriarchal society, are men. The novel is about the secrets of the brotherhood, of which it is said: "No woman can be a member" (Nebié 2017, p. 141).

From the perspective of feminist criticism, this novel serves then as a case of *écriture masculine*, as opposed to the feminist Cixous's *"écriture féminine"*.

This *"écriture masculine"* is also expressed in the fact that the writer does not think women are important enough to be named at all. Some female characters are nameless. The narrator refers to them as X's wife, or by using the possessive pronoun "his." It is the case with Claude's wife and Robert's wife, who are always referred to in this way (Nebié 2017, pp. 32–33, 58–59). Claude and Robert are two politicians and opponents. Their wives are under shadows, unknown. Only their worries about becoming widows sometimes come to the forefront, but they are quickly silenced by their husbands. They exist insofar as they contribute to give prominence to their husbands. Similar to Victorian women in England, their role is reduced to making their homes safe havens for their husbands, where the man could find strength to face the daily struggles of the workplace. Everything is focused on men.

Worse, women are sacrificed at the altar of men's social advancement. "The Djadjo demands the life of your wife...as condition for your initiation!" (Nebié 2017, p. 117) Gnama was told by his master, Old San, who also sacrificed his first wife for the initiation of his son Tiécoura (Nebié 2017, p. 137). Women are, in this *"écriture masculine"*, a prey that can be used by men for their ignominious purposes.

Lastly, women pay the price of the fraud involved in witchcraft and sorcery, which are reserved for men only. Old San, in a dialogue with Gnama, whom he newly initiated into sorcery, indexes patriarchy to explain the plight of women, who are the only people being accused of witchcraft:

> *In patriarchal societies, women find themselves in a fragile position: they are considered to be strangers both in their own immediate families and in those of her [sic] husbands. Just like everywhere else, when a community is faced with a major difficulty, the first suspected culprit is almost always the stranger.* (Nebié 2017, p. 152)

Women are seen as nomads by nature because marriage is deemed to play an important role in their self-fulfilment in patriarchal societies.

Yet, though being an *"écriture masculine"*, Nebié's novel as a whole makes a feminist point that there are no (female) witches, but only (male) sorcerers. This feminist statement follows a deconstruction of the patriarchal conception that there are mainly (female) witches. In the novel, Old San explains to Gnama that women cannot be witches, members of the brotherhood of men-lions because they do not meet the profile physically speaking, and cannot stand the rigors of the rules of witchcraft, emotionally (Nebié 2017, p. 141). To belong to the brotherhood of men-lions requires that one hold feminine qualities in contempt, as in any

Chapter 4

patriarchal society. Women in this patriarchal society have their own body in which the old ones initiate the younger ones into the sex life of a home (Nebié 2017, p. 141). But one wonders whether this *"écriture masculine"* was the price to be paid to come to such an outcome. The point reached is a message in the direction of men, holders of patriarchal traditions. Women are passive listeners. For sure, to have things change positively, men's mentalities should change. In this perspective, one can understand the focus on the male genre. Yet, in this novel, as well as in Tinguiri's, women have not been provided role models to imitate, other than the patriarchal ones. Women readers are then more than likely to consider these portrayals of female characters as ideal, which would be counterproductive to well-intentioned writers. Yaogo takes a stance that is opposite to these novels by adopting a style that is akin to *"écriture féminine"*.

The Odds Are Against Cycling as *"écriture féminine"*

In *We Should All Be Feminists* (2014), the Nigerian feminist critic Adichie observes that "gender as it functions today is a grave injustice" (p. 21). She is angry. This work, as well as her *Dear Ijeawele, or A Feminist Manifesto in Fifteen Suggestions* (2017), are her means of fighting against this injustice. Like her, Noëlie Yaogo in her first novel in French, *Les plaisirs du Mal... Les plaisirs du Mâle* (2007) (Evil's pleasures...Male's Pleasures), delves on women's issues of injustice. She revisits the patriarchal role assigned to women, showing women busy cooking and finding pride in procreating many children in polygamous families. Aware of how these age-long traditional laws and beliefs play against women's wellbeing, in *The Odds Are Against Cycling*, the author bemoans the fact that women, "Unlike their male counterparts, getting into and staying in a position of power is somewhat awkward because of customs. Such beliefs are so deep-seeded that women in critical leadership positions are often hampered by various obstacles and pervasive moods" (Yaogo 2012, p. 110).

Yaogo is committed, as a novelist, to taking effective actions against these deep-rooted customs and beliefs, so as to break through the glass ceiling to create equality and pave the way for gender mainstreaming. She does so by using biking as a metaphor for women's emancipation – a means for fighting against the patriarchal world order that traditionally stood against women's cycling. This good idea finds an echo in Adichie's feminist suggestion, in her feminist manifesto, of girls' "participation in sports" (Adichie 2017, p. 42) as a step forward in women's empowerment. Like Adichie, Yaogo is personally convinced of the importance of sports in woman's emancipation. She goes as far as saying that in the sport of cycling, "the bike movement is a medicine for creating change in one's physical, emotional, and mental states" (Yaogo 2012, p. 67). Women's cycling can bring about physical, emotional, and mental changes that will help effect equality between women and men.

Cycling is Yaogo's response to feminists' invitation to "write through their bodies" (Cixious 1976, p. 886), insofar as she is "convinced that the engine for [her bike] is [her] body – always fuelled by food" (Yaogo 2012, p. 58), with the muscles providing the power and energy to write or cycle. Cycling is the "impregnable language" Yaogo invented to use feminists' discourse, "wreck partitions, classes, and rhetorics, regulations and codes...submerge, cut through, get beyond the ultimate reverse-discourse...sweeping away syntax, breaking that famous thread... which acts for men as a surrogate umbilical cord" (Cixious 1976, p. 886). Her writing is strangely peculiar: the narrative, similar to postmodernism, has no thread, or has a broken one, and weird syntax at times, which makes its reading rebarbative. Maybe she has done this on purpose to look more feminist. If so, it plays against her, as so far as nobody seems to have read her novel: internet websites specialized in selling books still appeal for first comments on this work.

For sure, she responds to feminists' call by showing a concern for women in general. The French feminist Cixious (1976) says:

> *Woman must write herself: must write about women and bring women to writing, from which they have been driven away as violently as from their bodies – for the same reasons, by the same law, with the same fatal goal. Woman must put*

Chapter 4

herself into the text – as into the world and into history – by her own movement (p. 875).

Yaogo is responding to this feminist call. *The Odds Are Against Cycling* is actually about Noëlie Yaogo as a woman who likes cycling, and who is striving to assert herself in a man-ruled society. The synopsis of the novel written by its author – which is peculiarly unusual – presents it as her biography. She introduces herself as a Burkinabe woman, an English teacher at a secondary school, and a person who is eager to produce creatively. She attests that though she owns a master's degree in English, she has no mastery of the English language, which explains the poor quality of her English expression, unless it is done on purpose to look feminist. Comparing her work to those of Nigerian, Ghanaian, and Kenyan writers, she says that "[hers] would just be a newness…a break to a wordy routine" (Yaogo 2012, p. 159). She means that her work is strikingly different from the others. Her novel is strangely so, though the novels of her predecessors are more than "a wordy routine." She does not even explain why she says so. Nonetheless, her novel, which is born out of her own creative mind, is primarily all about herself. Most of the characters are women, and men appear only as shadows, putting her and the other women into brighter light.

In her narrative, Yaogo shows a deeper concern for the woman's body. She criticizes the systematic exploitation of sexuality, whereby teenagers use their bodies for profit, where on streets, "bodies are competitively priced" (Yaogo 2012, p. 60). To this end, these girls preen and maintain their bodies as commodities to enable them to entice men into matrimony for money or material gain. Their attention to their bodies, therefore, takes the form of producing them as objects for others' appraisal.

Wollstonecraft saw in this strategy, some dangers which have been echoed in feminist work up to the present day. In *A Vindication of the Rights of Woman (*1792), Wollstonecraft provides a clear example of the *disciplining* of the female body:

To preserve personal beauty, woman's glory! The limbs and faculties are cramped with worse than Chinese bands, and the sedentary life which they are condemned to live, whilst

> boys frolic in the open air, weakens the muscles…artificial notions of beauty, and false descriptions of sensibility have been early entangled with her motives of action. (p. 55)

Feminists usually regard embodiment with suspicion, choosing instead to stress the rational powers of the female mind, trying to break any suggested deterministic connexion between bodily characteristics and social role and mental faculties. They require a distinction between sex as fixed by biology, and gender, as the variable social and cultural meanings attached to such biology.

Acknowledging the fact that men and women are different in the sense that they have different hormones and different sexual organs and different biological abilities – women can have babies, men cannot – and that men have more testosterone and are physically stronger than women, the Nigerian feminist Adichie (2014) calls for an evolution in the ideas of gender by laying emphasis on the rational powers of the female mind when she underlines that "a man is as likely as a woman to be intelligent, innovative, creative" (p.18). Man and woman alike are qualified to lead the world today because physical strength is not anymore the most important attribute for survival, as it was the case thousand years ago. Because of this historical evolution, ideas of gender should evolve.

It is in this context of difference between biology and gender that Beauvoir's famous claim that "one is not born, but rather becomes, a woman" (p. 295), is usually quoted. Beauvoir claims that "woman" is not a natural fact, but a historical idea. She makes a distinction between sex, as biological facticity, and gender, as the cultural interpretation of that facticity. Following this distinction, to be female is a facticity, but to be a woman is to have become a woman, by compelling the body to conform to an historical and cultural idea of "woman." So the gendered body acts its part in a culturally restricted space, and enacts interpretations within the confines of already existing directives.

Beauvoir and Adichie actually explain that in childhood, the young girl's body is experienced in a different way from that of the young boy. She is encouraged to treat her whole person as a doll, "a passive object…an inert given object" (Beauvoir p. 306), mainly

Chapter 4

to please others. At the opposite, the boy is encouraged to climb trees and play rough games. In the African context, "baby girls are given less room and more rules, and baby boys more room and fewer rules" (Adichie 2017, p. 19). Beauvoir says that this state of facts explains the situation that women live their bodies as objects for another's gaze, something which has its origin not in anatomy, but in "education and surroundings" (p. 307). Likewise, being aware that "gender roles are absolute nonsense" (p. 14), Adichie (2017) invites women to question the Igbo culture's selective use of biology as "reasons" for social norms (p. 49), so as to allow men and women alike to do everything that biology allows. There is nothing one should do because one is a boy or a girl. Cycling is not an exception.

The Burkinabe woman, Noëlie Yaogo, also attempts, in her writings, to contribute to giving women's bodies a positive value. She is on the footsteps of Irigaray, a proponent of *écriture féminine*, a movement to produce writing reflective of female embodiment. From her personal and social experience that male bodies are those that have identity, power, and authority, and that female bodies are defective male bodies, Irigaray argues for the need to reconstruct a positive imaginary and symbolic of the female body.

Like Irigaray, Yaogo wants to restore the female body. She proposes that women use their bodies the hard way like men, to earn their living. Cycling against all the odds, she paves the way for women. She is a model that many can imitate in order to free themselves from traditional boundaries. She wants to teach the other women, from what she learned through the hardships of cycling, that nothing worthy can be achieved without struggling and sweat.

> *Biking is struggling, and it will still be emancipating women. In any case, the bicycle was the foundation of women's freedom, too. Indeed in the past, they were wrongly not allowed to cycle because of the so-called frailness of their female constitution. Were the male privates also examined? It would be a funny belief if a comparison were tried! Fortunately, the bike hurried disillusionment and other awakenings. Humans grew in wisdom; so were events. Furthermore, with the right new turn of mind in history, some long heavy-dressed women*

> and others with tight bone corsets had been liberated from these outdated things in society, thanks to the bicycle. These women still applaud the bicycle. Social virtue, freedom, and self-reliance always take profit. (Yaogo 2012, p. 11)

The author is thus engaged in a task of deconstruction, questioning the traditional conception of women regarding cycling, and drawing awareness to it as being not "natural" or "normal," but a social construction. Cycling helps to free women from these outdated traditions. She shows, by her experience, that women's emancipation is to be achieved by women themselves. Nobody can do it for them. The efforts involved in cycling symbolize the ordeals women should be ready to endure if they wish to gain freedom. She knows from experience that in cycling "one must always be ready to overcome wind resistance" (Yaogo 2012, p. 58), both physical and symbolic of traditions against women's cycling.

Cycling enables Yaogo to become like a man by acquiring manly physical strengths. It helps her build up her body physically, exercise her back and leg muscles, increase her cardiovascular fitness, and improve her blood circulation. With this gained extra strength through efforts willingly made, she can take revenge on abusive men like Wotike, whose fourth wife gave him a lesson in the following anti-patriarchal account:

> [Wotike] pushed the woman into the house, locked the door and put the key into his pocket. He hit her once. He was about to deal her a second blow when the woman stepped back, tied her loincloth tight, gathered strength, lifted Wotike and threw him onto the hard cement floor. The man could not believe what was happening to him.... She stepped aside, collected Wotike and smashed him against the wall before letting him down. She joined him there and began to mash him up like potatoes, pounding him like yams. Only then did Wotike realize that he was not dreaming. He started screaming for help. (Sawadogo 2000, p. 8)

Such an account is smashingly feminist. The possibility of a woman turning her husband into a thing that can be cooked like food, palatable to the eater, which the two similes powerfully convey, can help women to gather momentum against abusive husbands. It is by developing their physical strength that such a thing can be done.

With extra strength through efforts willingly made, Yaogo shows that woman can do works so far reserved for men, because requiring additional strength, like emptying the depositories for the Church Charitable Works Committee, with men watching her to see if she can do the job as well as men do (Yaogo 2012, p. 8). She says that her unusual stout constitution and hard work always earn her comments from people. In the area of Pawamtore, for example, she is known as a master grass cutter, brick collector, and cement bag supplier (Yaogo 2012, p. 9). Through such works, she becomes financially self-sufficient, financing her own further studies, and feeding her family.

In her English novel, Yaogo (2012) confides that she has been influenced by the cycling and hardworking life experience of other women. She has been "amazed by bikesick women, forcing the pedals, with uneasy carrying of earthenwares on their racks or loads on their heads. Fruits and vegetables constitute these loads. Well done!... The bicycle seems as good company as a husband.... I'm always witnessing that the bicycle is the right master of several issues" (p. 58).

The comparison of the bicycle to a husband is telling. It shows the strong link between the woman and her bicycle. They are as inseparable as a good husband and wife. The bike is shown as a necessary means of transport, entertainment, and sport. Yaogo says she uses it to get to her office, to perform errands, or to enjoy life outdoors. This simile also reveals that the bicycle makes a woman acquire, through hard work, what her husband can provide for her and the family, and thus contributes to her financial self-sufficiency. It is toward this end that she encourages her fellow women to embark on biking in an attempt at blanking out their "natural guilt" on this issue and reducing the gender gap (p. 111).

In addition to the focus on women characters, gender issues occupy more space in Yaogo's novel. Even the names given to political parties are gender-related: Gender Neutral, Gender Blind, and the Grange of Assertive People (GAP) is said to be a gender sensitive party (Yaogo 2012, p. 112). The GAP is a women's party that tries to boot out the ruling party because it fails to solve socio-economic troubles in the nation where "the international UN target of 30 percent female representation in positions of power" is not yet reached (Yaogo 2012, p.111). The writer tries to get her fellow women engage in the fight toward achieving equality between men and women, or empowering women in society.

She is preoccupied about getting women to work hard or undertake men's works, in a way that recalls Sojourner Truth's famous speech to the Ohio Women's convention, calling on women to compete with men in work:

> *I have as much muscle as any man, and can do as much work as any man. I have ploughed, and planted, and gathered into barns, and no man could head me! And ain't I a woman? I could work as much and eat as much as a man – when I could get it – and bear de lash a well! And ain't I a woman?* (Truth 1851, p. 117)

Like Sojourner Truth, Yaogo (2012) is cycling like men. She invites women to forgo some morally debasing jobs or activities, like prostitution and idleness in civil service. In fact, she mentions several types of professions in which women are involved: prostitution, secretariats, trade, teaching. She says that "prostitution, an old profession, goes well and enslaves deep" (p. 60); it has become a "modern enslaving work" (p. 62). She sees it as being "more privileging and empowering to the male on the one hand, but rather quietening and enslaving the female on the other" (p. 63). She implies that this is not a profession women should look for if they want to become free, to be considered equal to men, and not like objects used by men. Yaogo also criticizes women secretaries, whose concern is more about appreciating clothes, discussing about tailors, playing cards, and tattling too much on their men than doing their jobs (p. 78). She praises women who, like herself, engage in income-generating activities.

All these reasons, especially the focus on herself, on women in general, on gender, and the specific syntax and narrative line, coalesce to highlight the transgressive nature of Yaogo's English novel, which contributes to its being *écriture féminine*, which is "transgressive, rule-transcending, intoxicated" by its nature (Barry

Chapter 4

2009, p. 128). She emphasizes femininity as a social construction, and invites her fellow women to imitate her through hard work. Yet it can be observed that Yaogo (2012) unconsciously reinforces patriarchal ideology in her use of *man* and *he* in her novel, to represent humanity or *man and woman*, be they traditional sayings or proverbs she is using unapologetically. For example:

> "When a man does not know what harbor he is making for, no wind is the right wind" (a first century Roman philosopher, p. 4).
> "The best way to a man's heart is through his stomach" (p. 38).
> "Life is a foreign language; everybody speaks his own" (p. 160).

Yaogo strengthens patriarchal ideology by using the gendered language of the past, *man* and *he*, to refer to members of both sexes, as it was the practice in the old days. The feminist critic Tyson reports that feminists claim that "we should not use the masculine pronoun *he* to represent both men and women" because such use "reflects and perpetuates a 'habit of seeing,' a way of looking at life, that uses male experience as the standard by which the experience of both sexes is evaluated" (Tyson 1999, p. 82). Feminists argue that the use of the inclusive *he* is part of a deeply rooted cultural attitude that contributes to ignoring women's experiences and viewpoints in favor of men's (Tyson 1999, p. 82).

In addition, Yaogo (2012) uses *Mrs.* instead of the feministic *Ms.* For example, "I shall name you 'Mrs. Hulk' to remind me" (p. 8). And many times, pupils are calling their female teacher *Mrs.* An example is the case of Rita, one of the narrator's friends, who reverted to her maiden name, Rita, and "preferred to be called 'Miss Rita' rather than 'Mrs'" (p. 42).

Yaogo is not strongly feminist with such gendered language. The feminist Adichie explains that "the value we give to *Mrs.* means that marriage changes the social status of a woman but not that of a man" (Adichie 2017, p. 35). It is the reason why feminists prefer *Ms.*, which is similar to *Mr.* in the sense that it applies invariably to both married and unmarried persons.

Furthermore, Yaogo (2012), in her English novel, corroborates the popular idea according to which women do not have math brains (p. 97). She then tells a joke, in the form of an acrostic, that shows a low-esteem for women:

> Do you know what the word 'woman' means now?
> Yah! For me, it's a World of falsification!
> An Origin of appropriate retirement! And of sinning!"
> A Mind of weakened knowledge!
> And still an Area of entertainment!
> It's also the Name of an experiencing bull! (p. 97)

Such ideas are expressive of a patriarchal woman who has internalized patriarchal norms and values according to which "men are rational, strong, protective, and decisive," while women are "emotional (irrational), weak, nurturing, and submissive" (Tyson 1999, p. 83). For feminists, the opposition between body and mind has become an opposition between male and female, with the female regarded as enmeshed in her body in a way that she can barely reach rationality. "Women are somehow *more* biological, *more* corporeal, and *more* natural than men" (Grosz 1994, p. 14).

Reviewing the data of biology in the first chapter of the *Second Sex*, Beauvoir goes on to describe what are claimed as biological characteristics of the female *body,* which, in addition to differences in reproductive role, includes claims that "woman is weaker than man, she has less muscular strength…can lift less heavy weights" (p. 66). Yaogo is not sufficiently challenging such assumptions which require feminists to confront constructions of sexed difference. Woman is thus presented as 'other,' in reference to man. This ambivalent position of Yaogo towards women issues, both undermining and unconsciously reinforcing patriarchal ideology, makes her novel ideologically conflicted.

Conclusion

In comparing these three novels that represent the three main trends in Burkinabe English literature, we see similarities and differences come to the fore in the treatment of feminism. First,

Chapter 4

traces of patriarchal ideology are observable in all three selected literary works, sometimes despite the author's explicit opposition to it. My analysis shows that all three authors may be seen fighting against it, but using different means and strategies. Tinguiri, like an anthropologist, describes the state of facts, which can make the reality known so that adequate measures be taken for a solution. Nebié is, rather, preoccupied with men, the tradition holders, whose mentalities need change if a worthwhile improvement of women's issues has to be effected. Yaogo, at the opposite of the other two, focuses on women, showing herself as a feminist example.

Second, the differences in all three novels lie in the role models provided to women readers to look up to in everyday life. The role models offered to people of each sex vary significantly from Tinguiri's novel to Yaogo's. *The Tribulations of the Sahelian Traveler* provides no other feminist role model than the patriarchal one. Patriarchy is strongly emphasized in *The Secrets of the Sorcerer,* to the detriment of women who live under oppression. The novels of Tinguiri, Nebié, and Somé have a patriarchal agenda, reinforcing patriarchal ideology. Tinguiri, Nebié, and Somé either advocate women's situation as natural part of Burkinabe age-long tradition, or are silent about it, or just reproduce these gender roles in their works in an attempt to perpetuate it. It is only in *The Odds Are Against Cycling* that the narrator gives herself as a feminist role model that women can imitate. Yaogo's novel actually bears a feminist agenda, as its author is trying to fight against traditional beliefs and customs that are contrary to women's empowerment, showing that the roles traditionally assigned to women, as well as the women-related mores, are socially constructed. Focused on feminism of the body, she shows that gender is neither passively scripted on the body, nor is it determined by nature, but is historically and culturally added on. For example, the unpopularity around woman cycling is culturally related. Yaogo thus deconstructs gender issues and empowers women by fighting against patriarchal norms, going against the current.

Third, this study shows the degree to which traditional representations of women in Burkinabe English literature cannot be a representation that mobilizes social constructivism in modern times. Few educated women would be ready to play the role patriarchy assigns to women. Yet, despite Yaogo's strong feminist stand, it can be observed that the gendered language she sometimes uses – *Mrs., he*, and *man*, as inclusive language – is detrimental to women's empowerment and full emancipation.

Finally, there are divergences between the three selected writers as regards the bearing of gender upon style of writing. Tinguiri's style is more descriptive as he straightforwardly exposes the traditions and customs of villagers to foreign readership. Nebié's style, on the other hand, is thought-provoking, gory, and anti-feminist at times, to the extent that it can be called *écriture masculine*. As for Yaogo, the linguistic expression of her "écriture féminine", contrary to that of the other writers, is repulsive to the readership. One wonders if she could not have reached her target through better syntax construction instead. Her writing style may then account for the fact that the public and the critics have ignored her novel so far, unless there is a hidden operation of patriarchy behind the history of its reception.

References

Adichie, C. N. *Dear Ijeawele, or A Feminist Manifesto in Fifteen Suggestions*. New York and Toronto: Alfred A. Knopf, 2017.

Adichie, C.N. *We Should All Be Feminists*. London: Fourth Estate, 2014.

Barry, P. *Beginning Theory: An Introduction to Literary and Cultural Theory*. Manchester: Manchester University Press, 2009.

Bertens, H. *Literary Theory: The Basics*. Third edition. London and New York: Routledge, 2014.

Butler, J. "Performative Acts and Gender Constitution: An Essay in Phenomenology and Feminist Theory," Katie Conboy, Nadia Medina, Sarah Stanbury, editors. *Writing on the Body: Female Embodiment and Feminist Theory*. New York: Columbia University Press, 1997, pp. 401–417.

Chapter 4

CIA. *Burkina Faso Country Studies: A Brief, Comprehensive Study of Burkina Faso*. Kindle version, 2016.

Cixous, H., Cohen, K., Cohen, P. "The Laugh of the Medusa," *Signs*, vol. 1, no. 4 (Summer 1976), pp. 875–893.

Kousse, M. *Reap What You Sow and 28 Poems*. Ouagadougou: IPRESS Imprimérie, 2012.

Nebié, B. *Secrets of the Sorcerer*. Translated by Njoaguani, Francis Chuks. Ouagadougou: Editions Poun-yaali, 2017.

Ouadrago, A. *Burkina Faso Art and Culture: Tradition, Ethnic Group, Tribes, History, People*. Sonit Education Academy, Kindle version, 2016.

Sanou, S. *La littérature Burkinabè: l'histoire, les hommes, les œuvres*. Limoges: PULIM, 2000.

Sawadogo, M. *Neither in Heaven, nor in Hell and Other Stories*. Ouagadougou: Self-published, 2000.

Somé, M.P. *Of Water and the Spirit: Ritual, Magic, and Initiation in the Life of an African Shaman*. New York: Penguin Books, 1994.

Tinguiri, M. *The Tribulations of a Sahelian Traveler*. USA: Self-published, 2014.

Truth, S. "Speech at Women's Rights Convention in Akron, Ohio," Stanton, EC, Susan Anthony, and M.J. Gage, *History of Woman*, vol. 1, pp. 116–117. New York: Fowler & Wells, Publishers, 1851/1881.

Tyson, L. *Critical Theory Today: A User-Friendly Guide*. New York and London: Garland, 1999.

Yaogo, N. *Les Plaisirs du Mal...Les Plaisirs du Mâle*. Ouagadougou: Imprimerie SOGIF, 2007.

Yaogo, N. *The Odds Are Against Cycling*. Pittsburgh, PA: Dorrance Publishing, 2012.

Zoungrana, E. (2014). *The Ace of Spades in Disarray*. Translated by Bonkoungou, P. G. and Zaidi, S. Paris: EDILIVRE, 2014.

d) Creation Myths in Burkinabe and Biblical Literatures: A Comparative Approach

Introduction

Among the works of Burkinabe literature in English, Mathieu R. Ouédraogo's collection of stories, *A Deal is a Deal, or How Much for Your Head and Other Stories: A Reader for Burkina Faso Secondary Schools* (1989), contains creation myths. It was written to supply the lack of locally based textbooks for teaching the English language at Burkinabe secondary schools. The first three stories in this collection are stories authored by secondary school students, about God's creation of humanity. They are "The Origin of Humanity" by Gilbert Kaboré, "The Origin of Man" by Jean-Pierre Tiendrebeogo, and "The Origin of White and Black Men" by Laurent Nikiema. All of the students are from the same school and in the same class, and are all Christians. The author of the fourth creation story, "How Woman Was Created From Man," is anonymous.

These myths coexist with the biblical ones and trigger questions: Considering that, for a long time, the Moose, the main tribal group in Burkina Faso, rejected foreign influences by adhering to war-like isolation (Sissao, p. xi), how can we explain the presence and necessity of these myths alongside the biblical ones, and written by Christians, especially by teenagers, more than eighty years after the arrival of the first missionaries in Burkina Faso?

One hypothesis is that the authors of these creation stories, identifying the Bible with the Western colonization, attempt, by means of the creation myths they offer as alternative, to move away from Eurocentrism, or the monolithic way of presenting creation myths, and thus question the system of values that supported Western imperialism in Africa.

Using the postcolonial theory, this paper shows that, these myths were written to prevent the suppression of forms of "otherness" (Gayatri Spivak) that postcolonial writers, namely Mathieu R. Ouédraogo and his former students, engage in with

Chapter 4

their works. As both these stories, and the biblical ones, are nature-focused, ecocriticism will also be used. Hence, postcolonial ecocriticism. Examining the creation accounts in Mathieu R. Ouédraogo's collection of short stories from these theoretical lenses, the definition of which will come first, reveals attempts at preserving them from suppression or annihilation, as well as the hybrid nature of Burkinabe Literature in English.

Postcolonial Ecocriticism

The theory of postcolonial criticism can be seen as a way of "writing back" against the Eurocentric way, or canon, that is used by Western colonists (missionaries, educators, etc.) during and after the colonization of Africa and other territories to maintain their domination. Postcolonialism aims at destabilizing the intellectual, linguistic, economic, and social theories by means of which colonialists perceive the world, and so to establish intellectual spaces for non-Western people to speak in their own voices and for themselves, and thus produce a literature that is culturally expressive. It reveals and fights all discourse strategies used by colonialism to spread its hegemony through narratives that instill the colonizers' ideologies in and through the colonized people.

In his introduction to postcolonial studies, Lane expounds the different ways in which the "writing back" involved in postcolonialism operates: By way of intertextuality, through the writing of intertextual literature that goes against Western literary canon at the level of the very fabric of the texts. Or by rejection through deliberate refusal of religions, values, and symbols brought into Africa by Western people, in favor of precolonial African cultures, values, practices, religions, and beliefs, including creation myths (Lane, p. 487).

Though there are many postcolonial theories, emphasis will be laid here on Ngugi's approach to postcolonialism. Ngugi Wa Thiong'o shows his rejection of European culture in the change of his Christian name, James, to Wa Thiong'o, and in his preferential choice, to write his fictions no more using the colonial

Introduction to Burkinabe Literature in English

language, English, but his mother tongue, Kishiwahili, to express African values and culture. In most of his writings, he explains mythologically how white colonizers used the Christian religion to alienate Kenyans from their lands.

In Ngugi's novel *Weep Not, Child* (1964), through the powerful speech of the freedom fighter Kiarie, to the assembled folk, it is explained how the land given to the mythical ancestors, Gikuyu and Mumbi, has been taken away through the Bible and the sword, the first paving the way for the second (65). Later, in *A Grain of Wheat* (1967), through the political speech of the hero of deliverance, Kihika, a small man with a strong voice, the masses learn of the history of the tribe about the coming of colonizers and their confiscation of Kenyan lands:

> *We went to their church. Mubia, in white robes, opened the Bible. He said: Let us kneel down to pray. We knelt down. Mubia said: Let us shut our eyes. We did. You know, his remained open so that he could read the word. When we open our eyes, our land was gone and the sword of flames stood on guard. As for Mubia, he went on reading the word, beseeching us to lay our treasures in heaven where no moth would corrupt them. But he laid his on earth, our earth.* (15)

The confiscation of lands in this strategy is soon followed by the substitution of Kenyan languages and cultural practices with foreign ones. Ngugi tries to restore all that has been stolen from him and his country folk.

As far as myths are concerned, in his postcolonialism, Ngugi uses intertextuality in drawing parallelism between biblical accounts and Kenyan traditional ones. He equates Gikuyu to the biblical Adam, and Mumbi to the biblical Eve, and Murungu to Yahweh. Thus, he narrates in his fictions that the earth belongs to Gikuyu (Adam) and Mumbi (Eve), and their posterity. Gikuyu and Mumbi are created by Yahweh (Murungu), who put them under the sacred tree of life called Mukuyu, and told them: "This land I hand over to you. O Man and woman, it's yours to rule and till in serenity, sacrificing only to me, your God, under my sacred tree" (*Weep Not, Child,* p. 28).

This narrative, coming from a Christian, like the authors of

Chapter 4

the creation myths under study, is reminiscent of the biblical story where God entrusted His creation to Adam and Eve, giving them permission to eat of the fruits of any tree except that of the tree of knowledge of good and evil (Genesis 2:4–15). Ngugi resorts thus to intertextuality in his "writing back" against Western literary canon, putting side-by-side biblical characters and Kenyan mythological ones. A similar strategy is used in Ouédraogo's collection of short stories, which makes Ngugi's postcolonial approach ever-relevant to the analysis. Furthermore, Ngugi and many other postcolonial theorists (Said, Spivak, Findley, etc.) are committed to a fight against any pretention to universalism, through which the discourse of other cultures appear like "other."

Now, it is usually taken for granted that biblical creation stories translated into European languages impose themselves universally. Therefore, the presence of "other" creation stories relativizes this pretention to universalism, which is at the heart of the works of many postcolonialist critics. For example, in *Beginnings: Intention and Method* (1975), Edward Said argues against any metaphysical universalizing. In his novel *Not Wanted on the Voyage*, Timothy Findley also mentions some Western colonial and imperialist practices that are associated with what Gayatri Spivak refers to as "Othering." Taking the example of the Bible as a book brought by Europeans to other nations, he says that through colonialism and imperialism, biblical accounts become codes of reference, thus destroying the existing codes (Ashcroft, p. 97). For example, the story of Noah and the flood in the biblical book of Genesis, becomes the reference against which similar existing accounts are sanctioned as being radically "Other." European thinking based on the Bible, which is not European per se, becomes thus authoritative by comparison to the existing tribal ones.

As the critic Ashcroft points outs, imperial discourse, in its attempt to maintain authority over the Other in a colonial context, strives to describe the latter as radically different from the self, yet at the same time maintaining sufficient identity with the Other to valorize control over it, which leads the colonial subject into hybridization or colonial mimicry (102). This ambivalence, or hybridization, can be highlighted through the similarities and contrasts that exist between the biblical myths and Burkinabe creation stories.

The postcolonialist critic Findley also concludes that the building or preservation of any civilization, or tradition, as authoritative, prohibits "other" developments. "The 'rise' of any culture is not just coincident with the demise of other forms and possibilities, it involves the active suppression and/or annihilation of forms of 'otherness.' It closes off alternative tropes or modes," including even the processes of interpretation of reality, namely here, of God's word (Ashcroft p. 97).

By analyzing Ouédraogo's collection of short stories, namely those dealing with creation myths, especially with Ngugi's approach to postcolonialism, the objective is to explain how writing back to colonialism, and of using strategies to establish intellectual spaces for Burkinabe people to speak in their own voices and for themselves, leads to the production of a literature that expresses Burkinabe culture and contains some European cultural aspects.

The literatures under study deal with creation, nature, the environment. That is why, in addition to postcolonialism, ecclesial ecocriticism will be used. Kaboré (2016), tracing the roots of literature to the hermeneutics of religion, and displaying the immense ecological literature produced by recent popes and Catholic bishops on the protection of the environment, namely *Laudato Si* (2016), *Caritas in Veritate* (2009), *Centesimus Annus* (1991), *Sollicitudo Rei Socialis* (1987), *Laborem Exercens* (1981), devises, in comparison to literary ecocriticism, the theory of ecclesial ecocriticism, which is applicable especially to religion-based literature (156). He enunciates four characteristic features of this theory that its user should keep in mind: The inclusion of human nature in nature; the interdependence of natures within the environment; the attribution of a common author, namely God, to all natures, which calls for "universal fraternity" between all created beings; lack of faith in God, and belief in nature's origin as the result of mere chance or evolutionary determinism, lead to nature's destruction without somebody to blame.

Chapter 4

The Creation stories in my corpus fall within this category of religion-based literature. Hence the choice of this theory in the current postcolonial study of stories about creation.

Postcolonial ecocriticism, which is also implemented by Isiguzo Chikwurah Destiny when analyzing Ngugi's *I Will Marry When I Want,* and Fugard's *Sorrows of Rejoicing*, looks at both people and the environment they live in, as both are interconnected. Depiction of an overused environment in some works can be symbolic of the exploitation and moral decadence of society.

Ecclesial ecocriticism explores the impact and legacy of colonization on both humans and nonhumans, as does postcolonialism. It shows the juxtaposition in these stories, of oppression and freedom, right and wrong, blacks and whites, European and African mentalities, all of which are linked to ecocritical concerns, and are expressive of hybridity in the process of writing back to colonialism.

Ontological Signs of Hybridity: Semitic, African, and Western Mentalities

There are some similarities between the biblical or Semitic worldview as highlighted by John L. Mckenzie, in his "Aspects of Old Testament Thought," and the African one. This fact makes it possible for J.C. Bayeux to compare and contrast the African mindset to the biblical and the Western ones, in his article "Mentalité noire, mentalité biblique" (black mentality, biblical mentality). He concludes that the African thinking process and worldview are similar to the Hebraic, or Semitic, ones and different from the Western ones. He believes, therefore, that the Bible reveals a world, some conception of life, and thinking process with which Blacks can sympathize because they feel comfortable with it (59).

The points of comparison and contrast I can gather from Mckenzie and Bayeux are so important for discussion and comments that I synthetically summarized the seven main ones in the following table:

Introduction to Burkinabe Literature in English

	Western Mentality	Biblical/Semitic Mentality	African Mentality
1	Importance of the individual, e.g. Aristotle is the author of *Physics*. Thomas Aquinas wrote *Summa Theologica*, and Descartes, *Discourse on Method*.	Importance of the collectivity: Most Biblical books are anonymous. The Bible is a nation that tells the story of its sufferings, joys, and contradictions.	Importance of the collectivity: songs, dances, stories, tales, and proverbs are anonymous productions.
2	Separation of the religious from the secular: Focus on reason and the rigor of science. History is the result of series of causes. The secular is more important than the religious.	No separation of the religious and the secular: Supernatural explanation of natural events. e.g. In *Genesis*, everything comes into being from divine will: thunder, Sarah's sterility, fecundity, etc.	No separation of the religious and the secular: Supernatural explanation of natural events. e.g. The Haitian man seeks the charlatan, then the doctor when his child is sick.
3	Importance of scripture/writing as a tool.	Importance of orality: The Bible is the product of an oral civilization told from one generation to the next, before being written.	Importance of orality: prevalence of an oral tradition that uses songs, dances, stories, tales, and proverbs.
4	Repetitions are avoided whenever possible.	Hebraic poetry likes repetitions. Use of tom-toms and dances: King David dances before the Arch, accompanied with tambourines.	Lot of repetitions in African songs. Dances at the sounds of tom-toms and tambourines are part and parcel of African culture.
5	High consideration for metaphysics: thinking process is remote from Nature.	Little metaphysics: Thinking process is closer to Nature. The Bible is full of proper nouns, specific places, dates and stories to be metaphysical.	Little metaphysics: Thinking process is closer to Nature. Césaire's and Leon-Damas' poems are similar to the prophets Isaiah and Jeremiah.
6	Aloofness and individualism as characteristics of Western culture: everybody minds his/her own family and business.	Hospitality as characteristics. e.g. Abraham spontaneously welcomes three travelers as soon as he sees them.	Hospitality is a legendary characteristic of black society.

Chapter 4

| 7 | Meaninglessness of given names: they do not forcibly reflect reality. | Meaningfulness of given names: they reflect reality, e.g. Sarah means *princess*; Moses means *drawn from the waters*. Other names are theophanous: Isra-El; Shmu-El (Samuel); El-ijah; Immanu-El; Jo-El; Dani-El; Beth-El. | Meaningfulness of given names: they reflect reality. Are often theophanous: e.g. Wênd-kûuni in Moore means *God-given*, Sid-be-Wêndê means *Truth is in God*. |

This nonracist table of comparison helps decipher what, in the texts under study, is inspired from imitating the mindset of the colonizer, and what is drawn from Burkinabe traditional lore. For example, concerning the importance of individual authors versus anonymity or collectivity, it can be pointed out that three of the creation myths are authored – only one is anonymous – like the biblical book of Genesis. The mixing in this collection of two (colonial and Burkinabe traditional) worldviews is already a sign of hybridity. The story in Appendix 4 rightly presents the white man individualistically alone, while the blacks constitute a couple.

A synoptical comparison of the biblical story with the students' stories reveals further interesting parallels and contrasts, as can be seen in the following table.

Source	Genesis 1:1 to 2:3	Ouédraogo's collection
The author of creation	A single God, YHVH.	A single God, Wênnam.
Initial state of the earth	Darkness	Emptiness
First step	Creation of light	Creation of the world
Second step	Creation of the firmament	Creation of trees
Third step	Creation of dry land	Creation of animals
Fourth step	Creation of sun, moon, stars	Thinking of a king.
Final step	Creation of men and women.	Creation of man.

From this table, one can notice that the beginning and the end coincide. The creator is one God/Wênnaam, who made everything exist out of nothing, darkness, and crowned his work with the creation of human species. Comparing these made-up stories to the precolonial one in Appendix 1, it can be noticed that there is one common point: God as Creator at the beginning. The aim of the Burkinabe precolonial creation story is to explain why the

121

heaven and the clouds are far from the ground, and why the clouds are fat-looking. The story is set after the creation of heaven, earth, and human beings, and builds on this to explain the separation of heaven from the earth. It can be argued that this precolonial story has served as the basis for elaborating the other stories under the influence of the new details found in the biblical version brought by the colonizers. The stories in the collection are then a combination of two sources (native and colonial), creating hybridity.

Second, the cause of the man turning black (Appendix 4) is scientifically explained. There is no supernatural explanation, as would be the case in Semitic and Burkinabe thinking process.

Third, these made-up stories from Ouédraogo's students did not circulate orally before being written down: the reader knows them from reading them.

Fourthly, some authors tried to avoid repetitions, but others could not afford repeating some words and phrases: *alone* and *big* (Appendix 2), *think* (Appendix 3), *thought* (Appendix 5), which are marks of oral culture.

Fifthly, the man who turned white in Appendix 4 is aloof, minding only his own business, characteristic of Europeans' individualism, while the other one shows signs of the legendary African hospitality, having a wife in his home, staying with her, eating and talking with her, working together. The author of this story, Laurent Nikiéma, can be seen as unconsciously creating hybridity by mixing elements of European and African cultures.

Sixthly, the stories are not metaphysical, removed from nature, but about down-to-earth realities (land, trees, animals, men, and women), as shown in the similarity between the Semitic and African mindsets, which may explain the relative easiness for the Burkinabe authors to borrow elements from the biblical/Semitic culture and elaborate on them in their creativity.

Finally, all three known authors bear European first names (Gilbert, Jean-Pierre, and Laurent), while their Burkinabe surnames are more meaningful: Tiendrebeogo means *think of tomorrow* (Forebears).

Thus, Bayeux's comparison from an ontological perspective makes it possible to see the hybridity inherent in the different

Chapter 4

stories and any aping or mimicry involved, as regards colonizers' mentality.

Besides the similarity between the biblical, or Semitic, mentality and the African one, especially in the importance given to the collectivity and orality, the fusion of the religious and the secular, the closeness to nature, and the legendary hospitality, leads to the conclusion that Africans should have no problem understanding the Bible. It also cautions us to be aware of Eurocentrism while using translations of the Bible into European languages, as the difference between the biblical mindset and the Western one may have caused some difficulties. In fact, there is room for discussing the process of European modernist ideals being foregrounded in biblical translation into English. For example, the Hebrew word *El*, translated as *God* in English, means any god in general, including Hadad, Moloch, or Yahweh. It comes from a root word meaning "might, strength, power" (Summer). It is used in proper names, in compound forms (e.g. Isra-El). Yet *El*, or its derivative name *Elohim*, in the English Bible, is normally translated as God. Why didn't the English keep *El*, but use *God* instead?

Such a question is importantly relevant because, as Summer explains, *El*, in its plural form, *Elohim*, which is a form of majesty and honor, is found 2602 times in the Hebrew Bible, where it is used for: the true God, false gods, supernatural spirits (angels), and human leaders (kings, judges, the messiah). The fact that the English use the singular *God* to translate the Hebrew majestic form *Elohim*, for example, means that something is lost in the translation, and that the translation carries Eurocentrist aspects. In fact, translating the four Hebraic words *El, Elah, Elo'ah, Elohim*," to the one word *God* in English, means that many things are lost in the translation.

Concerning the etymology of the word *God* itself, the philologist Max Müller argues that there is perhaps "no etymology so generally acquiesced in as that which derives *God* from *good*. In Danish, *good* is *god*, but the identity of sound between the English god and the Danish *god* is merely accidental" (Kavanagh 155). After considering the same distinction of sound between *good* and

123

Introduction to Burkinabe Literature in English

god in other European languages, namely English (God and good), in Gothic (Gut and god), in German (Gott and gut), in Dutch (God and goed), Müller acknowledges the impossibility of giving a satisfactory etymology of either *God* or *good*, and concludes that the two words cannot be traced to one central origin. He claims that "God was most likely an old heathen name of the Deity, and for such a name the supposed etymological meaning of *good* would be far too modern, too abstract, too Christian" (Kavanagh 155). The process of European modernist ideals are thus foregrounded in biblical translation into English.

If the origin of the English *God* is heathen, the colonizers should consider the native Africans as heathen relatives and stop "othering" them, demanding they get rid of their religious practices they labeled "heathen." Their heathen past should have helped them to be more understanding and welcoming toward the native Africans. Yet "othering" the ones they colonized brings the latter to ape or mimic the colonizers in view of getting better consideration. This mimicry appears in three authors of the creation stories using the English word *God* instead of the Moore word *Wênnaam*, for the Creator. Only one is using it (Appendix 5). Yet, even he deems it necessary to put *God* in parenthesis at the first occurrence of the term *Wênnaam*. This word may come from *Wîniga* (the Sun), or *Wênd naam* (like majesty or kingship), which is closer to the etymological meaning of the Hebrew *El*.

Moreover, colonization is held responsible for the hybridity in the concomitant use of both *God* and *Wênnaam*. At colonial time, it was strictly forbidden to speak indigenous languages at school. Students were expected to speak only colonial languages, especially in the French colonies. Those who infringed that law were laughed at and punished. But as the students wrote in English and not in French, this may explain their taking the chance of concomitantly using some words from their mother tongue. Such hybridity expresses their desire to write back to postcolonialism, and to make their mother tongue survive in writing, in its ontological, as well as in its cultural, aspects.

Chapter 4

Hybrid Cultural Aspects in Creation Stories

Analyzing Burkinabe creation stories under study, cultural facts are to be taken into consideration for a deeper understanding. In Kaboré's account (Appendix 2), the first cultural element to pay attention to is the binarity of the Moose worldview, in which the world is divided into two opposite spheres: the home and the bush (Dévérin 2004). In the culture of the Moose people, whenever somebody is not at home, s/he is in the bush, even though that person may be in Paris, New York, or Dublin. In this context, one can understand the binary presentation of wild animals (elephant and reptiles) versus domestic ones (sheep) in Kaboré's creation story. Such a presentation is particular to the Moose perception of the universe, which colonization did not succeed to change. Hence, the hybrid nature of the colonized.

The second characteristic is that the Moose people are predominantly a farming population, like Israel's society, which remained agricultural throughout Biblical times. In the days of the Biblical patriarchs, agriculture included the farming of land and rearing of animals. Livestock farming and cattle breeding are also the main activities of Burkinabe people (World Bank 2017). Burkinabe farmers usually complain of cattle eating their plants and crops. The anthropomorphism in God as a farmer, and imageries on farming in the creation stories in Ouédraogo's collection are clearly understandable in this context. For example, the animals are presented in Kaboré's story as eating God's plants and crops.

The age-long opposition between farmers and cattle breeders also appears in the stories. The antagonism between these two categories is being depicted in this creation myth: animals are not good because they eat crops; man is good simply because he does not eat plants. The same agricultural-pastoral conflict exists in the Bible following the creation of the family of Adam and Eve, with their children Cain, a tiller of the soil, and Abel, a cattleman. But the sociologist Lynn Smith observes in his analysis of agricultural-pastoral conflict in the cradles of civilization: "As might be expected in a chronicle derived from a pastoral people, the Lord was offended by the smell of scorched grains and vegetables, and gratified by the odours given off by burned lamb" (18). By contrast, the Moose people are predominantly agricultural. Hence, the disfavor of pastoralism in the stories. The students adapted borrowed biblical elements to Burkinabe cultural context, which produced hybridity.

The third cultural element to be considered for a deeper understanding of the hybridity in Kaboré's story is the importance of kingship in Moose tradition. Even now, the Moose king plays an important role as mediator in crises, for which he won the 2017 Macky Sall Prize for Dialogue in Africa (Jamah 2017). This importance of kingship explains that in all of the creation stories in Ouédraogo's collection, man is made a king of the world. Gilbert Kaboré's account shows that God "decided to make [man] the king of the world and ruler of all animals," (Appendix 2) whereas the absence of a king is the worry at the center of Jean-Pierre Tiendrebeogo's creation story:

> *At the beginning, the world was empty. Then God created trees and animals. But there was no* king. *One day, God thought and thought. He said to himself: "I have created the world. I have created all the trees and animals that exist in the world. I am a very intelligent being. But I haven't created a* king *for the world. The world needs a* king.
>
> *Then God decided to create the* king *of the world. He created man.* (Ouédraogo p. 4, emphasis mine)

The teller of this story is obsessed with the idea of kingship, which rhythmically punctuates the narrative. This not exactly the case in the biblical account. In fact, the concept of kingship is completely absent in the first two chapters of *Genesis, which is about Adam's* "dominion" over all animals (Genesis 1:26, 30). The Hebrew word the English translated as *dominion*, also means *command*, which is one the king's attributes. From the point of view of ecocriticism, *dominion* can lead to mistreatment of other creatures in the environment, while the role of the king is to govern and take care of what is given to him. The king is called to rule the population as a subordinate king underneath God, the true King over all. Thus, through the witty adaptation of biblical elements to local context, in view of preserving the Burkinabe culture without rejecting the

Chapter 4

Bible in English cultural translation, Burkinabe creation stories are then a melting pot of both traditional and biblical elements about creation, and constitute Burkinabe people's response to the biblical stories brought to them dressed in European culture.

Ecocritical Considerations in Creation Stories in English

Nature is the subject of conflict in both Burkinabe and biblical creation stories: the environment being destroyed by one man's wickedness through the use of fire (Appendix 1); humans preferred to animals in the running of everything in the environment (Appendix 2); opposition between animals and man (Appendix 3); whites against blacks in the use of water (Appendix 4); lack of happiness when only one species of animals (man) is living in solitude (Appendix 5); and in the Bible, Adam and Eve are punished for eating the forbidden fruit.

So all these stories call for the protection and preservation of the environment through fights against forest fires; overuse of natural resources (plants, crops, water, etc.); and the fight for biodiversity in the prevention against disappearance of animal species, because humans would not live happily if they were the only one species left in the world. All stories are ecologically-minded, as they underline that the world's problems come from disobedience to the Creator.

In fact, from an ecclesial ecocritical point of view, one Creator made all that exists. The environment is then not man-made. Nature is just given to man to look after (as a king does), not to destroy it (as in the exercise of dominion). In order to encourage man in this noble task of caretaking, all stories underline man's goodness and superiority in the midst of the whole of creation. The Genesis stories are punctuated by, "And God saw that it was good." Man is created good.

Gilbert Kaboré's story (Appendix 2) contends that after creating all types of animals, which turn out to be naughty, "One day, God decided to create an animal very different from the other animals. He gave him a kind heart and a lot of intelligence. He called this animal man. Man did not disappoint God. So God was happy with man" (Ouédraogo 3). Man is an animal like the others – as stipulates the first characteristic of ecclesial ecocriticism theory – yet an intelligent and a kind one. In all stories, the couple man and woman is created after all the other creatures. However, the biblical accounts differ from the others because it is not explicitly stated therein that the human couple was created after the other animals created turned naughty. So the Burkinabe stories make explicit some aspects of the biblical account in European robe by writing back to it.

Another major point of similarity between biblical creation stories and the other ones is the idea of separation. The idea of separation is seen several times throughout Genesis. Genesis 1:4 reads: "God saw light was good; and God separated the light from the darkness," indicating the creation of night and day. The idea is also in Genesis 1:6: "God said, let there be a dome in the midst of the waters, and let it separate the waters from the waters." Likewise, Laurent Nikiéma's story, within Ouédraogo's collection, is about the separation of races, explaining "The Origin of White and Black Men," or that of the colonizer from the colonized (Appendix 4). It tells of the separation of humanity from a colorless unnamed race into two separate races, black and white, due to the wasting of a precious natural resource – water. The number of characters (two men), and the presence of the river, makes one liken this mythical village to the biblical Eden, with its garden and river watering it (Genesis 2:10). Yet the biblical creation myth does not explain the multiplicity of races, and the presence of this explanation in Nikiéma's story is undoubtly due to colonization. He is involved in the process of writing back, due to the influence of colonization: the different races appeared accidentally in time, as did colonization, and both wreaked similar havocs on the environment.

Furthermore, in both accounts of creation, laws or prescriptions are laid down for the protection of the environment, and to ensure order for a peaceful coexistence. In the biblical story, permission is given to Adam and Eve to eat of any fruit except one. In Nikiéma's story, the two men are allowed to use the water of the river, but prohibited to waste it. So in both narratives, freedom is

Chapter 4

not devoid of any laws and regulations. Yet the regulations have been transgressed. In all accounts, the disobedience of one person brings about negative consequences upon future generations. Yet, unlike the biblical story, where Adam and Eve share the same punishment after eating of the forbidden fruit, in Nikiéma's narrative, the whole family of one of the two men from the same village is punished (turned black) because of the disobedience of his colleague, who unexpectedly, is blessed (turned white). It is not told what their skin color was like prior to becoming white out of washing, or black due to the accumulation of dirt. Yet the presentation of blackness as the result of laziness and passivity, and whiteness as the recompense of active endeavors, serves the politics of colonial agenda. Such a negative representation of the origin of the black race by a black boy bears the influence of colonialism, which has instilled an inferiority complex in him, leading him to present the white race in a brighter light. The pupil appears then like a colonial product through this story, in which black people appear as objects of dupery from white people, who excel in tricks and subterfuge, like Mubia in Ngugi's allegory on the dispossession of black people's land by white colonizers (Ngugi, *A Grain of Wheat,* p. 15). Even today, the poor people suffer from the consequences of climate change caused by the rich.

The man who turned white out of washing is revealed to be too greedy in his use of water. The water was meant for drinking and washing. But he overused it, while his peer villager and his wife remained dirtier, and eventually black, as a result of staying home eating and gossiping, wasting time, instead of showing concern for more important matters. Such story perpetuates the colonial cliché of the white as witty and clever, and the black as lazy people. In fact, if water is symbolic of African natural resources, the story holds white people responsible for the spoiling of natural reserves when black people are inactive, and will eventually pay the price of their laziness, because by the time they wake up, they find that nothing of their God-given resources is left, but looted, plundered by others, like Mubia and the like in Ngugi's aforementioned allegorical story.

In both accounts, God pre-existed his creation. The fourth

characteristic of ecclesial ecocriticism requires that attention be paid to this aspect. The Creator lived alone before calling creation into existence: creation is not the result of mere chance. In the first biblical account of the creation, it is written: "In the beginning, God created the heavens and the earth" (Genesis 1:1). The second biblical account says: "At the time Yahweh made earth and heaven, there was as yet no wild bush on the earth, nor had any wild plant yet sprung up, for Yahweh God had not sent rain on the earth, nor was there any man to till the soil" (Genesis 2:5). Gilbert Kaboré's story also indicates that God lived alone in the world. Loneliness made him be bored. To solve his problem of solitude, he makes up his mind to create things and animals (Appendix 2). But though in both accounts, God makes himself known by creating – *Creator* is his name – in Burkinabe stories, creation is done out of need. Whereas, in the Bible, it is only out of love: the act of creating is presented as part of God's nature. This is a metaphysical explanation, proper to the European mentality. Whereas, the Burkinabe mindset expresses it differently. In fact, creation comes as a result of a need, in Kaboré's story, for God himself rather than for his creators. This need is another way of expressing love, because the lover is always in need of the loved one. Kaboré's account is thus a cultural adaptation and expression of the biblical one.

Next, in Kaboré's story, God starts creating the elephant, and sees that it is not good. Then he created the sheep, and was also dissatisfied. Successive disappointments lead God to create all the animals and plants, one after the other. The biblical version names only categories of animals: "God made every kind of wild beast, every kind of cattle, and every kind of land reptile. God saw that it was good" (Genesis 1:25). The two accounts corroborate, as the elephant belongs to the "kind of wild beast," and the sheep to the "kind of cattle." Kaboré's account writes back to, and elucidates, the biblical one. However, the apparent difference between the two stories is that, while the biblical account is rhythmically punctuated by the phrase, "And God saw that it was good," after the creation of each category, it is the opposite in Kaboré's story, where every specimen is created because the preceding ones are faulty. Yet a thorough analysis reveals that Kaboré's story is writing back to and adapting ideas expressed in different parts of the Bible. In fact, in the Bible, the divine exclamation at first sight, "It is good," will be soon followed by disappointment, which leads to God taking further actions. What is actually made explicit in Kaboré's story, is told in other parts of the Bible (Genesis 6:9–9:17) where God destroys his first creation to replace it with a new one. The universe was created perfect, but degenerated to the point where God had to kill every person, from the newborn to the elderly, in the flood of Noah. He destroys what was deemed perfect to initiate more perfect ones. Kaboré's account can then be seen as writing back under the influence of the different biblical accounts related to creation.

All creation stories reveal God's search for perfection in creation, the move from the imperfect to the perfect. The human being is the perfection par excellence, so that once man is created, God stops his work as the creator. Human beings' perfection is judged by the care given to the environment, in the protection of the natural eco-system.

Conclusion

From the similarities and differences between the biblical and Burkinabe creation stories shown through the comparative approach and the postcolonial ecocriticism theory, a certain number of conclusions can be drawn. First, traditional creation myths existed among the Burkinabe people, as they existed everywhere. With the influence of Christianism, the students created hybrid stories, expression of their new identities. Postcolonialist critics would say that their "twoness gives way to a bilateral sense of parallel cultures, and to a sense of multiple belongings, plural identities with no one more standard or normal or appropriate than another" (Rivkin and Ryan, p. 1101). The similarities and contrasts come from the adaptation of biblical elements dressed under European culture to Burkinabe context in a postcolonial period. The Burkinabe pupils' stories are thus a combination of old biblical themes with new twists due to new cultures and current realities such as colonialism.

Second, the presence and necessity of Burkinabe myths alongside the biblical ones, and written by Christians, have many sources of explanation. On the one hand, these mythical accounts respond to Burkinabe colonized people's refusal to let their creation stories be annihilated by the biblical versions of creation which spread in Africa during the colonial period. The authors of these creation stories in Ouédraogo's collection attempt, through their writings, to dismantle Eurocentric imperialism in Africa by moving away from the European monolithic way of presenting creation myths. On the other hand, the hybrid identity of the authors of these stories strongly impacted their writings, which bear the marks of hybridity and intertextuality.

Third, this study reveals that concern for the protection of Nature and the environment is not a modern innovation, but is mythologically grounded: all creation myths bear environmental concern. Myths and stories have been used, in places where orality prevails, as means of drawing people's awareness to the care for Nature. The diagnosis in all creation stories is that greediness destroys the harmony and peaceful coexistence of all creatures in Nature. All the myths didactically, then, call for a change in attitude for the protection of the environment, the common home to all animals, including men and women.

Works Cited List

Alliance Biblique Universelle. *Ancien Testament interlinéaire hébreu-français avec le texte de la Traduction œcuménique de la Bible et de la Bible en français courant*. Villiers-le-Bel: Société biblique française, 2007.

Ally Jamah. "Traditional King in Burkina Faso wins Africa Peace Award," https://www.standardmedia.co.ke/article/2001270911/traditional-king-in-burkina-faso-wins-africa-peace-award, Accessed August 19, 2019.

André Kaboré, "Theorizing Ecclesial Ecocriticism: Pathetic Fallacy in Ecclesiastical Literature on Climate Change," *Environment and Ecology Research*, vol. 4, no. 3 (2016), pp. 155–160.

Chapter 4

Ashcroft, Bill, Griffiths, Gareth, Tiffin, Helen. *The Empire Writes Back: Theory and Practice in Post-Colonial Literatures*. Second edition. London and New York: Routledge, 2002.

The Bible of Jerusalem. London: Darton, Longman & Todd, 1966.

Dévérin, Yveline. "Facteurs culturels et représentation de l'espace en pays mossi," Dulucq Sophie et Pierre Soubias, editor, *L'espace et ses représentations en Afrique* subsaharienne: Approches pluridisciplinaires. pp. 14–31. Karthala, 2004.

Findley, Timothy. *Not Wanted on the Voyage*. London: Penguin Books, 1996.

Forebears, https://forebears.io/surnames, Accessed November 3, 2020.

Gilbert Kaboré, "The Origin of Humanity," Ouédraogo, Mathieu R. *A Deal is a Deal, or How Much for Your Head and Other Stories: A Reader for Burkina Faso Secondary Schools*. p. 3. Ouagadougou: Self-published, 1989.

Isiguzo, Chikwurah Destiny. "Postcolonial Ecocriticism and the African Response to Human Experience and the Environment," *Localities*, vol. 7 (2017), pp. 43–74.

Kavanagh, Morgan Peter. *Origin of Language and Myths*. vol. 1. London: Sampson Low Publishers, 1871.

Lane, J. Richard. *The Postcolonial Novel*. Cambridge: Polity Press, 2006.

Mckenzie, John L. "Aspects of Old Testament Thought," *The Jerome Biblical Commentary,* edited by Raymond Brown, et al. pp. 736, 737. London: Chapman, 1970.

Ngugi, Wa Thiong'o. *A Grain of Wheat*. London: Heinemann, 1967.

Ngugi, Wa Thiong'o. *Weep not, Child*. London: Heinemann, 1964.

Nikiema, Laurent. "The Origin of White and Black Men," Ouédraogo, Mathieu R. *A Deal is a Deal, or How Much for Your Head and Other Stories: A Reader for Burkina Faso Secondary Schools*. p. 5. Ouagadougou: Self-published, 1989.

Ouédraogo, Mathieu R. *A Deal is a Deal,* or *How Much for Your Head and Other Stories: A Reader for Burkina Faso Secondary Schools.* Ouagadougou: Self-published, 1989.

Ouédraogo, Mathieu R. "How Woman was created from Man", Ouédraogo, Mathieu R. *A Deal is a Deal,* or *How Much for Your Head and Other Stories: A Reader for Burkina Faso Secondary Schools.* p. 6. Ouagadougou: Self-published, 1989.

Rivkin, Julie and Ryan, Michael. "English Without Shadows: Literature on a World Scale," *Literary Theory: An Anthology*, edited by Julie Rivkin and Michael Ryan. pp. 1099–1106. Malden: Blackwell, 1998.

Said, Edward W. *Beginnings: Intention and Method.* London: Granta Books, 1997.

Said, Edward W. *Culture and Imperialism.* London: Vintage Books Editions, 1993.

Said, Edward W. *Orientalism.* London: Vintage Books Editions, 1978.

Sissao, Alain Joseph. *Folktales from the Moose of Burkina Faso.* Translated by Tanti, Nina. Bamenda: Langaa RPCIG, 2010.

Slemon, Stephen, "Post-Colonial Allegory and the Transformation of History," *The Journal of Commonwealth Literature,* vol. 23, no.1 (1988), pp. 157–168.

Smith, T. Lynn, "Agricultural-Pastoral Conflict: A Major Obstacle in the Process of Rural Development," *Journal of Inter-American Studies*. Vol. 11, no. 1 (1969), pp. 16–43.

Summer, Paul. "'Elohim' in Biblical Context," http://www.hebrew-streams.org/works/monotheism/context-elohim.html. Accessed July 3, 2020.

Tiendrebeogo, Jean-Pierre. "The Origin of Man," Ouédraogo, Mathieu R. *A Deal is a Deal,* or *How Much for Your Head and Other Stories: A Reader for Burkina Faso Secondary Schools.* p. 4. Ouagadougou: Self-published, 1989.

World Bank, "Burkina Faso: Agriculture as a Powerful Instrument for Poverty Reduction," June 29, 2017, www.worldbank.org, Accessed August 19, 2019.

Chapter 4

Appendix 1

Moore Language	Translation into English
Sɪngr wẽndẽ kibare Sɪngr wẽndẽ, Wẽnnaam naana saaga la sawat da pẽ tẽnga, tɪ Wẽnnaam yeele: "Mam maana woto n kõ neba. La sawat na n lebga nemd tɪ neb wãbdẽ," la zĩig a yembr bee be n ya taok n yɪɪda, tɪ Wẽnnaam yeele: "Zĩ-kãnga yaa kaam zĩiga, bugum da pɛneg-a ye." La neb fãa sakame la b wãba nemd daar fãa la nemd zãaga zĩiga la ra keta taokã zĩigẽ bala. La wãoor n da be neb sʋka, la a pa tõe n paam nemd daar fãa ye. La a sũur puuga ne neba t'a yeele: "Mam pa tõe n paam nemd la wã sẽn pẽ tẽnga, mam na mok bugum n vulg tɪ yẽneg tɪ mam me paam," tɪ neb yeele: "Ayo, fo pa wʋm Wẽnnaam sẽn yeel tɪ d na ning bugum ka," t'a yeele, "Yẽe, la ya bõe yĩnga tɪ mam ka be nusi la naoa n tõog n paam tɪ yãmb yãkd daar fãa la y pa kõt maam, mam nan ninga bugum bala." La wãorã ning bugum zĩ-kãnga, la saaga zẽka sawatã n kul yĩngri. La rẽ yĩng la saaga be yĩngri tɪ sawat wend nemd kaam. Yaa wãor n maan neb pʋto-kãnga. Sãn pa rẽ saaga ne sawatã da bee tẽngre, la marsã saaga ne sawatã kula yĩngri. (R.P. Alexandre, *Moos soalma*, sebre III, Self-published, 1953, p. 32.)	**A story about the beginning** At the beginning, Wênnaam created heaven and the clouds were close to the ground, and Wênnaam said, "I have done this for people. And the clouds shall become meat for people to eat." But there is one part in it that is harder than the others, and Wênnaam said, "This part is fat meat, fire should not go near this part." And all people agreed and they were eating meat every day and meat was far from the ground except the part with fat meat. And a leper was among the people, and he was not able to have meat every day. He became angry with the people and said, "I am not able to reach the other part of meat, but the fat meat that is close to the ground. I'll fetch fire and burn the fat in order to have some." And the people said, "No, haven't you heard that God said we should not bring fire near it?" and he said, "Yes. But why, I have no hands and feet and cannot reach the meat but you take it every day and do not share with me, I am going to put fire to it." And the leper put fire to this part, and heaven removed the clouds and went up. It is because of this that heaven is up and the clouds are like fat meat. It is the leper who wickedly caused this to people. If not, heaven and the clouds were close to the ground, but now heaven and the clouds went up. (Translation mine)

135

Appendix 2
The Origin of Humanity

At the beginning, there was only God in the world. He lived alone in the big, big world. He was not very happy, because he felt lonely. One day, he said that he had enough of living all alone. He decided to create things and animals.

So he created the elephant. But the elephant destroyed his crops. God was not happy with the elephant. Then he created the sheep. But God was not happy with the elephant or the sheep. The sheep ate his plants and crops. So he was angry with the sheep.

Then he created all the animals, one after the other. But he was not satisfied with them. They were all very naughty. One day, God decided to create an animal very different from the other animals. He gave him a kind heart and a lot of intelligence. He called this animal man. Man did not disappoint God. So God was happy with man. He decided to make him the king of the world and ruler of all animals. (Gilbert Kaboré, Collège de la Salle, classe de 3e)

Appendix 3
The Origin of Man

At the beginning, the world was empty. Then God created trees and animals. But there was no king. One day, God thought and thought. He said to himself: "I have created the world. I have created all the trees and animals that exist in the world. I am a very intelligent being. But I haven't created a king for the world. The world needs a king."

Then God decided to create the king of the world. He created man. Unlike the other animals, he could think and talk. All the animals feared him because he looked different, and he had manners that they could not understand.

But man was not very happy, because he felt lonely. No animal came to talk to him. God did not always have time to come and sit and talk with him. But he took time to think, think, and think. Then one day, he found the solution. He created woman and gave her as a wife to man. When man saw her, he was very

Chapter 4

happy. He thanked God very much for his kindness. (Jean-Pierre Tiendrebeogo, Collège de la Salle, classe de 3ᵉ)

Appendix 4
The Origin of White and Black Men

Once upon a time, there lived two men in a village. The village had a river, but there was not much water in the river. God warned them that they could use the water of the river, but he told them that they should not waste it.

But one hot day, one of the men went to the river. He took a lot of water. He drank and washed himself. He became white.

The second man stayed at home with his wife. He ate some rice and talked with his wife. Then he, too, went to the river to fetch some water. But when he arrived there, he found that there was no more water in the river. He called his wife. They both went in the riverbed. But there was no water. They dug the mud, but could not find any water. In the end, they were covered with mud. They were angry because they could not find water to drink and wash themselves. The dark clay dried on their skin and they became black. (Laurent Nikiema, Collège de la Salle, classe de 3ᵉ)

Appendix 5
How Woman was Created from Man

At the beginning, the world was empty. One day, Wennam (God) decided to create man. But he did not know how to begin. So he thought and thought and thought. One day, Wennam took some wet clay and shaped it into man. This was the first man that God created.

Man was alone. He had nobody to talk to or laugh with or tell stories to. So he was very unhappy. Wennam saw that man was not happy. And Wennam was not happy.

Then Wennam decided to create woman. He said: "I have created man from clay. I am not going to use clay again. I must find something else, something new." So Wennam thought and thought and thought for a long time. Then one day, he took a bone from man and made woman. So woman was like man, but was not man. When man saw woman, he was very happy. Woman saw man and was happy. Wennam was happy to see them happy. (Anonymous)

Chapter 4

e) Nature and Peaceful Religious Coexistence in Thiobiany's *Before the Fires I was Black*

Introduction

Framed in the context of an African oral storytelling environment around the hearth or the tree of palavers, Thiobiany's novel, *Before the Fires I was Black: A Blueprint for a Brighter Future* (2018), is organized as a collection of sixteen talks from a father, Yaldia, to his three children, Hounteni, Talar and Pala. The talks are about the African continent and its descendants, discussing the different foreign invasions' effects on African and black societies. The narrator takes readers on a journey to different African countries, sharing the experiences he had in each country. The novel is a portrayal of the complexity and intricacy of African cultures and environments. The author addresses all African people through Yaldia's children, who, like many Africans, are "cultural hybrids" whose "roots are slipping from under [them]." Moreover, these children, and Africans in general, are eager to know their cultural and historical background, and even keen on exploring painful narratives of fragmentation, such as Achebe's "Things Fall Apart."

The novelist yields to the audience's desire to know about their precolonial past. The cultural hybridity in which the three children live is actually the main reason why the father undertakes to spend sixteen evenings during the summer vacation to tell his offspring about their origins. Colonization and devastation of African forest and fauna are blamed throughout the novel, the purpose of which is to free people from colonization's grip, and to provide more care of the environment; hence, the relevance of the adoption of a postcolonial ecocritical approach to this fiction.

During the fourth and sixth evening talks, the subjects are respectively about "Spirituality and the Invisible World," and "Our Relationship with Mother Nature." Realizing that the world today is in a high level of cultural and ecological conflicts because some politicians promote environmental, cultural, and religious intolerance as a means of domination (82), the narrator, a master storyteller, promotes himself as a peace builder. What means does the narrator use to reach his objective of religious cohesion and peace among the diversity of people and natures? This is the question this research paper sets out to answer. It looks at Thiobiano's presentation of the history of the human and environmental crisis confronting Africans, and shows that the rehabilitation of African Traditional Religion (ATR), respect for Mother Nature and other religions, and inculturation (the use of African cultural practices into Christianity) are the main methods the author strongly puts forward to bring about peace in social living, as well as in the environment.

Postcolonial Ecocriticism

The theory of postcolonial ecocriticism is a combination of postcolonialism and ecocriticism: the first being concerned with culture, and the second with nature. Postcolonialism ignores the environmental exploitation of former colonies and ecological concerns that underpin the colonizers and the colonized. Ecocriticism also does not consider cultural and civilizational concerns. Yet, apart from this strict nature-culture dichotomy, combing them into social justice for the environment is possible. In Isiguzo's (2017, p. 51) definition of postcolonial ecocriticism, while applying it to his analysis of two works from African literature, this theory emphasizes "the interdependence and interconnectedness of human survival and environmental change, and the sustainment of a relationship between cultural survival and a viable environment."

The recent outbreak of the coronavirus actually calls to mind this interconnectedness of human life and environmental change. As a matter of fact, studies have shown how in recent decades, the interconnectedness of humans with the animal kingdom has come to the forefront as transmission of such illnesses as SARS, Ebola, and coronavirus have been spread to humans. In fact, human activities are causing major upheavals in biodiversity in many places on the planet. These diseases occur in a context of an ever-globalized world with an intense international connectivity. Likewise, colonization and neocolonization, in the context of globalization, bring many cultures into contact, thus favoring the

Chapter 4

possibility of the stronger cultures absorbing the weaker ones, similar to humans preying on other species in the environment.

Young (2001, p. 57) contends that it is the nature of postcolonialism to be both contestatory and committed toward ideals of social justice, of political and transnational nature, attacking the status quo of hegemonic economic imperialism for the advent of new forms of political identity. "Identity" is central to both postcolonial and ecological discourses, as it challenges oppression based on cultural identity, or dissemination of biodiversity. The notion of identity, specifically in the postcolonial register, focuses on "colonial and neo-colonial oppression, on resistance to colonialism, on the respective identities of colonizer and colonized," as well as on "the patterns of interaction between those identities, on postcolonial migration to the metropolis, on the ensuing hybridity of culture, and so on" (Hans Bertens 2001, p. 202). Postcolonialism basically counters the "center," or those dominating, in order to give the "margin," or the dominated, its own true voice and identity. It is then a "counter-hegemonic discourse" in which "the empire writes back to the centre," in the words of Rusdie Salman (Ashcroft, Griffiths & Tiffin 1989, p. ix), to dismantle the Western notion of superiority and assert its identity.

Postcolonialism is a body of thinking that questions Western hegemony through the examination of literary and cultural productions. It tries to subvert the notion of white people's superiority over the so-called Third World inferiority. Postcolonialism also questions the notion of universalism, through which Westerners maintain their hegemony, and the use of the notions of "alterity," or otherness, "of the margin", through "hybridity." Hence, Ashcroft, Griffiths, and Tiffin (1989, p. 2) submit that postcolonial theory deals with old and new issues of various kinds, such as "migration, slavery, suppression, resistance, representation, difference, race, gender, place, and responses to the influential master discourses of imperial Europe." Ecocritics also deal with these issues, mainly with the migration of species, their mistreatment, eradication, and the measures of resistance undertaken to ensure the representation of species in respect of race, gender and place in the universe.

Ecocriticism is actually the transposition of postcolonialism to the field of ecology, as it is about the preservation of the identities of species of animals and plants, which make up biodiversity. Human-centeredness, or mono-identity, does not make up biodiversity. Human nature is one among many others in Nature (Francis 2015). It is the dominating nature that should be countered in order to give the other "marginal" natures and environments their own identities. Like postcolonialism, ecocriticism aims at doing social justice to the environment and its inhabitants. So it questions the notion of human hegemony over the other creatures, "othering" them, as though human beings are not just one of the creatures. It questions the natural independence of the human species formerly subjected to the general natural rule.

To sum up, ecocriticism deals with the protection of the environment, which is an aspect of the universe. Postcolonialism is concerned with anything regarding the colonized and his/her culture in a globalized world. What is at the core of each of these theories is, then, the protection of an element, out of a whole, from destructive predators. The theory that will be used in this paper, postcolonial ecocriticism, considers African people and culture as threatened to disappear due to greedy foreign forces. It looks at both the environment and people, how both are interconnected. A critical analysis of Thiobiany's *Before the Fire I was Black,* reveals the author's perception of the impact of slavery, colonialism, and neocolonialism in Africa, and the strong solutions he proposes, as well as the literary devices he uses to call for a retrospective reformation of Africans and their environment.

Use of Environmental Metaphors in the Criticism of Colonization

Two strong metaphors in Thiobiany's novel draw the reader's attention to the havocs caused by colonialism and the misuse of the environment: the tree as symbolic of culture and knowledge, and the fire for colonialism. Talking to his children, Yaldia claims that "the disaster of the foreign fires that moved over our continent have burned many roots in the ground, the roots of many ancient,

Chapter 4

endemic trees," causing them to lose most of their leaves, and to be "in the state of prolonged coma because of the heat from these fires" (p. 300).

The "ancient, endemic trees" are metaphors for African culture and folklore. These trees have not been substituted by foreign ones, but simply suppressed, burned from the leaves down to the roots in the ground. Substitution is deemed impossible because the African ground and climate are not suitable for foreign trees. In other words, foreign cultures can hardly thrive in Africa. These metaphoric trees are so old, and with well-grounded roots, that it is impossible to deracinate them unless through burning. Even the effect of the fire on them is a slow death, starting from the leaves and going slowly down to the roots.

The narrator posits that in such a context, there are basically two available options for the preservation of our metaphoric trees of culture and knowledge: One consists in giving up and watching powerlessly as an outsider, the irreversible burning of "the ancient forests of our very being." And the other is to actively "struggle to maintain and revitalize the trees that still have lost most of their leaves, and to nurture the seedlings of rare species of cultural values and information that can then be anchored to contemporary science and other valuable kinds of knowledge" (p. 300). The leaves are metaphors for cultural values. The values that are still hanging, resisting to the effects of the destructive fires, need care and maintenance for survival. As for those which have already been burnt, but whose seeds have been kept, these can be replanted to add to the biodiversity of universal knowledge, or to constitute what Senghor (1963) calls the "Civilisation of the Universal."

The main second ecologic metaphor appears right in the title of the novel: *Before the Fires I was Black*. The forest-devastating "fire" is a metaphor for colonization. The "fires" are the different periods of colonization. The foreword to the novel states that the "book discusses the myriad of ways that foreign invasions have affected African and Black societies, and how we must accelerate the healing process – because we were burnt" (p. vii). Encapsulated in the "we" are black people and their environment.

Introduction to Burkinabe Literature in English

This idea is made more explicit in the first chapter, entitled, "We Are Stronger Than Colonization's Grip." The omniscient narrator has Yaldia explain to his children that "there have been several foreign fires that have burned and are still burning the land in our continent, bringing disaster to our hearts and the lives of those who live in our communities" (p. 2). The burning concerns both the land and its inhabitants inseparably. In all these instances, and throughout the whole novel, emphasis is placed on the negative and destructive nature of fires, overshadowing the positive aspects of brightness suggested in the subtitle, *Blueprint for a Brighter Future*.

The antidote to the fires, which can bring about a brighter future to both people and the land, is "the journey to the world of our Ancestors to better understand our culture" (p. 3). The "world of the Ancestors" refers to both the living and their habitat, including forests and rivers. The solution is easy – it is in close reach, as the Ancestors do live in the spiritual world, as well as in that of the living. As the Senegalese poet Birago Diop (1960) asserts, the Ancestors are not dead and buried underneath the earth:

> *The dead are not under the earth:*
> *they are in the tree that rustles,*
> *they are in the wood that groans,*
> *they are in the water that sleeps,*
> *they are in the hut, they are in the crowd,*
> *the dead are not dead...*
> *they are in the whimpering rocks,*
> *they are in the forest, they are in the house,*
> *the dead are not dead.*

There is, then, no separation between the world of the living and that of the dead. Both living and dead live together in harmony, in the same nature. The destruction of this prevailing symbiosis with the arrival of the binary vision of life during colonization constitutes an ecological havoc. To solve this problem, the narrator recommends a return, or spiritual journey, to the past to learn to live in harmony with the environment. This is what the narrator means with the closing words of the novel, "using our cultural values as a foundation" (p. 339), creating thus an *inclusio* as both beginning – "to better understand our culture and move towards a brighter future" (p. 3) – and end of the novel are all about the same issue.

Inclusio (also known as bracketing, or an envelope structure) is a literary device based on a concentric principle which consists of creating a frame by placing similar material at the beginning and end of a book. In the novel under study, this literary device alerts the reader to the particularly important theme of the metaphoric fires destroying African cultural values developed within the bracketed inclusion or the entire novel.

The strong metaphor of "fires" for colonization and its aftermath of neocolonialism powerfully depicts the bitter encounter of two civilizations and the devouring nature of colonialism, which attempts to swipe anything in its way. The fire metaphor is in the plural because it stands for, not only "the flames of the slavery, colonial, and postcolonial periods, and the fires of globalization" (p. 100), but also the environment-destructive fires. Many examples of the plights produced by the fires are given. The narrator contends that the overexploitation of African natural resources and the plight of the colonial war veterans are some of "the many examples of the impact of colonial fire…a fire that burned over the continent and sent most of its strong and valorous men for the building of foreign peace and welfare," with no compensation in return (p. 180).

Accordingly, the objective of this novel, as the author states in the preface, is to "celebrate our resilience and resistance despite the number of fires that we have endured and the trials that we are still experiencing" (p. ix). This fiction constitutes by itself a way of resisting being burned. It aims at making the readers come to the knowledge of African cultural values which have been wiped out by colonial fires, hoping that this knowledge will operate like balm to heal the wounded parts and stop further fires from having any destructive effect. The author is confident that transmitting the best of our African values to the African youth contributes to taking the fire away from their skins, and paves a way for a brighter future for them.

Introduction to Burkinabe Literature in English

The narrator makes Yaldia tell his children of his conviction that African intellectuals trained by Westerners have their "cultural values hidden under layers of fake "white" cultural behaviours" (p. 100). The fires have touched only the epidermis of their bodies. We move thus from the metaphoric fire that can reduce the trees of culture and knowledge into ashes, to a new fire that can bring about a postcolonial hybrid identity, white and black at the same time. Or rather, African and European/Asian. The metaphoric fire is able to camouflage one's true identity in the same ways as dust covers one's body.

The fire is also not a black-smoke-producing, or darkening, fire, but a whitening one. One does not become black as a result of undergoing such fires, but one loses one's blackness and becomes white on the surface as a consequence. Being not irreversibly burned, but just covered with white soot or ashes, a good shake off can reveal one's real black identity, which is hidden under a white mask. Yaldia, the storyteller, presents himself to his children as belonging to this "new generation of 'Whites with Black skin'" (p. 240).

All these elements coalesce to lead readers into taking this novel as another version of Frantz Fanon's *Black Skin, White Masks* (1952), both in its symbolic form, as well as in its contents. Actually, even though a comparison of the two books is not the object of this study, it can be observed that both books are written in the style of auto-theory, in which the authors share their own experiences in addition to presenting a historical critique of the effects of colonialism on the human psyche. Both Fanon and Thiobiany call upon historical interpretation, and the concomitant underlying social indictment, to understand the complex ways in which African identity is constructed.

Furthermore, religiously speaking, the narrator resorts to the metaphor of "burning" to explain the appearance of the black race. He explains that God is a potter. God makes all races out of clay. The narrator claims that newly converted Africans to foreign religions, in the early days of colonial occupation, were told that "God's forgotten clay became burned by fire. As God didn't want to throw this clay away, he decided to create Black people" (p.

139). This is a mythical colonial explanation of the appearance of different races that can but bring conflict of races. How can the black race be accidentally created? How can God be careful in the creation of white races and the like, but careless for black people? In a postcolonialist perspective, such biased myths are inventions aiming at "othering" all that is not white. The narrator further highlights that a similar strategy of "poisoning and things like that" have been used to "condemn traditional religion and present it as evil" (p. 153), "othering" it from the Christian religion.

To counter such religious misrepresentation in favor of peaceful coexistence among religions, as well as between humans and the environment, the master storyteller raises his children's awareness to the fact that bad practices exist in any society, by giving them the example of a former Russian spy poisoned in London with polonium-210, and so invites them to never lose sight of the positive aspects of ATR, which is respectful of Mother Nature.

Strategies for Peaceful Coexistence

The strong simile between trees and African values and knowledge requires that the advent of peace comes from care and respect for the environment. The other strategies the storyteller presents to his listeners in favor of peace between religions are also a rehabilitation of ATR, which has been ignored during colonial time. Then there is the presentation of the features in all religions to help mutual understanding; and lastly, the examples of the examples of inculturation to encourage religious syncretism.

Care for Mother Nature

At the opening of the novel, Yaldia informs his audience that Africa is an old continent rich in thousands of societies and cultures that all have something in common – that is, "a respect for Mother Nature and the value of the relationship between her and humans" (p. 4). Africa has different environments – from the forests to the savannah and deserts – but there is harmony and peace when people give due respect to the different environments. For example, Africans know that the Ancestors live with humans, as well as in the wild: in most villages, a sacred patch of vegetation, or a sacred grove, known as "sacred forest," is consecrated to the Spirits and Ancestors (p. 102). So once in the wild, people should show respect by greeting the visible and invisible creatures, using special songs. And in that way, show that they are coming there in peace to praise their "wisdom of coexistence with animals" (p. 89). The narrator says that environmentalists nowadays acknowledge that the preservation of the original biodiversity of flora and fauna is due to the taboos (animal or plant) surrounding these sacred groves or forests, which saved them from human and livestock pressure and wildfires (p. 102).

Conflicts arise when Mother Nature is not respected. Yaldia tells his children that the banning of traditional taboos and other rules as "satanic," by colonizers and foreign religious leaders, has consequently led to a "large-scale environmental 'apocalypse'" (p. 103). Young people and civil servants started overthrowing the old environmental values, which led to free and unregulated access and use of natural resources, and destruction of protected tree species. As a result, humans are left to themselves with no environment to learn knowledge from when they face problems of hunger and diseases.

However, the narrator stresses that when the thousands of ethnic groups, nations, and nationalities who live in Africa "tailor their lives, their philosophical approaches, and social organizations according to their physical environments" (p. 101), the overwhelming result is peace and harmony. The reader is told that the millennial survival of the African continent is due to its traditional wisdoms, as well as "the useful information that [what] anyone is able to learn is closely linked to the environment in which he or she is living" (p. 16). The environment, then, deserves respect because it is a master teacher, showing people how to "find food and medicines from Mother Nature" and other solutions to their specific problems (p. 16). This respect for the environment paves the way for the respect of the Ancestors who have their sacred abodes in it, according to the rules of the traditional religion.

Chapter 4

Rehabilitation of African Traditional Religion (ATR)

The advent of peace in everyday living requires a rehabilitation of ATR. Yaldia tells his children that the minds of African people have been disturbed during colonial time because of attempts at "othering," or calumniating their religious practices. The narrator explains that because African people were told that their traditional religion was nothing but evil, they lacked "sufficient confidence and interest in taking stock of their own African values" (p. 249), and younger generations started expressing their disbelief in ATR (p. 323). It is understandable that communication and dialogue are not possible in this utter denial of one's true nature. Dialogue is only possible when all religions are recognized in their own rights. Therefore, African religion has to be resuscitated or rehabilitated if peace is to be restored.

The narrator gives lessons girded on the rehabilitation of ATR. First, he gives the indigenous religion a name: animism. Then he bemoans that, during colonial and neocolonial periods, "none of the major world religions acknowledge[d] animism as our motherland religion, yet this is the religion that flourished in the past, nourished our spirituality, and led to the innovations created by generations of Africans" (p. 68). He explains that it is a religion which believes that "there is only one God who can be reached through respective Ancestors" (p. 67). In this sense, it is like the revealed religions. In this religion, adherents also believe in life after death (238). The narrator strongly posits that it is also a religion whose "philosophy prescribes tolerance for various religious beliefs and cultural background, fully recognizing that intolerance can bring societies, countries, and the overall world close to destruction" (p. 67). He then urges people to believe in this religion, as in any other. It is a religion in which "spirituality *is* life" (p. 68), not separated from life but a component of it.

After rehabilitating ATR so that it can participate in the world system of "give and take," the narrator proceeds to strike a comparison with the other world religions to pave the way for mutual understanding and peaceful coexistence.

Similarities Between Religions

After studying the novel, one realizes that belief in one God, and in the mediation of the Ancestors or saints, constitutes the main similarity between revealed religions – such as Judaism, Christianity, and Islam – and ATR. All religions are at par in terms of the oneness of God. They differ in how to approach him. The storyteller informs his audience that in its different initiation practices, the adherents of ATR do not "other" or discriminate against anybody based on his or her official religion (Christian, Muslim, or Animist) or financial status (rich or poor), but strive to preserve unity in the community (p. 92, 93). This unity is inspired from Nature's wisdom.

The former state forester, Peter Wohlleben (p. 2016), makes the case that the forests are a social network: trees are social creatures that talk to each other, experience pain, have sex, and mother their young, just like humans. In Nature, there is a place for any plant to grow, and any animal to live, without discrimination on any basis; hence the injunction not to "destroy the vegetation simply for pleasure" (p. 24). If this is done, humans will be deprived of food, medicines, and inspirational wisdom. Likewise, religions should coexist peacefully in society.

One of the differences between ATR and the revealed religions is that, as the storyteller explains it to his audience, "For Christians, Jews, and Muslims, God's precepts are written in sacred books, while, in the pure African religion, there is no written sacred book, yet there are sets of concepts, rules, and laws with taboos transmitted orally from generation to generation" (p. 95). That is why Christians make oaths with their hands on the Bible, and Muslims on the Holy Koran. Whereas, in ATR, "sacred sayings or speeches are vows to be kept as a sign of respect to God and the Ancestors" (p. 259). Some of the rules in ATR are in respect of the devotion to God and the Ancestors, and are taught to children, particularly during sacred initiation ceremonies. The moral and religious values they contain help men and women to maintain hope and courage despite the challenges before them.

The narrator further expounds that, whereas in Christianity, angels and devils exist in the spiritual world, in ATR, it is a

Chapter 4

question of *tuur* (for the *Serere* people in Senegal) or *boolo* (for the *Gourmantché* in Burkina Faso), which are presented as a key feature of African theology. The *tuur* or *boolo* is described as "a good spirit who serves as a medium...[a] spirit in permanent connection with the Ancestors, who guides you and provides you with the best alternatives and wisdom" (p. 76). A guardian angel's role is to give advice, in enigmatic language, to anybody, every day. Initiation is required to decipher the codes of its language (p. 76).

Yaldia also makes his children aware that solidarity is stronger in ATR. Whereas individualism tends to characterize the revealed religions:

> *Foreign religions* tend *to focus on* individuals *rather than* communities *or* families. *In a traditional system...the chief would encourage everyone to interact with each other as a large family...prays for the family, not for his individual interests.* (p. 281, Emphasis mine)

The choice of words is important here: the two main comparative terms are repeated, while the use of the verb *tend* in the description of foreign religions shows caution. It is in fact an oversimplification to see that revealed religions are individualistic. From its etymology, *church* comes from *ecclesia*, which means *gathering, assembly*. People gather to offer Mass and pray for the whole community, even though individually, people should pray and live as Christians. But by using the verb *tend*, one can perceive the desire to simplify for comparison sake, paving the way for peaceful religious coexistence through inculturation, without "othering" or causing prejudice to the revealed religions. Comparisons enable believers of the different religions to know each other in order to live together peacefully.

Inculturation

After establishing the similarities and differences between the religions, the narrator proceeds to show that they are compatible by way of syncretism, which is inherent in ATR. He argues that adherents of ATR can take part in any other religion, provided they "pay tribute to the Ancestors spirits by all means" (p. 70).

He gives the example of the northern part of the Republic of Senegal, where Muslims and Christians alike practice ancient ancestral ceremonies involving paying tribute to the Ancestors. He draws the conclusion that "calls for help to the Ancestors are embedded in the fabric of societies throughout the continent" (p. 70), regardless of belonging to any new religion. Despite being either a Christian or a Muslim, African men and women are still fundamentally attached to the Ancestors. He does not conceive of any pure Islamists, or pure Christians in Africa, as most Africans who converted into Christianity or Islam still pay tribute to the Ancestors' spirits by all means. Such syncretism gives no room for "othering prejudices," or religious extremism or radicalism.

Furthermore, once on the African soil, some foreign religions tried to incorporate some traditional practices. The narrator claims that many Muslims, though they do not sing and dance in their religious rites, many of their Muslim practices do integrate other African traditional practices. He gives the example of the "important presence and role the Marabou play in traditional societies as an illustration of the synergy between African Islam and animist spirituality" (p. 82). Marabou are traditionally Muslim religious leaders and teachers.

Finally, in addition to syncretism, attempts of inculturation are also found, especially in Christianity. Inculturation, especially in the Roman Catholic Church, refers to the adaptation of the way Church teachings are presented to non-Christian cultures, and to the influence of those cultures on the evolution of these teachings. Examples are the incorporation of drummed songs and dances in some Protestant and Catholic churches as an important part of the service (p. 90).

Yaldia gives the example of the celebration of the feast of the Epiphany in Addis Ababa, Ethiopia, highlighting how much he was transported during the celebration, by the processional music, and at contemplating Christian Orthodox priests dancing, with their crosses moving up and down. He also strongly commends the decision made by the Episcopal Conference of Churches in Africa "to amend the Roman style of preaching by adding the rich African spiritual dimension" (p. 91). The amendments include the use of drums and tam-tams, made from wood taken from some special trees of African forests, and melodies from the depths of African traditional richness. In this way, mutual mistrust or hatred yields to mutual acceptance and peaceful coexistence, helping Africans, as Yaldia puts it, "to keep their spiritual traditions while practising exogenous religions" (p. 91).

Conclusion

With his novel, *Before the Fires I was Black* (2018), Prince Lamourd Thiobiany shows serious concerns for peace in the African environment and culture, inviting the current generation of Africans to stop aping foreigners and be proud of themselves and their identities. With the mastery of African storytelling eloquence, the narrator succeeds in convincing readers that taking care of nature and "promoting cultural and philosophical diversity and respect for the religions of others builds cohesion and peace" (p. 82).

To come to this conviction, my critical analysis of this novel has been aided by the postcolonial ecocritical theory defined and used to expose the literary techniques the writer resorts to in order to fight for the protection of Mother Nature and African folklore. Through the metaphors of "tree" for African traditional culture and knowledge, and "fires" for external foreign aggressive invaders, the author blames colonization for "othering" and firing away African culture and age-long traditions, and looting its natural resources, regardless of the existing taboos. He shows that there can be no peace between religions and nations if people are not living in harmony with their environment.

Resorting to comparative strategies in postcolonial perspective, he also pleads for the protection of the environment, for the rehabilitation of ATR, and the incorporation of its values in the foreign religions to ensure peaceful coexistence. It is within this religious and cultural symbiosis that the Eden tree of knowledge of good and evil (Genesis 2:17) can grow amid the other trees in the "civilisation of the Universal," where "the give and take" system of life takes precedence over self-centrism and "othering."

Works Cited List

Ashcroft, Bill; Griffiths, Gareth & Tiffin, Helen. *The Empire Writes Back: Theory and Practice in Post-Colonial Literatures*. London: Routledge, 1989.

Ashcroft, Bill, Griffiths, Gareth and Tiffin, Helen, editors. *The Post-Colonial Studies Reader*. London and New York: Routledge, 2006.

Bamgbose, Gabriel Sunday. "The Black Man's Ordeals: A Post-Colonial Reading of Kofi Anydoho's *Ancestrallogic and Caribbean Blues*," *The African Symposium*, vol. 13, no. 1 (2013), pp. 34–41.

Bartens, Hans. *Literary Theory: The basics*. London: Routledge, 2001.

Diop, Birago. *Leurres et Lueurs*. Paris: Présence Africaine, 1960.

Francis, Pope. *Encyclical Letter 'Laudato Si' of the Holy Father Francis On Care for Our Common Home*. Rome: St. Peter's, 2015.

Isiguzo, Chikwurah Destiny. "Postcolonial Ecocriticism and the African Response to Human and the Environment," *Localities*, vol. 7 (2017), pp. 43–74.

Klages, Mary. *Literary Theory: A Guide for the Perplexed*. London: Continuum, 2006.

Selden, Raman and Widdowson, Peter. *A Reader's Guide to Contemporary Literary Theory*. New York: Harrester Wheatsheaf, 1993.

Senghor, Léopold Sédar. "Négritude et Civilisation de l'Universel, " *Présence Africaine*. vol. 2, no. XLVI (1963), pp. 8 à 13.

Tyson, Lois. *Critical Theory Today: A User-Friendly Guide*. New York and London: Garland Publishers, 1999.

Thiobiany, Prince Lamourd. *Before the Fires I was Black: A Blueprint for a Brighter Future*. Self-published, 2018.

Wohlleben, Peter. *The Hidden Life of Trees: What They Feel, How They Communicate – Discoveries from a Secret World*.

Translated by Jane Billinghurst. Vancouver: Greystone Books, 2016.

Young, Robert J.C. *Postcolonialism: A Historical Introduction.* Oxford: Blackwell Publishers, 2001.

End Notes

1 This paper was first published in *Revue du Cames*: *Littérature, Langue et Linguistique*, no. 6, 2017, pp. 1–14.
2 This paper was first published in *Journal de la Recherche Scientifique de l'Université de Lomé* (Togo), Volume 21, Numéro 4, Spécial, 2019, pp. 147–159. Actes du colloque de l'INSEPS 2019 sur le thème: "Sport et développement durable en Afrique francophone."
3 This paper first appeared in *Revue Africaine et Malgache de Recherche Scientifique (RAMReS): Littérature, Langues et Linguistique* No. 9, 2020, pp. 32–49.

CHAPTER V

Overview of Burkinabe Literature in French

Burkina Faso is a country of culture in which literature holds an important place. Salaka Sanou's *La Littérature Burkinabé: l'histoire, les hommes, les oeuvres* (2000), and Yves Dakouo's *Emergence des pratiques littéraires modernes en Afrique francophone* (2011), provide an overview of Burkinabe literature produced in French and local languages from 1960 to 2000. The literary productions in the last twenty years are missing in their works. This current work fills in this gap.

Below is a chart that shows the different writers and the titles of their productions, from 1960 to 2020, with translations into English to guide the non-French reader. The classification is done in alphabetical order of the writers' family names, written in capital letters.

Introduction to Burkinabe Literature in English

Biographical Details	Titles of Works	Genre	English Meaning of Titles
De Bascorma ABDOULAYE (1981)	L'autopsie de Soamba le lièvre (2017)	Tales	The Autopsy of Soamba the Hare
K. Frédéric AMOURAZANE	Le calvaire de Sali (2017)	Short Story	Sali's Hell
Association humanisme et culture	La parole raconte (2002, 2005) A la santé des poètes (2003)	Tales Poetry	The Word Tells To the Health of Poets
Frédéric Assomption AYEREOUE (1962)	Larmes de mon flamboyant (1994)	Poetry	Tears of My Flamboyant
Africa no. 1 et Sépia	Kilomètre 30: L'Afrique, 30 ans d'indépendance (1990)	Short story	Kilometre 30: Africa, 30 Years of Independence
Befer Hassane BAADHIO	Hommage à la femme africaine (1994)	Poetry	Tribute to African Women
Honorat BADIEL	Murmures d'un soleil solitaire (1994)	Poetry	Whispers of a Lonely Sun
Laurent K. BADO	Journal d'un vacancier (2012)	Short story	Diary of a Holyday Man
Noufou BADOU	Au fond du fond, le fond (2014)	Poetry	At the Bottom of the Bottom, the Bottom
Serge H. BADOUN	Destinée solitaire (2007)	Novel	Solitary Fate
Clément Odou BAKYONO (1959)	Soupir et sourire (1991)	Poetry	Sigh and Smile
Régis Kévin BAKYONO	Et si la victime devenait juge (2014)	Short story	And if Ever the Victim Becomes the Judge
Armand BALIMA	Voiles marines (1979)	Poetry	Sea Sails
Calliste Wendé BAMBARA	Encore Fatou (2014)	Novel	Fatou Again
Claire BAMBARA	Plumes du sahel (1971)	Poetry	Feathers of the Sahel
Jean Robert L. BAMBARA	Suppliques (2005) La mosaïque hors-temps (2016)	Poetry Poetry	Petitions The Timeless Mosaic
Yves Arsène Boulgouhon BAMBARA	L'enfant prodige (2016)		The Wonder Child

Chapter 5

Babou Paulin BAMOUNI (1950–1987)	Luttes (1980) Burkina Faso, Processus de la revolution (1986) Obou, l'étudiant journaliste (1986)	Poetry Essay Novel	Struggles Burkina Faso, Process of the Revolution Obou, the Student Journalist
Harouna BANDE (1987)	Au nom d'un rêve (2005) Innimme (2014)	Novel Novel	In the Name of a Dream Innimme
Priscille BANSE	Du paradis à l'enfer (2018)	Novel	From Paradise to Hell
Mamadou BARRO	Le Cahier de souvenirs (1995)	Novel	The Book of Memoirs
Sirre Christophe BARRO (1950)	Nouvelles du village…réalités d'ailleurs (2018)	Short story	Village News… Facts of Elsewhere
Pierre BARROT	Bill l'espiègle ou l'extraordinaire aventure d'une pompe à eau en Afrique (1992)	Novel	Bill the Mischievous Man, or, The Extraordinary Adventure of a Water Pump in Africa
Angèle BASSOLE-OUEDRAOGO (1967)	Ode pour un rêve brisé (1998) Burkina Blues (2000) Avec tes mots (2003) Sahéliennes (2006) Les Porteuses d'Afrique (2007) Yennenga (2012)	Poetry Poetry Poetry Poetry Poetry Poetry	Ode to a Broken Dream Burkina Blues With Your Words Sahelians African Carriers Yennenga
Alfred Jean Michel BATIONO	L'amour en poésie: recueil de poèmes (2008) Le démon au prénom d'ange (2009) Le Coma politique: recueil de nouvelles (2011) La liberté enivrante: théâtre (2012) Du ministère au mystère: Recueil de poèmes (2014) La résurrection de Tonta ou l'ange au prénom de démon (2016) Fabliaux d'une vie nacrée (2018)	Poetry Novel Short stories Drama Poetry Novel Short Story	Love in Poetry: A Collection of poems The Devil Under an Angelic Name Political Coma: Collection of Short Stories Intoxicating Freedom: Theatre From Ministry to Mystery: A Collection of Poems The Resurrection of Tonta, or, The Angel with a Devilish Name Fabliaux of a Pearly Life

Introduction to Burkinabe Literature in English

Athanase Koazoma BATIONO (1977)	La maison brûle (2005)	Novel	The House is on Fire
Bédieryé Parfait BAYALA	D'Amhara à Mourmansk: une aventure planétaire (1999)	Novel	From Amhara to Mourmansk: A Worldwide Adventure
Cyr Prosper BAYALA	Afrique, réveille-toi (1995)	Poetry	Wake Up, Africa
Baya Blaise BAZIE	Les pages d'un voyage (2017)	Novel	The Pages of a Journey
Denis BAZIE (1953)	La sorcière de Bapu (2005)	Novel	The Witch of Bapu
Jacques Prosper BAZIE (1955–2014)	Orphelin des collines ancestrales (1983) L'agonie des greniers (1983) Poésie du Burkina (1983) La saga des immortels (1987) La dérive des Bozos (1988) Amoro (1988) Cantiques des soukalas (1987) Aux miradors de l'espérance (1992) L'épave d'Absouya (1994) Crachin de Rissiam (2002) Croquis de Panguin (2004) Parchemins migrateurs (2009) Pangée de campements (2009)	Poetry Short stories Poetry Poetry Novel Drama Tales Poetry Poetry Short story Novel Short story Novel	Orphan of Ancestral Hills The Agony of Food Store Poetry of Burkina The Saga of Immortals The Bozo Drift Amoro Song of Soukalas At the Watchtowers of Hope The Wreck of Absouya The Drizzle of Rissiam Penguin Sketch Migratory Scrolls Pangea of Camps
Jean Hubert BAZIE (1949)	Sally-Alima (1985) Chroniques du Burkina (1986) Champ d'août (1986) Lomboro de Bourasso (1988) Sally-Alima (1988) Zaka (1991) Le bossu et le candidat (1992)	Story Chronicle Novel Short story Story Novel Strip cartoon	Sally-Alima Chronicles of Burkina August Field Lomboro de Bourasso Sally-Alima Zaka The Hunchback and the Candidate
Vincent-Pascal BAZONGO	Un drôle de petit nuage (1997)	Novel	A Weird Small Cloud
Tidjeni BELOUME	Les Sany d'Imane (2006)	Novel	Imane's Sany
Joseph BEOGO (1968)	Le Chant du retour. Renaissance in Une saison d'amour et de colère: poèmes et nouvelles du sahel (1998) Curieux sorts (2001)	Poetry Short story	The Song of Return. Renaissance Curious Spells

Chapter 5

Françoise BIGIRIMANA	Femme Battante (2013)	Novel	Woman Fighter
Goubgou BILA	La corvée nocturne (1994)	Short story	The Night Shift
Lionel BILGO	Burkina Faso: du rêve à l'action (2019)	Essay	Burkina Faso: From Dream to Action
Fred BISSAHOU	Une vie à Mangueba (2009)	Novel	Life in Mangueba
Ram Georges BOGORE (1936)	Les animaux veulent un roi (1977) La chasse au serpent-boa (1977) Nini, Doudou et l'hyène (1977)	Tales Tales Tales	Animals Want a King Hunting a Boa Snake Nini, Doudou and the Hyena (1977)
Assan BONCOUNGOU	Rien ni personne (2009)	Short story	Nothing and Nobody
Nazi BONI (?1912–1969)	Crépuscule des temps anciens: Chronique du Bwamu (1962) Histoire synthétique de l'Afrique résistante (1971)	Novel Essay	Twilight of the Old Times: Chronicle of Bwamu Synthetic History of Resistant Africa
Bobo Nazi Jean-Luc BONKIAN (1955)	Les fils des crevasses (1992)	Novel	The Threads of the Cracks
Issiaka BONKOUNGOU	Echos du grenier magique : contes du Burkina Faso (2007)	Tale	Echoes from the Magic Granary: Tales from Burkina Faso
Doris BONNET, Moussa OUEDRAOGO et Désiré BONOGO	Contes et Proverbes mossi (1982)	Tale	Mossi Tales and Proverbs
Gnindé BONZI	Dix petites histoires de la légende Sankara (2017) Dix autres petites histoires de la légende Sankara (2018) Le collégien aux pieds nus: chronique d'une enfance villageoise (2018)	Short story Short story Chronicle	Ten Short Stories of Sankara's Legend Ten Other Short Stories of Sankara's Legend The Student in Bare Feet: Chronicle of Childhood in a Village
Chloé-Aïcha BORO et Claude-Nicolas LETERRIER	Paroles d'orphelines (2009)	Novel	Words from Orphan Girls
Elhadji BOUBACAR	Desseins contraires (2019)	Novel	Opposite Designs

Introduction to Burkinabe Literature in English

Seidou Guetwindsisa BOUDA	Les nuits des Fofana (2016)	Novel	The Fofana's Nights
Wennin Jacob BOUDA	Quand le courage se réveille (2019)	Novel	When Courage Wakes Up
Sarah BOUYAIN	Niararaye (1997) Les enfants du Blanc (2000) Métisse façon (2003)	Film Film Short story	Niararaye White Man's Children Weird Mulatto
Gaston CANU	Contes mossi actuels (1969) Contes du sahel: les récits de la calebasse de bière de mil (1975)	Tales Tales	Mossi Tales of Today Tales from the Sahel: Tales of the Millet Beer Gourd
Abdoul CISSE	N'Tolé la sorcière: conte (1997)	Tales	N'Tolé the Witch: Fairy Tal
Kamirini Marius Wenceslas COMBARI	Pressions (2018)	Short story	Pressions
Sibo Fernand COMBARY	Plus fort que la mort (2007)	Story	Stronger than Death
William Aristide Nassidia COMBARY (1980) ou Henri-Michel Nassaris	Les sept douleurs (2007) Hymne à l'amour (2008) A la croisée des chemins (2009) Sueurs froides (2012) Le Mariage militaire (2014) Le Verdict du sable (2015) Les Contes de mon père (2018)	Short story Poetry Short story Story Essay Short story Tale	The Seven Pains Ode to Love At the Crossroads Cold Sweats The Military Wedding The Sand Verdict My Father's Tales
François COMPAORE	Le vent emportait nos rires et les oiseaux nous répondaient en écho (2011)	Novel	The Wind Blew away Our Laughter and the Birds Echoed Back to Us
Rasmané COMPAORE et Rasmané ZOUNDI	Contes modernes et récits comiques du Moogo (2013)	Tales	Modern Tales and Comic Stories from the Moogo
Simporé Simone COMPAORE (1956)	Tu ne m'entendras plus	Play	You Will Not Hear Me Anymore
Inoussa CONGO	Les bons contes font de bons amis (2015)	Tales	Good Stories Make Good Friends
Issaka CONGO	Travers et revers (2018)	Short story	Crossbars and Reverses
Moumouni CONGO	La columbière (2015)	Short story	The Columbaria

Chapter 5

Tiga Mamoudou CONGO (1956)	Les aventures de Yembi (2015)	Novel	The Adventures of Yembi
Aboubacar D. COULIBALY	Contes et légendes (2004) La légende continue (2009)	Tale Tale	Tales and Legends The Legend Continues
Augustin-Sondé COULIBALY (1933)	Les dieux delinquents (1974) Poèmes pour enfants (1976) Le dossier de la littérature et de l'art africain (1976)	Novel Poetry Essay	The Delinquent Gods Poems for Children The Case of African Art and Literature
Isaïe B. COULIBALY	Ma joie en lui (1977) Les deux amis (1979)	Novel Short stories	My Joy in Him (1977) The Two Friends
Soumouni Faustin DABIRA (1946)	Le kiro (1985)	Short story	The Kiro (1985)
Der Laurent DABIRE	Chemin de croix (2008)	Novel	Stations of the Cross
Kpiélé Pierre DABIRE (1935)	Les aventures de Dary l'araignée Sansoa (1969) Recueil de nouvelles	Tales Drama Short stories	The Adventures of Dary the Spider Sansoa Collection of Short Stories
Léa Nadège DABIRE	La jeune fille (2003)	Novel	The Young Girl
Zakaria DABONE, Joseph SANOU, Odile SANKARA	Recueil de nouvelles (2004)	Short story	Collection of Short Stories
Ismaël Nestor DAHANI	Fragrance au crépuscule (2019)	Poetry	Fragrance at Dusk
Paul DAKUYO (1959)	Ce qu'il faut savoir sur la négritude (1986) Négroïde (1988)	Essay Poetry	What you Need to Know About Negritude Negroid
Dissara Mathias DALA	L'algue d'amour (2008)	Poetry	The Seaweed of Love
Toussaint Hènènè DAMAN	La Rivière aux mystères ésotériques (2012) Mélancolie des temps anciens (2015) La vertu chez nos ancêtres (2017)	Essay Novel Drama	The River of Esoteric Mysteries Melancholy of Ancient Times Virtue for Our Ancestors
Denis DAMBRE	Solitude et vibrations (2015)	Poetry	Solitude and Vibrations

Introduction to Burkinabe Literature in English

Author	Original Titles	Genre	English Titles
Danini Geoffroy DAMIBA (1952)	Patarbtaale, le fils du pauvre (1990) Le geste interdit (1993) Papa, je te pardonne tout (1994)	Novel Novel Novel	Patarbtaale, the Son of the Poor The Forbidden Gesture Daddy, I Forgive You of Everything
François-Xavier DAMIBA	Dieu n'est pas sérieux La douceur du dieu-à-mère (200)	Tales Tales	God Cannot be Serious The Softness of God to Mother
Joseph DAMIBA	Poèmes Moore-Français (1983)	Poetry	Moore-French Poems
Bernadette DAO/ SANOU (1952)	Parturition (1986) Emeraudes (1987) Quote part et symphonie (1992) La dernière épouse (1997) La femme de diable et autres histoires (2003) Avance mon peuple et autres nouvelles (2005) Pour Fabienne et Cie (2009) Le charme rompu (2014)	Poetry Poetry Poetry Short story Short story Short story Nonfiction Short story	Parturition Emeralds Quote Part and Symphony The Last Wife The Devil's Wife and Other Stories Go Forth, my People and Other Stories For Fabienne and Others Broken Spell
Sabari Christian DAO	Afrique: mon pays (2014) Aimer (2015)	Prose Poetry	Africa: My Land To Love
Bernard DELMOND	Retour à Dori : Burkina Faso (2007)	Novel	Back to Dori: Burkina Faso
Karim DERME	Un cœur entre deux frères de sang (2004)	Novel	A Heart between Two Blood Brothers
Daouda DERRA	Un rêve brisé (2017) Florilège de sentiments (2019)	Novel Poetry	An Unfulfilled Dream Anthology of Feelings
Frédéric DE-SION	Lambeaux et espoir : poésie de la vie (2007) Trésor pour enfants (2011) Dormez, parents!	Poetry Poetry Novel	Shreds and Hope: Poetry of Life Treasure for Children Sleep, Parents!

Chapter 5

Abdoulaye DIABATE	A la rencontre de Mokembo et autres nouvelles (1991)	Short story	Meeting Mokembo and Other Short Stories
Arouna DIABATE	Les sillons d'une endurance (2006)	Novel	The Furrows of Endurance
Abdoulaye DIALLO	Le bonheur retrouvé (2005) Nafissa ou l'illusion d'une vie (2014)	Novel Novel	The Recovered Happiness Nafissa, or, An Illusive Life
Boubacar DIALLO (1962)	Le mendiant (1985) Le totem (1993) La nuit des chiens (1999) Un fils du pays (2000) Amnesty Fumée noire (2000)	Story Tales Novel Novel Drama Novel	The Beggar The Totem Pole The Night of the Dogs A Son of the Country Amnesty Black Smoke
Ibrahim DIALLO	Contre vents et marées (2011)	Short story	Against all Odds
Mamadou Hama DIALLO (1936)	Le chapelet de Dèbbo Lobbo (2006)	Novel	The Rosary of Dèbbo Lobbo
Yacouba DIARRA	De Koutab à la Sorbonne: itinéraire d'un talibé (1999) La terre, cette grande arène (2005)	Novel Novel	From Koutab to the Sorbonne: Itinerary of a Talibé The Earth, This Great Arena
Kadiata DICKO	L'affranchie (2020)	Novel	The Affranchised
Aly DIONI (1968)	Long songe (1990	Short story	Long Dream
Founawiré Kiri S. DIONOU et al.	Poésie du Burkina Faso (2005)	Poetry	Poetry from Burkina Faso
Ousmane DJIGUEMDE	Shekina : le rêve inachevé (2005)	Novel	Shekina: The Unfinished Dream
Edmond Manégré DJIGUEMKOUDRE	Songes et mensonges (2017)	Essay	Dreams and Lies
Félicité DONDASSE	Petit Gars, grands rêves (2012)	Novel	Little Friend, Big Dreams
Abi Fenne DONINOAR (1983)	Journal de Nido (2010)	Story	Nido's Diary

165

Introduction to Burkinabe Literature in English

Justin Stanislas DRABO	L'autopsie (2014) La magie des lucioles (2014) Les confessions d'une muette (2014) Les terres amères: recueil de poésie (2017)	Drama Poetry Short story Poetry	Autopsy The Magic of Fireflies The Confessions of a Dumb Woman Bitter Lands: A Collection of Poetry
Adama DRAME	Cesirijala (2013)	Poetry	Cesirijala
Karidia DRAME	Rompre le silence (2018)	Novel	To Break the Silence
Adelaïde Edith H. FASSINOU	Pour cinq indignes mille francs (2014)	Short story	For Five Thousand Unworthy Franc Notes
FRYDA (1986)	La danse de Myhiti (2017)	Novel	The Dance of Myhiti
Gnissa Muller GANOU	Poésie à l'école primaire (1997) Chants d'oiseaux (2001) Wati, j'y ai cru (2003) Voyages (2007)	Poetry Poetry Poetry Short story	Poetry in Primary School Birds' Songs Wati, I Believed In It Journeys
M. René GNALEGA	Pampres (2017)	Poetry	Vines
Edoxi Lionelle GNOULA	Legs (2017)	Drama	Legs
Etienne GNOUMOU	Nécrose à Koufa (2018)	Novel	Necrosis in Koufa
Issou GO (1954)	Les Voix dans le roman islamique d'Afrique Occidentale d'expression Française Essai d'études critique (1984) Les Arènes nuptiales (2008) La princesse de Konkoliba (2009) Les murmures de la nuit: recueil de nouvelles (2010) La marâtre redouble de férocité (2013) Poétique et esthétique magiques (2014)	Essay Novel Novel Short stories Novel Essay	Voices of Islamic Western French Africa: Critical Study Essay The Bridal Arena The Princess of Konkoliba Whispers of the Night: Collection of Short Stories The Stepmother Redoubles Her Ferocity Magical Poetics and Aesthetics
Zassi GORO	Le dernier des Sîm-bon (1997)	Novel	The Last of the Sîm-bon

Chapter 5

Jacques Boureima GUEGANE (1941)	"Nativité" in Poèmes voltaïques, (1978) La guerre des sables (1979) L'an des criquets (2001) En mémoire d'un tambour de guerre (2003) Chanson du mal inconnu (2004) Du yin et du yan (2009) Terres promises (2015)	Poetry Poetry Poetry Poetry Poetry Poetry Novel	"Nativity" in Voltaic Poems The Sand War The Year of the Locusts In Memory of a War Drum Song of a Forgotten Illness Of Yin and Yan Promised Lands
Zakaria GUENGANE (1978)	Débâcle et espoir d'une République (2017)	Novel	Debacle and Hope for a Republic
Somlawende Rasmani GUIGMA	Afrique contemporaine et autogoalisme	Essay	Contemporary Africa and Autogoalism
Daogo Jean Pierre GUINGANE	Le fou (1986) Papa, oublie-moi (1990) Le cri de l'espoir (1992) La grossesse de Koudbi (1996) Les lignes de la main (1996) La savane en transe (1997) La musaraigne (1997) Le baobab merveilleux (2007) La malice des hommes (2008) La danseuse de l'eau (2009)	Drama Drama Drama Drama Drama Drama Drama Drama Drama Tale	The Madman Daddy, Forget about me The Cry of Hope Koudbi's Pregnancy Handlines The Savannah in Trance The Shrew The Wonderful Baobab Tree Men's Malice The Water Dancer
Maurice GUIRE	De la savane au désert (1998)	Novel	From the Savannah to the Desert
Frédéric GUIRMA	Princesse Kiug Peulgo (1994)	Tales	Princess Kiug Peulgo
Zarra GUIRO (1957)	Au pays de Zarra: Contes et légendes de Namissiguima (1992) Zarra, Accoucheuse en Afrique. (1994)	Tale Autobiography	In the land of Zarra: Tales and Legends of Namissiguima Zarra, Midwife in Africa

Introduction to Burkinabe Literature in English

Author	Works	Genre	English Title
Baba HAMA (1959)	Batane (1986) L'homme de Wouro (1987) Le passage (1994) Lamordè (2005) Encens et myrrhe (2007) Lamordè (2008) Kalahaldi: la patte de charognard (2008) Atikou, le revenant de Bafélé (2016)	Story Story Story Novel Short story Short story Novel Novel	Batane The Man of Wouro The Passage Lamordè Frankincense and Myrrh Lamordè Kalahaldi: The Paw of the Scavenger Atikou, the Ghost of Bafélé
Héba Henriette HAMMUDA	Nady sauve le monde (2014)	Short Story	Nady Saves the World
Abdouramane HAROUNA	Le Mal d'aimer (2001)	Novel	The Evil in Love
Missa HEBIE	Kouka (1993)	Short story	Kouka
Aimé Désiré HEMA	Le monarque démocrate (2003)	Novel	The Democratic Monarch
Ansonwin Ignace HIEN (1952)	L'enfer au paradis (1988) Secrets d'alcôves (1989) Au gré du destin (1988) La queue de guenon (1989) Chich-choc (1993) Poésie pour enfants (1994) Le conte de la Volta Noire: contes dagara (1995) Larmes de tendresse (1997) La nuit des tout-petits (1996) Je veux la lune (2000) Au coin des tout-petits (2000) Itinéraires (2005) Mouka et le petit avion du blanc (2006) L'enfant et l'œil de Dieu (2007) Le plus beau cadeau de Noël (2007) Pourquoi l'âne n'a-t-il pas de cornes? (2008) Bouba et Boubou (2008)	Novel Short story Novel Tales Story Poetry Tales Novel Tales Poetry Poetry Tale Short story Tale Short Story Tale Tale	Hell in Heaven Secrets of Alcoves As Fate Would Have It Guenon's Tail Chich-Choc Poetry for Children The Tale of the Black Volta: Tales from the Dagara Tears of tenderness Toddlers' Night I Want the Moon Toddlers' Corner Itineraries Mouka and the White Man's Small Plane The Child and the Eye of God The Most Beautiful Christmas Present Why the Donkey Has not Horns? Bouba and Boubou

Chapter 5

Faartio Flore HIEN	Oh my God!!! Chronique de souvenirs américains (2016)	Chronicle		Oh my God!!! Chronicle of souvenirs from America
Sansan Tori HIEN	Le prix de la trahison (2014)	Novel		The Price of Treason
Joel Jérôme HOUANGRE	Adjaratou la servante (2011)	Story		Adjaratou the Maid
Clémentine ILBOUDO	Robert ou l'enfant modèle (2000)	Novel		Robert the Model Child
Gomdaogo Patrick ILBOUDO (1951)	Les toilettes (1985) Le procès du muet (1987) Les carnets secrets d'une fille de joie (1988) Les vertiges du trône (1990) Le héraut têtu (1991)	Story Novel Novel Novel Novel		The Toilets The Trial of the Mute The Secret Notebooks of a Girl of Joy Dizziness from the Throne The Stubborn Herald
Hamado ILBOUDO	Veneg-yaoba ou l'histoire du royaum mossi (2016)	Essay		Make it Clear to the Young, or, The History of the Moose Kingdom
Monique ILBOUDO (1959)	Le mal de peau (1992) Muraketete (2000) Une histoire d'œufs (2001)	Novel Novel Short story		Skin Disease Muraketete A Story About Eggs
Pierre Claver ILBOUDO (1948)	Le fils aîné (1985) Mariage de Tinga (1985) Adama ou la force des choses (1987) Le retour de Yembi (1994) Madame la ministre et moi (2007) L'éveil (2017)	Novel Short story Novel Novel Novel		The Eldest Son Tinga's Wedding Adama The Return of Yembi Madam Minister and I The Awakening
Tiraogo Maxime ILY	Maximes africaines (2011)	Maxims		African Maxims
Inades-Formation	Contes de Tanlili (2003)	Tale		Tales from Tanlili
Fredy Magloire IVIGA	Des roses et des ronces (2005)	Poetry		Roses and Brambles
Adama KABORE	Faste désastre (2017) Possibo la diabolaise (2020)	Short story Novel		Great Desaster Possibo the Devilish
Armand Joseph KABORE	Le pari de la nuit (2004)	Novel		The Bet of the Night

169

Introduction to Burkinabe Literature in English

Author	Title	Genre	English Title
Bila Roger KABORE (1954)	Forces obscures (1985) La princesse Yennega (1983) Les indésirables (1990) Sous l'arbre à palabres (1994) L'épopée de Boukary Koutou (1997) Au clair de la lune (1999)	Poetry Legend Novel Legend Legend Legend	Dark Forces Princess Yennega The Undesirable Under the Palaver Tree The Epic of Boukary Koutou In the Moonlight
Florent KABORE (1990)	Le troisième monde (2012) Vive la jeunesse (2014) Les élections arrivent (2014)	Novel Poetry Novel	The Third World Long Life to the Youth Elections are Coming
Harouna KABORE	Mémoire d'un combat (2018)	Poetry	Remembering a Fight
Issa Barthélemy KABORE	Des clones-zombis pour le sahel (1998)	Novel	Zombie Clones for the Sahel
Julien KABORE	Mieux vivre sa jeunesse : roman épistolaire (2008)	Novel	To Better Live One's Youth Epistolary Novel
Madeleine de Lallé KABORE (1955)	Arc envolé (2006) La voix (2009) Poulemde (2013) Bruits de silence (2013) Héritage (2014)	Poetry Novel Poetry Poetry Poetry	Soaring Bow The Voice Promise Noise of Silence Heritage
Nazi KABORE	Gouyaks chauds (2006)	Stories	Hot Guavas
René Emile KABORE	Burkina Faso: et si enfin on se disait la vérité	Essay	Burkina Faso: What if We Tell Each Other the Truth
Théophane KABORE	Les trésors sacrés: éloges à l'amitié et l'intégrité (2020)	Short story	Sacred Treasures: Praise to Friendship and Integrity
Timothée H. KABORE	Histoires pour enfants (2013) Amour à mort (2015) Voyage de nuage (2017) Je n'oublierai jamais (2018)	Short story Short story Novel Short Story	Stories for Children Love to Death Journey of Cloud I Shall Never Forget
Edouard KABRE (1966)	L'autre enfant (2013)	Novel	The Other Child

S. Issouf KABRE (1975)	L'affaire du car de Rakaye (2009) Lien singulier (2000)	Novel Novel	The Rakaye Bus Affair Singular Link
Diandé KADRE (1982)	La réussite scolaire de Rachid, fils de pauvre (2013)	Novel	The Academic Success of Rachid, Son of the Poor
Lamoussa Théodore KAFANDO (1943)	A l'école du conte (1986) Contes (1986) La vieille femme et la vieille vache (1988) Dualité (1988) La femme de mon père n'est pas ma mère (1995) Laafi-nooma ou la santé (1993) La handicapée de taabgninga (1996) Recueil de chansons pour enfants (1998) Je t'aime à la folie (2008)	Tale Tale Tale Poetry Drama Drama Tale Poetry Tale	In Storytelling School Tales The Old Woman and the Old Cow Duality My Father's Wife is Not My Mother Laafi-nooma or Health The Disabled Woman of Taabgninga Children's Songbook I Love You to Madness
Izak KAGAMBEGA (1988)	Fruits incomestibles (2017)	Short story	Inedible Fruits
Louis KALMOGO (1952)	Raogo ou le destin du mogho (1996) Du fond du cœur (1998)	Novel Novel	Raogo or the Fate of the Mogho (1996) From the Bottom of my Heart

Introduction to Burkinabe Literature in English

Sophie Heidi KAM (1958)	Ecrire, Sérénité, Résolutions, Trouble in Une saison d'amour et de colère: poèmes et nouvelles du sahel (1998) Pas d'ici, pas d'ailleurs: Anthologie poétique francophone de voix féminines contemporaines (2012)	Poetry	Writing, Serenity, Resolutions, Trouble in A Season of Love and Anger: Poems and Short Stories from the Sahel Not From Here, Not From Anywhere: Poetic Anthology of Contemporary Francophone Female Voices
	Podium Doppelheft, Afrika (2011)	Poetry	Podium Doppelheft, Afrika
	Pour un asile (2009)		For an Asile
	Quêtes (2005)	Poetry	Quests
	Sanglots et symphonies (2005).	Poetry	Sobs and Symphony
	Offrande (2009)	Poetry	Offering
	Paroles partagées: Poésie des 1000 continents – Anthologie composée et présentée par la Maison africaine de la poésie internationale (MAPI) à Dakar (2005)	Poetry Poetry	Shared Words: Poetry of the 1000 Continents – Anthology Composed and Presented by the African House for International Poetry (MAPI) in Dakar
	Poésie du Burkina Faso: Les grands traits caractéristiques de la poésie écrite du Burkina Faso – La revue Estuaire, no. 114, (2003).	Poetry	Poetry of Burkina Faso: The Main Characteristics of the Written Poetry of Burkina Faso – La Revue Estuaire, no. 114.
	Saison d'amour et de Colère: poèmes et nouvelles du Sahel (1998)	Poetry Poetry	Season of Love and Anger: Poems and Short Stories from the Sahel.
	Qu'il en soit ainsi (2013).		So Be It.
	Et le soleil sourira à la mer, (2008).	Novels	And the Sun Will Smile at the Sea.
	La rentrée des classes (2010), Le devoir de classe (2011), Le suspect (2012), L'anniversaire (2012). Ce sont des romans pour enfants, adaptations de L'As du lycée, série télévisée de Missa Hébié (2012).	Sketches Drama Poetry	Back to School, Classroom Duty, The suspect, The Birthday: All are children's novels, adaptation of *L'As du lycée*, television series by Missa Hébié.
	Senghor Cent ans – la BD burkinabè rend hommage au Poète-président (2006).		Senghor One Hundred Years – the Burkinabè comic strip pays homage to the Poet-President.
	Nos jours d'hier (2013) Florilège (2019)		Our Days of Yesterday Anthology

Chapter 5

Author	Work	Genre	Translation
Sophia KANGAMBEGA	Une affaire d'anges (2017)	Short story	A Matter of Angels
Adamaou L. KANTAGBA	La femme du président et autres histoires (2012)	Short story	The President's Wife and Other Stories
Edjou Djomniyo KANTIEBO (1970)	Djomniyoh (2007)	Poetry	Djomniyoh
Sandra Pierrette KANZIE (1966)	Les tombes qui pleurent (1987)	Poetry	The Weeping Graves
Windetongo Jean KEBRE	La chance de naître et d'exister (2005)	Novel	The Chance of Being Born and To Live
Sanhouba Gildas KERE	Victime d'amour (2014)	Short story	A Victim of Love
Etienne Nicolas KIBA (1961)	Moi, la sorcière (2005) Sonorités sahéliennes (2006)	Novel Poetry	I, the Witch Sahelian Sonorities
Philippe KIENDREBEOGO	Le cri de mon cœur (2018)	Poetry	The Cry of My Heart
Oualilaï KINDO	Contes de pays des noirs (2014)	Tale	Tales from Countries of the Black
Théodorat de KIRITENGA	L'homme-qui-vient-après-le-président (2004) La fileuse du coton (2005) Le sceau des revolutions (2017)	Short story Tale Novel	The Man That Comes After the President The Cotton Weaver The Seal of Revolutions
Désirée Aimée KI-ZERBO	Coupable (2019)	Novel	The Culprit
Joseph KI-ZERBO	Le Monde africain noir (1964) A quand l'Afrique? (2003) Afrique Noire (2005)	Essay Essay Essay	The Black African World When Will Africa? Black Africa
Judith KOALA	Baasnéré (2013)	Short story	To End Well
Françoise KOAMA	La vie d'un père (2005)	Short Story	The Life of a Father
Noaga KOLLIN (1944) (Nongma Ernest OUEDRAOGO)	Dawa à Abidjan (1975), ou, Le retour au village (1978) Haro! Camarade Commandant (1977)	Novel Novel	Dawa in Abidjan, or, Back to the Village Haro! Comrade Commander
Prospère KOMPAORE (1950)	Les voix du silence (1998) Faire du théâtre pour développer (1998) La porteuse d'eau (2011) Etranger (2011) La commande (2011)	Drama Essay Drama Drama Drama	Voices of Silence Making Theatre for Development The Water Carrier The Stranger The Order

Introduction to Burkinabe Literature in English

Dramane KONATE	Sahela (2017) La triade de sang L'antédestin (2004)	Short story Novel Novel	Sahela The Blood Triad The Antedestin
Moussa KONATE (1956)	Le caïman, le chasseur et le lièvre, ou, le prix de l'ingratitude (1986) Le chat et la souris, ou, le danger de l'ignorance (1987) Le mari infidèle (1988) Le lièvre et les autres animaux de la brousse, ou, l'effet de la musique (1990) Le lièvre, l'hyène et les pintades, ou, les méfaits des feux de brousse (1990) Le lièvre, l'éléphant et l'hippopotame, ou, l'avantage de l'intelligence sur la force (1991) Les trois chiots et leur maman, ou, le devoir des enfants (1998). Bibata et les génies des collines (2000) Les enfants qui plantent des arbres (2011)	Tale Tale Tale Tale Tale Tale Tale Tale	The Crocodile, the Hunter and the Hare, or, the Price Ingratitude The Cat and the Mouse, or The Danger of Ignorance (1987) The Unfaithful Husband The Hare and Other Bush Animals, or, The Effect of Music The Hare, the Hyenas, and the Guinea Fowl, or, The Misdeeds of Bush Fires The Hare, the Elephant, and the Hippopotamus, or, the Advantage of Intelligence Over Strength The Three Puppies and Their Mother, or, The Duty of the Children Bibata and the Geniuses of the Hills The Children who Plant Trees
Otozanga KONATE	Les élucubrations d'un fou (2013)	Short Story	Rantings of a Madman
Gael KONE (1976)	Poussière de mots et d'images (2000)	Poetry	Dust of Words and Images
Lara Barthélemy Kondadjé KONE (1967)	L'ombre ensoleillée (1996)	Novel	Sunny Shadow
Mariam KONE	Landolo et le grand caïlcédrat: Contes du Burkina Faso en pays San (2006) La fille qui ne voulait pas se marier (2012) Les crocodiles de Bangrewéogo (2013)	Tale Tale Tale	Landolo and the Great Cauliflower: Tales from Burkina Faso in the Country of San People The Girl Who Didn't Want Get Married The Crocodiles of Bangreweogo
Naby Isidore KONE et al.	Nouvelles du Burkina (2005)	Short Stories	Short Stories from Burkina

Chapter 5

Author	Title	Genre	English Title
Christophe KONKOBO	La pratique du théâtre moderne au Burkina Faso (2017)	Essay	The Practice of Modern Theatre in Burkina Faso
Agathe KOUAKOU	Métamorphose (2013)	Short story	Metamorphosis
Dede Rose Gloria KOUEVI	Le parcours d'une femme battante (2013) Vengeance fatale (2018)	Novel Novel	Life of a Fighting Woman Deadly Revenge
Emmanuel KOURAOGO	Bitiirga (2015) Et la terre refleurit (2017) Une filiation en question (2018)	Novel Novel Novel	A Good Son And the Earth Blooms Anew A Filiation on Debate
Mamadou KOUSSE	Poèmes humoristiques et thérapeutiques du Burkina (2014)	Poetry	Humorous and Therapeutic Poems from Burkina
Angelina Marie Laurentine KY/ KANKYONO	La nuit des noces (2012) Etre président là-bas (2016) Lucia, ou, le bout du tunnel (2017) Et si on était fait l'un pour l'autre (2018)	Short story Novel Novel Short story	The Wedding Night To Be a President There Lucia, or, The End of the Tunnel And If We Were Made One For the Other!
Lydie Marie Innessa KY (1982)	Mon fils jumeaux (2001)	Short story	My Twin Son
Mathias KYELEM	L'épine de la rose (1996) L'envers du décor (1999) Les espiègles (2005) Le courage des autres (2011)	Novel Novel Novel Novel	The Thorn of the Rose Behind the Scenes The Mischievous Ones The Courage of Others
Massa LANDY (1959)	Zedy (2005)	Novel	Zedy
Daniel LANKOANDE (1984)	Anita, la petite fille sacrifiée (2017)	Short story	Anita, the Sacrificed Little Girl
Hamidou Ange Djehn Massiack LANKOANDE (1980)	Culte d'un poète (2014)	Poetry	Worship of a Poet
Didier LEZIN	Amertume Souvenir (1989) La mendiante et 9 autres nouvelles (1993)	Short stories Short stories	Bitter Remembrance The Beggar Girl and 9 Other Short Stories
Mazono Djadamné LORO	Le Placenta (1998)	Short story	The Placenta
Théohanni MADOPAR (1990)	La sagesse des ancêtres (2015)	Tales	The Ancestors' Wisdom
Yaya Inoussa MAIGA (1982)	Wangari, un trône pour deux chefs (2017)	Novel	Wangari, a Throne for Two Chiefs

Introduction to Burkinabe Literature in English

Stéphanie Lydie MAMIAKA	Le rêve brisé du poète combattant (2018)	Prose poetry	The Broken Dream of the Fighting Poet
Honorine MARE	Traces croisées, Hélas, Etranges compagnons, Le Pays d'amour in Une saison d'amour et de colère: poèmes et nouvelles du sahel (1998)	Poetry	Crossed Traces, Alas, Strange Companions, The Land of love in A Season of Love and Anger: Poetry and Short Stories from the Sahel
Gilles MAROUE	Femmes d'ici, filles de là (2018)	Poetry	Women of Here, Girls from There
Bob-Zié Wilfried MEDA	De la prison à la bière (2017) Bienvenue à Sodome et Gomorrhe (2019)	Novel Short story	From Prison to the Beer Welcome to Sodom and Gomorrah
F. Lucien MILLOGO	Le Reportage: les geôles du temps (1999) Soupirs de calliope (2011)	Novel Poetry	The Report: the Jails of Time Sighs of Calliope
Léopold N. MILLOGO (1957)	Promesse fatale (2011)	Novel	Fatal Promise
Samuel MILLOGO (1946)	Savannah Blues (1996) Récits de ma vallée (2000) Pays-là (2017)	Poetry Poetry Novel	Savannah Blues Stories from My Valley This Country!

Chapter 5

Ministère de la culture	Poèmes-Théâtre français-mooré (1983) Anthologie de la jeune poésie burkinabé (1984) Poésie du Burkina (1985) Pièces théâtrales du Burkina (1985) Nouvelles du Burkina (1985) France laureates au Grand Prix national des arts et lettres (Bobo 86) Contes: France laureates au Grand Prix national des arts et lettres (Bobo 86) Pièces théâtrales du Burkina (1988) Poésie pour enfants (1987) Poésie du Burkina (1987) Nouvelles du Burkina (1987) Contes du Burkina (1987) Le miel de la tradition (recueils de proverbes) (1988) Soirées enchantées (1994) Poésie pour enfants (1994) Humus: recueil de nouvelles (2001) La fille et le génie: contes de la troisième région culturelle (2004) Recueil de neuf nouvelles (2017)	Poetry Drama Poetry Poetry Drama Short Stories Novel Tales Drama Poetry Poetry Short Stories Tales Proverbs Drama Poetry Short Stories Tales Short Stories	Poems and Plays in French and Moore Anthology of Young Burkinabé Poetry Poetry of Burkina Theatrical plays from Burkina Short Stories from Burkina France laureates at the Grand Prix national des arts et lettres Tales: France laureates at the Grand Prix national des arts et lettres Theatrical plays from Burkina Faso Poetry for Children Poetry of Burkina Short Stories from Burkina Tales from Burkina The Honey of Tradition (Collection of Proverbs) Enchanted Evenings Poetry for Children Humus: Collection of Short Stories The Girl and the Ghost: Tales from the Third Cultural Region Collection of Nine Short Stories
Ministère de l'éducation nationale	Recueil théâtral de l'Atelier Théâtre burkinabè (1986) Recueil théâtral: pièces de théâtre forum (1988)	Drama Drama	Theatrical Collection of the Burkinabè Theater Workshop Theatrical Collection: Forum Plays
Etienne MINOUNGOU	Madame, je vous aime (2008)	Drama	Madam, I Love You
Pegdawende Pélagie NABOLE (1993)	Le péril (2012)	Novel	The Peril
Henriette Philomène NANA/NIKIEMA (1959)	L'histoire de Pendo, la petite paresseuse (1994)	Tales	The Story of Pendo, the Little Lazy Girl
Kietagniga Vincent NANA	Souvenirs vivaces (2016)	Poetry	Vivid Remembrance
Rosalie NANA (1962)	L'homme de minuit (2001)	Short story	The Midnight Man

Introduction to Burkinabe Literature in English

Author	French Title	Genre	English Title
Julien B. NAON (1974)	Une vie d'albinos (2016)	Novel	The Life of an Albino
Niadiyé NAON (1973)	Histoires mystérieuses du Burkina: contes et légendes (2013)	Tales	Mysterious Stories of Burkina: Tales and Legends
Issouf NASSA	Les chemins du cœur (2020)	Short story	The Ways of the Heart
Bali NEBIE	Le crépuscule des ténèbres (2004) Le roi Djadjo (2013) Les secrets du sorcier noir (2015)	Novel Novel Novel	The Twilight of Darkness King Djadjo The secrets of the black sorcerer
Songo NEER	Mon beau pays, le Burkina Faso (2011) Les dix devoirs de l'enfant (2011) Les dix droits de l'enfant (2011) Contes poétiques d'Afrique (2017)	Tales Drama Drama Poetry	Poetic Tales from Africa The Ten Duties of a Child The Ten Rights of a Child My Beautiful Country, Burkina Faso
Babou dit Michel NEYA	Le villageois (2013)	Short Story	The Villager
Marie N'GUESSAN/ KABORE (1945)	Dieu écrit droit sur des lignes courbes (2018)	Short story	God Writes Straight on Curved Lines
Charles NIAMBA	Le retour à Massala (2016)	Novel	The Return to Massala
Adèle NIKIEMA	La mangeuse d'âmes (2006)	Novel	The Eater of Souls
Ousseni NIKIEMA	Les contes de Dunia (2000) L'honneur du Buudu (2011) L'âge d'or (2013)	Tales Drama Short stories	Tales of Dunia The Honor of Buudu The Golden Age
Roger NIKIEMA (1935)	Dessein contraire (1966) Les deux adorables rivales (1971) Les Soleils de la terre (1971) Le rêve de Macalou (1976) Mes flèches blanches (1981) L'Hier de Koss Yam (2012)	Novel Short story Poetry Poetry Poetry Novel	Counter Fate The two Adorable Rivals The Suns of the Earth Macalou's Dream My White Arrows Yesterday of Koss Yam
Suzy Henique NIKIEMA (1983)	L'homme à la bagnole rouge (2001)	Novel	The Man in the Red-Hot Jalopy.
Timbila Roger Théodore NIKIEMA (1935)	L'hier de Koss-Yam (2012)	Short story	The Past of Koss-Yam
Tinga Issa NIKIEMA (1957)	Daniel, ou, le salaire de l'ambition (1983) Troisième poétique (1987) Poèmes sur le marché (1985)	Drama Poetry Poetry	Daniel, or, The Wage of Ambition Third Poetics Poems in the Marketplace

Chapter 5

Oumar NITIEMA	Maladie d'amour (1996) La dernière confession (2000) Un voyage dans le monde (2003) Le verdict des jupons (2004)	Novel Novel Novel Novel	Love Disease The Last Confession A Journey in the World The Verdict of Petticoats
Alphonse NONREGMA (Alphone Nongrema OUEDRAOGO) (1958)	L'apatride (1996) Périphérie (2009)	Novel Novel	The Stateless Person Periphery
André NYAMBA (1952)	Avance, mon peuple (1973)	Short story	Go Forth, My People
Sam OLEY	Le chemin de la sagesse (2019) Djélideni: l'enfant griot (2019)	Tale and Slam Novel	The Road of Wisdom Djélideni: The Child Griot
Nadia ORIGO	Le bal des débutants (2012) La valse des initiés (2014)	Novel Novel	The Beginners' Ball The Initiates' Waltz
Gilbert OUANGRAWA	Père avant l'âge	Tale	Underage Father
Lona Charles OUATTARA	Les dessous de la révolution voltaïque ; la mélancolie de la victoire (2017) Mon engagement (2020)	Essay Essay	The unsaid part of the Voltaic Revolution: Melancholy of Victory My Commitment
Moussa OUATTARA	Le grin: rires et blagues à Bobo-Dioulasso (2003).	Story	The Grin: Laughter and Jokes in Bobo-Dioulasso
Sou Emmanuel OUATTARA (1978)	Biba la Bella: les déboires d'un amour matériel (2015)	Novel	The Beautiful Biba: The Disaster of a Materialist Love
Vincent OUATTARA (1960)	L'aurore des accusés et des accusateurs (1994)	Novel	The Dawn of the Accused and the Accusators
Yvonne OUATTARA et Jean-Luc POULIQUEN	En souvenir de l'Arbre à palabres: Lettres de France et du Burkina Faso (2009)	Story	In Memory of the Tree of Palavers: Letters from France and Burkina Faso
Adama OUEDRAOGO	Hymne à la jeunesse (2016)	Poetry	Hymn to the Youth
Albert OUEDRAOGO	Les braises du plaisir (2018)	Poetry	The Embers of Pleasure
Bambingnélé Philippe OUEDRAOGO (1987)	Un innocent en enfer (2019)	Novel	An Innocent Man in Hell
Bibata Sotissi OUEDRAOGO	Sous le ciel de la savane (1999)	Tale	Under the Savannah
Bibiane OUEDRAOGO/ BONI	Revirement (2015)	Novel	Turnaround

Introduction to Burkinabe Literature in English

Cyrille OUEDRAOGO	La grève des étudiants (2005) Festival ténébreux (2008) Les empreintes antinomiques (2008) Des quittances obligatoires (2011)	Short story Shot story Short story Novel	Students' Strike Dark Festival The Antinomic Fingerprints Mandatory Receipts
Didier OUEDRAOGO	Poubelles de la ville (2014)	Novel	City Garbage Bins
Dim-Dolobsom OUEDRAOGO	Maximes, pensées et devinettes mossi (1934)	Tale	Maxims, Thoughts, and Riddles of the Mossi
Elie Justin OUEDRAOGO	Recueil de poèmes du Zandoma (2005)	Poetry	Collection of Poems from Zandoma
Emmanuel S. OUEDRAOGO (1974)	Le destin cruel de Wendpoulumdé (2012)	Novel	The Cruel Fate of Wendpoulumde
Hamadé Yaya OUEDRAOGO (1950)	Rumeurs de pluie et chant d'espérance (1985)	Poetry	Rumors of Rain and Song of Hope
Hamado OUEDRAOGO (1955)	L'Ahuri de Oualga (2012) Conseils révolutionnaires de discipline (2012)	Short story Novel	The Bewildered Man from Oualga Revolutionary Disciplinary Advice
Ignace Guietwendé OUEDRAOGO	Une flamme dans le noir (2007) Le charme de l'innocence (2016) Cri d'espérance: sur les syllabes de mots en rage (2020)	Poetry Poetry Poetry	A Flame in the Dark The Charm of Innocence Cry of Hope: On the Syllables of Words in Anger
Jacqueline W. OUEDRAOGO	Ma gratification pour toi, Mère (2018)	Novel	My Gratitude for You, Mother
Jean-Baptiste OUEDRAOGO	Ma part de vérité (2020)	Essay	My Truth
Jean-Emile OUEDRAOGO	Union Tabou (2013) Errements et tourments (2012)	Novel Novel	Taboo Union Errings and Torments
Joël OUEDRAOGO	Le vent de l'amour (2016)	Novel	The Wind of Love
Lassane OUEDRAOGO	Sotigui le nouveau prophète (2007)	Novel	Sotigui the New Prophet
Madi OUEDRAOGO	Le totem (2018)	Short story	The Totem Pole
Mahamadou OUEDRAOGO	Sur le pont (2016) L'impair d'or (2016)	Novel Novel	On the Bridge The Golden Odd
Mahamoudou OUEDRAOGO	Roogo (2003)	Novel	Roogo
Marc OUEDRAOGO	Gris bonbons (1984)	Poetry	Gray Candies

Chapter 5

Nakaosgnimbdi Youssouf OUEDRAOGO	Destin à trois chemins (2011) Discours d'une jeunesse insurgée (2015)	Short story Essay	Fate to Three Paths Speeches of an Insurgent Youth
Nobilo B. OUEDRAOGO (1936) et Fati SABA (1942)	Le ringou de Naaba Kiiba (2010)	Novel	Naaba Kiiba's Kingdom
Ouamdégré OUEDRAOGO	L'avare Moaga : comédie des mœurs Moaga Miser: a Comedy of Manners	Drama	The Stingy Moaga: Comedy of Manners
Ousmane OUEDRAOGO	Adieu (1994)	Novel	Farewell
Pakisba Ali OUEDRAOGO (1976)	Une lune rouge	Novel	A Red Moon
Paul Tenoaga OUEDRAOGO	Du collier de braises (1994) Bras de fer pour l'avenir (1994) Echos d'hier (2008)	Short story Short story Short story	The Necklace in Embers Fight for the Future Echoes from Yesterday
Raymond Edouard OUEDRAOGO	Paradis infernal (2012)	Novel	Infernal Paradise
Saïdou Zembendé OUEDRAOGO	Palébédébé laï laï (2010)	Drama	It is Not Going Well at All
Sidi Mohamed OUEDRAOGO (1973)	L'étoile des fleurs (2006) Le grenier de la sagesse (2012)	Poetry Poetry	The Star of Flowers The Granary of Wisdom
Théodore OUEDRAOGO (1971)	Soleils jaunes (1998) La fuite des reptiles (2002) Silences de miradors (2006) Les contes de Noël à partir de ceux de la savane (2007) Christianisme aux prises avec les fétiches (2007) Sauveurs d'Afrique (2007)	Poetry Poetry Poetry Tales Essay Poetry	Yellow Sons The Flight of the Reptiles Silences of Watchtowers Christmas Tales from the Savannah Christianity against Fetishes Saviors of Africa
Wend-Kogonda Maxime OUEDRAOGO	Demain… (2020)	Poetry	Tomorrow
Wendyam Salifou OUEDRAOGO (1976)	L'ombre des jours (2012) L'exil ou la patrie (2020)	Poetry Poetry	The Shadow of the Days Exile or Patriotism

Introduction to Burkinabe Literature in English

Yamba Elie OUEDRAOGO (1952)	Coopération ou conspiration: la part du lion (1976) Tam-tam au ciel (1978) On a giflé la montagne (1991) Falagountou suivi de Le rire (2015) La dynastie maudite (2016) Temps de campagnes (2020) Vautours enchantés (2020)	Drama Drama Novel Novel Tale Essay Novel	Cooperation or conspiracy: The Lion's Share Tom-tom in Heaven The Mountain Has Been Slapped Laugh The Cursed Dynasty Times of Electoral Campaigns Enchanted Vultures
Youssouf OUEDRAOGO	Le fils de la terre (2006) Discours d'une jeunesse insurgée (2015)	Novel Essay	The Son of the Earth Speech of a Risen Youth
Zounogo Léandre OUEDRAOGO (1978)	La terre ne ment pas (2013) Parcours d'un combattant (2016)	Novel Novel	The Earth Does Not Lie The Life of a Fighter
Jérôme OUOBA (1985)	L'incivisme n'est pas la solution (2015)	Short story	Incivism is not the solution
Katrine de l'Or REBEOGO (Catherine Tiendrebeogo)	Discours de votre Présidente (2015)	Essays	Speech of Your President
Titinga Fréderic, PACERE (1943)	Refrains sous le Sahel (1976) Ça tire sous le Sahel: satires nègres (1976) Quand s'envolent les grues couronnées (1976) La poésie de griots (1982) Poème pour l'Angola (1982) Du lait pour une tombe (1984) Poème pour Koryo (1987) Des entrailles de la terre (1988) Poème pour le Sahel (1988) Saglego, la poésie du tam-tam (1994) Poésie du Burkina Faso: anthologie francophone (2012)	Poetry Poetry Poetry Poetry Poetry Poetry Poetry Poetry Poetry Poetry Poetry	Refrains under the Sahel Shootings in the Sahel : Negro Satires When the Crowned Cranes Take Flight The Poetry of Griots Poem for Angola Milk for a Grave Poem for Koryo From the Bowels of the Earth Poem for the Sahel Saglego, the Poetry of the Tam-Tam Poetry from Burkina Faso: French-Language Anthology
Augustin PALE	O paysages, délices et douleurs	Poetry	O Landscapes, Delights, and Pains

Chapter 5

Suzanne PLATIEL	Des animaux et des hommes: Contes sanan de Haute-volta (1971)	Tale	Animals and Men: Tales from the Sanan People in Upper Volta
	La fille volage et autres contes du pays San (1984)	Tale	The Fickle Girl and Other Tales from the Region of San People
Patrick Z. M. POADIAGUE	Le Fou in Une saison d'amour et de colère: poèmes et nouvelles du sahel (1998)	Short story	The Madman in A Season of Love and Anger: Poems and Short Stories from the Sahel
	La prochaine escale (2013)	Short story	The Next Stop
Etienne POULET (1934)	Pondre de la crapaudière: essai sur des proverbes, sentences, contes et mythes des Mossi du Burkina Faso (2011)	Essay	Toad-laying: An Essay on Proverbs, Sentences, Tales, and Myths of the Mossi of Burkina Faso
Pawindbè Fidèle ROUAMBA (1966)	Le carnaval de la mort (1995)	Novel	Carnival of Death
	Pouvoir de plume (2003)	Novel	Feather Power
	L'insurgée (2005)	Novel	The Insurgent
Stéphane A. SABA	L'imprudent (2014)	Novel	The Imprudent
Sid-Lamine SALOUKA	Nouvelles du Kuntaara (2014)	Short story	Short Stories from Kuntaara
Jean-Bernard SAMBOUE	Halombo: Chronique romancée du pays bwamu (2001)	Novel	Halombo: Fictionalized Chronicle of the Bwamu Country
SAINTE-MEULE (Nérée Zabsonré)	Les perles de l'humanité, ou, Les dix commandements de l'enfant (2005)	Drama	The Pearls of Humanity, or, Children's Ten Commandments
	Le prix de l'excellence (2005)	Novel	The Price of Excellence
	La termitière, ou, l'odyssée d'un jeune migrant (2005?)	Novel	The Termite Mound, or, The Odyssey of a Young Migrant
Brahima SAMOU, Jean-Pierre FOURNAT et André CARREE	En passant par Bobo-Dioulasso (1998)	Short story	Going Through Bobo-Dioulasso
Hamidou SAMPEBGO (1984)	Carte de Séjour (2017)	Novel	Where is the World Going?
	Où va le monde (2018)	Novel	Residence Card
Amadou SANFO (1971)	Contes d'Afrique (c. 2010)	Tales	Tales from Africa
	Le grand livre des comptines africaines (2011)	Poetry	The Great Book of African Nursery Rhymes
Issouf SANKARA	Le sage qui eduquait les enfants (2017)	Tales	The Wise Man Who Educated Children

Introduction to Burkinabe Literature in English

Author	Original Title	Genre	English Title
Lazare Tiga SANKARA (1953)	Les aventures de Patindé (2005) Le retour du mort : nouvelles atypiques (2010)	Short story	The Adventures of Patindé The Return of the Dead: Atypical News
Cyriaque Membéré SANON	Sur les sentiers épineux de la démocratie (2013)	Essay	On the Thorny Paths of Democracy
François Xavier SANON	La pensée et les proverbes voltaïques (1978) L'enfant noir et le conte de la savane (1981)	Proverb Tale	Voltaic Thought and Proverbs The Black Child and the Savannah Tale
K. B. Jules SANON (1952)	Ténèbres de lumière (1981) Regard intérieur (1984) L'enfant noir et l'acquisition linguistique du français (1988)	Poetry Poetry Essay	Darkness of Light Inner View The Black Child and French Language Acquisition
Fatoumata SANOU	Tiiga (1994)	Novel	Tiiga
Joseph Bakhita SANOU	Il était une fois aux feuillantines (2014)	Novel	Once upon a Time in Feuillantines
Noël Sangouan SANOU	La clameur des cymbales (2000) Excellence (2001)	Poetry Short story	The Clamor of the Cymbals
Adiza SANOUSSI (1960)	Les deux maris (2001). Devoir de cuissage (2005) Sopam, le duc de Liptougou. (2012). Ciel dégagé sur Ouaga (2012) Et Yallah s'exila (2015)	Novel Novel Novel Novel Novel	The Two Husbands Firing Duty Sopam, the Duke of Liptougou. Clear Skies Over Ouaga And Yallah Went into Exile
Bassidou SARE	Joies et souffrances (1999) Les oubliés de l'histoire (2011)	Poetry Short Story	Joy and Suffering The Forgotten from History
Issouf SAVADOGO	Taryam (2017)	Novel	Taryam
Moussa SAVADOGO	Fille de la Volta L'oracle	Drama Drama	Daughter of the Volta The Oracle
Soumaïla SAVADOGO	Yonmada (2018)	Story	Yonmada
Youssouf SAVADOGO (1968)	Tristesse et louange (1995) La faute et le pardon (2001) Chemin de Gagnoa (2003) Au seuil de l'espoir Ce que femme veut, Dieu ne veut pas toujours (2006) Un héros de la foi (2006)	Poetry Novel Novel Novel Novel Novel	Sadness and Praise The Sin and the Forgiveness On the Road to Gagnoa In the Border to Hope God Does Not Always Want What Women Want A Hero of Faith

Chapter 5

Aboudou SAWADOGO	Le salaire du mensonge (2015)	Short story	The Wage of Lying
Adama SAWADOGO	Parcours d'un Diaspo (2020)	Novel	Itinerary of a Diaspora Man
Alfred Yambangba SAWADOGO (1944)	Le chien du roi n'est pas le roi des chiens du royaume (2012) Un âne étrange (2010)	Essay Short stories	The King's Dog is Not the King of the Kingdom's Dogs A Weird Donkey
Barthélemy SAWADOGO	Révolution (1987)	Drama	Revolution
Etienne SAWADOGO (1944)	La défaite du Yargha (1977) Contes de jadis, récits de naguère (1982) Le gigot de mouton (1987)	Novel Tale Tale	The Defeat of Yargha Ancient Tales, Tales of Yesterday The Leg of Lamb
Fidèle SAWADOGO et al.	Le chant du droit (2012)	Poetry	The Song of Law
François SAWADOGO	Franck: Loin des yeux, loin du cœur	Novel	Franck: Far From My Eyes, Far From My Heart
Issa SAWADOGO	L'homme a perdu la raison (2018)	Essay	Man Lost His Senses
Kelgwendé André SAWADOGO	La foi d'un clochard (2017)	Essay	The Faith of a Tramp
Latifatou Wendemanegueda SAWADOGO	Lourd secret de famille (2019)	Short story	Heavy Family Secret
Poussi SAWADOGO	Petit traité de sagesse: à travers l'histoire de Yangrin du Burkina (2008)	Story	Small Treatise of Wisdom: Through the Story of Yangrin of Burkina
R. David SAWADOGO	Les tuiles sur la tête (2017)	Novel	The Tiles on the Head
Serge Kango Rosaire SAWADOGO	Le retour de l'homme invisible, ou, Descartes à Pilimpikou (2007) Fumbe-Fumbe veut des galons (2010)	Novel Novel	The Return of the Invisible Man, or, Descartes to Pilimpikou Fumbe-Fumbe Wants Promotion
Somaïla SAWADOGO	Et demain…jeunesse africaine?:poésie (2012)	Poetry	What About Tomorrow… African youth?
Sougrinooma SAWADOGO	La revenante (2020)	Novel	The Ghost
Wendpouiré Assane Arsène SAWADOGO (1984)	Par le soleil et par l'éclipse ou les flammes d'une vie (2015)	Novel	By the Sun and by the Eclipse, or, Flames of a Life

Introduction to Burkinabe Literature in English

Zakaria SAWADOGO (1992)	Une plume de larmes (2017) Une lettre ouverte à ma fille (2017) L'orphéline, l'histoire tragique d'une fille (2017)	Novel Novel Short story	A Pen of Tears An Open Letter to My Daughter The Orphan: The Tragic Story of a Girl
Lamouzou Siméon SENI (1957)	Makoé (1991) La lutte contre la colonisation (1986) Sanglots du silence (1999)	Poetry Essay Poetry	Makoé The Fight against Colonization Sobs of Silence
Marie-Simone SERI (1954)	Mon enfant, mon cri, ma vie (1997).	Autobiography	My Child, My Cry, My Life.
Tiémiko Rémy SERME	Pleurs dans la nuit (2014)	Novel	Cries at Night
Philippe Roland SIB SANSAN (1985)	Poèmes de mon pays lobi (2014)	Poetry	Poems from My Lobi Country
Adama Jacques SIBALO (1975)	Au clair de lune (2013)	Tale	In the Moonlight
Roger SIDOKPOHOU (1948)	Le griot (2007)	Novel	The Griot
Boureima Jérémie SIGUE	Faut-il désespérer de l'Afrique? (2014) Media et gouvernance: le sel ou le poison (2015)	Essay Essay	Should We Lose Hope of Africa? Media and Governance: Salt or Poison
Adama Amadé SIGUIRE (1981)	Le Triomphe de l'amour (2013) Le crime parfait (2015) Epitre aux épigones, ou, leçons de vie (2017)	Novel Novel Essay	The Triumph of Love The Perfect Crime The Epistle to Epigones, or, Life Lessons
Pêgwendé Alphonse SILGA	Les infortunés, ou, la souffrance des gens bien (2019)	Short story	The Wretched, or, The Suffering of Good People
Alain Joseph SISSAO	Weoogo: poèmes d'exil (2005)	Poetry	The Bush: Poems from Exile
B. Dominique SISSO	Les assassins de mon mari (2020)	Novel	The Murderers of My Husband
Bwéni SOALMA	La case aux fétiches: Légende des savanes d'Afrique (2008)	Legend	The Fetish Hut: Legend of the African Savannas
Tinzanga SOGOBA (1962)	Tipoko, ou, les méandres du destin (2017)	Novel	Tipoko, or, The Meanders of Fate

Chapter 5

Author	Work (Original)	Genre	Work (English)
Jean-Baptiste Metouele SOMDA	Contes dagara du Burkina Faso: 72 contes recueillis et traduits (1991)	Tale	Dagara Tales of Burkina Faso: 72 Stories Collected and Translated
	Au pays de Zarra: contes et légendes de Namissiguima (1992)	Tale	In the Land of Zarra: Tales and Legends of Namissiguima
Marie-Ange SOMDAH (1959)	Demain sera beau (1989) Adjoa, l'aurore (1992) Campus blues (1993) Le nombril de la terre (1994) Seeds and Deep Season (1997) Rêves de la savane (2002) Un soleil de plomb (2003) One Wild Proposal: Where's She Going? (2020)	Poetry Novel Novel Novel Poetry Poetry Novel Novel	Tomorrow Will Be Beautiful Adjoa, the Dawn Campus Blues The Navel of the Earth Seeds and Deep Season Dreams of the Savannah Blazing Sun
	The Dream of Little Awa (2013)	Short	
	Pen & Dreams from My Students (2013)	Essays	
	Te amo (2013) Libertés, chocolat & cie (2005) Images de vie (2005) Un long fleuve (2005) Hôtel la Désirade & autres récits (2005) Scents of Love (2006)	Poetry Poetry Poetry Poetry Short story Poetry	Liberty, Chocolate & Co. Images of Life A Long River Desirable Hotel and Other Stories
Auxence Sotuo SOME	Ces chemins escarpés (2014)	Novel	These Steep Paths
Djinè Sié Emmanuel SOME	Nom de famille (2007)	Drama	Family Name
Firmin SOME	Elsa (1995) Elsa mon amie (2008)	Novel Novel	Elsa Elsa, My Friend
Iterre SOME et al.	Nouvelles du Burkina Faso (2005)	Short story	Short Stories from Burkina Faso
Jean-Baptiste SOME (1948)	Le miel amer (1985) Affaire de cœur (1990)	Novel Novel	The Bitter Honey Affair of the Heart

Introduction to Burkinabe Literature in English

Maxime Z. SOME (1959)	L'ombre de la vie (2011) Contes du Burkina Faso pour mes trois filles (2006) L'ombre de la vie (2005) Politique éducative et politique linguistique en Afrique (2003) La métamorphose de Zita (2000) Le prédateur venu du Sud (2000) Bouffe mortelle (1998)	Novel Tales Novel Essay Novel Novel Short story	The Shadow of Life Tales from Burkina Faso for My Three Daughters The Shadow of Life Education and Language Policy in Africa The Metamorphosis of Zita The Predator from the South Deadly Food
Sotuo Auxence SOME	Les compromis du citadin (2017)	Novel	The City-Dweller's Compromises
Valère D. SOME	Recueil de textes politiques, 2t. (2016)	Essay	Collection of Political Texts
Paul SONDO (1956)	L'aube du sort sacré (2019) Crépuscule du sort sacré (2020)	Novel Novel	The Dawn of the Sacred Fate Twilight of the Sacred Fate
Drissa SORE	Le destin tragique d'Angèle (2018)	Novel	Angela's Tragic Fate
Ouindpouiré Auguste Aristide SORE (1992)	Femme, sèche tes larmes! (2014) Descente aux enfers avec Ted (2014)	Short story Novel	Woman, Stop Weeping! Down to Hell with Ted
Elisé SORGHO (1982)	Le fils prodigue (2018) Lève-toi et porte tes sandales (2019)	Novel Essay	The Prodigal Son Get Up and Wear Your Sandals
Pascal SORGHO	Secrets de l'amour (2012)	Novel	Secrets of Love
Théodore SORGHO	Miroir: recueil de poèmes de Togossoba (2008)	Poetry	Mirror: Collection of Poems from Togossoba
Frédéric SOW	Notre effort de guerre (2017)	Novel	Our War Effect
Aadama Rosalie TALL (1941)	Poésie pour enfants (1987) Bouboukary Taïrou (1994) Djoubo (1994)	Poetry Short story Short story	Poetry for Children Bouboukary Taïrou Djoubo
Hamadoun TAMBOURA	Sur la route de l'école, la destinée (2016)	Short story	Fate on the Road to School
Dofini Wotuan TAMINI	Saisons de jeunesse (200?)	Poetry	Seasons of Youth
Samou Dieudonné TAMINI	A nous la galère (1990)	Novel	Trouble is Ours
Lamoussa TANGA	La Bâchée blanche (2007)	Novel	The White Tarpaulin

Chapter 5

Jacob TAPSOBA (1974)	L'amour interdit: recueil de nouvelles	Short story	Forbidden Love: Collection of Short Stories
Parfait TAPSOBA (1986)	La malheureuse pogpaala (2016)	Short story	The Unhappy Pogpaala
Thierry TAPSOBA (1993)	L'échange d'une vie contre la fortune (2013)	Novel	The Exchange of a Life for Wealth
Prince Lamourd THIOBIANY	L'île des dieux (2018)	Novel	The Island of Gods
Kontondia J. H. THIOMBIANO	Massaali en quête du monde (2014) L'initié du soleil (2019)	Tale Tale	Massaali in Quest of the World The Initiated with the Sun
Céline Nazihanko TIAHO	Tremplin des tourments (2017)	Short story	Springboard of Torments
Jean-Paul TIAMA	La femme asexuelle (2020)	Short story	The Asexual Woman
Jean Samuel TIENDREBEOGO (1962)	Petit-fils d'esclave, ou, le destin d'un esclave au Moogo (2017)	Novel	Grandson of a Slave, or, The Fate of a Slave in Moogo
Marie Bernadette TIENDREBEOGO/ OUEDRAOGO	La vengeance de Ruth et 8 autres nouvelles (1996) Dulcinée Victoria et huit autres nouvelles (1998) Le malheur des uns (1999) Les contes du terroir (2001)	Short story Short story Novel Tales	Ruth's Revenge and 8 Other Short Stories Dulcinea Victoria and Eight Other Short Stories The Misfortune of Some Tales from the Native Land
Rigobert TIENDREBEOGO (1967)	Les fantasmes de l'esprit: récit initiatique (2009) Le monde mystique qui nous entoure (2016)	Essay Essay	The Fantasies of the Mind: an Initiatory Narrative The Mystic World That Surrounds Us
Yamba TIENDREBEOGO (1907)	Contes du Larhalle (1963) O Mogo! Terre d'Afrique: contes, fables et anecdotes du pays mossi (1976) Contes et dictons du pays mossi (1980)	Tale Tale Tale	Tales from Larhalle O Mogo! Land of Africa: Tales, Fables and Anecdotes from the Mossi Country Tales and Sayings of the Mossi Country
Kiangoulé Evrad Bonaventure TOE	Les aventures de Bila songo (2014)	Tale	The Adventures of Bila Songo
Issa Dieudonné TOE (1962)	L'or brille pour une minorité (2014)	Novel	Gold Shines for a Minority
Harouna TOGUYENI (1955)	En quête de progrès social: combat d'un militant (2018)	Essay	In Quest for Social Progress: Fight of a Militant

Introduction to Burkinabe Literature in English

Jean-Philippe TOUGOUMA	La chute du sphinx de Koso-yam, ou, les secrets d'une insurrection (2016)	Novel	The Fall of the Sphinx of Koso-yam, or, The Secrets of an Insurrection
Bakary Christophe TRAORE (1933)	L'avaleur de cadavres (2000)	Novel	The Swallower of Corpses
Biny Jean-Claude TRAORE (1948)	La guerre des fourmis (2001)	Short story	The War of Ants
Frédéric TRAORE (1951)	La dent de l'aïeule (2011), 3 tomes	Novel	The Ancestor's Tooth, 3 volumes
Issaka Herman TRAORE	Le boa qui avale sa queue (2007)	Novel	The Boa That Swallows its Tail
Lassina TRAORE (1983)	Mon baptême de l'air (2017)	Short Story	My First Flight
Sayouba TRAORE (1955)	L'œuf (1993) Burkinabè: humeurs et rumeurs (1993) Loin de mon pays, c'est la brousse (2005)	Short story Novel Novel	The Egg Burkinabe: Humors and Rumors Far from my Country, It's the Bush
Serge Daniel TRAORE	L'ange déchu (2015) Le marabout de Kouta (2015) Le secret du roi (2015)	Novel Novel Novel	The Fallen Angel The Marabout of Kouta The King's Secret
Sy André TRAORE	Chaînes de libérations (1997)	Poetry	Chains of Liberation
Yacouba TRAORE	Gassé Galo: entre les lignes de mon journal (2012) Un monde de murs et de pas mûres (2018) Kroh! Les femmes ont déserté la maison (2016)	Essay Essay Novel	A World of Walls and Unmatured Gassé Galot: In Between the Lines of My Newspaper Kroh! The Women Abandoned the House
Hermann VALY (1970)	Grossesse désirée & autres nouvelles (2016)	Short story	Desired Pregnancy & Other Short Stories
Gilbert VIEILLARD	Récits peuls du Macina, du Kounari, du Djilgodji et du Torodji (1977)	Tale	Fulani Tales of Macina, Kounari, Djilgodji, and Torodji
Karim YABRE	Les malheurs de nos bonheurs (2014)	Novel	The Misfortunes of Our Happiness
Edith Max YAGUIBOU	Voyage en enfer (2012)	Novel	Journey to Hell
Alex YAMBA (1969)	Trahison conjugale (2013)	Novel	Marital Betrayal
Alexandre YAMEOGO (1970)	Douleurs de femme (2012)	Novel	Woman's Pains

Chapter 5

Bassirou YAMEOGO	Du rêve au cauchemar (2018)	Novel	From a Dream into a Nightmare
E. Brigitte YAMEOGO	Les dehors trompeurs (2015) La sernapiste (2016)	Novel Novel	The Deceptive Outdoors The Sernapist
L. Casimir YAMEOGO	Le paradis troublé (2017)	Novel	The Troubled Paradice
Sophie YAMEOGO/ KONTIEBO	Carlos (2019)	Novel	Carlos
Noëlie YAOGO	Les plaisirs du mal (2007)	Novel	The Pleasures of Evil
Jean Bosco Vinu Muntu YE (1949-2011)	Poèmes voltaïques (1977) Appels (1978)	Poetry	Voltaic Poems Calls
Roland YEHOUN (1976)	Histoires de vie (2013)	Novel	Stories of Life
Edouard YONI (1978)	Corinne en haut et Gildas en bas (2017)	Novel	Corinne Above and Gildas Under
Hado Paul ZABRE (1943)	Contes pour mon fils (2008) Jours sombres en Tagana (2010) Kabena, l'instituteur (2015)	Tale Story Novel	Tales for My Son Dark Days in Tagana Kabena, the Teacher
Richard ZANGRE	Ce que les enfants nous enseignent: Sous-rires (2020)	Stories	What Children Teach Us
Edmond ZEMBA (1979)	En quête de bonheur (2014)	Novel	In Search of Happiness
Drissa ZERBO	Eldorado (2015)	Short story	Eldorado
Yacouba ZERBO (1945)	Une jeunesse si pleine de vie (2005)	Novel	A Youth So Full of Life
ZÎ-HÂ	Sali (2013)	Novel	Sali
Wolfgang ZIMMER	Répertoire du théâtre burkinabè (1992)	Drama	Repertoire of the Burkinabè Theatre
Tanwi ZINGUE	Le sacre d'un Jambaar (2013) Les contes de tante Dagnan (2016)	Novel Tales	The Coronation of a Jambaar The Tales of Aunt Dagnan
Wéta ZINGUE (1948)	Fleur de rose (2006)	Short story	Rosy Flower
Clément ZONGO	Moah le fils de la folle (2020)	Novel	Moah the Son of the Mad Woman
Daniel ZONGO	Charivaris: poèmes (1977)	Poetry	Charivaris: Poems
Lézin Didier ZONGO (1951)	Amertume souvenir (1990) La mendiante et neuf autres nouvelles (1993) Contes du Burkina Faso (2005)	Short story Short story Tales	Bitter Remembrance The Beggar Girl and Nine Other Short Stories Tales from Burkina Faso

Introduction to Burkinabe Literature in English

Martin ZONGO (1957)	La nasse de Tinga (1985)	Drama	Tinga's Trap
Norbert ZONGO (1949–1998)	Le parachutage (1988) Rougbêinga (1990)	Novel Novel	Parachute's Drop Rougbêinga
Wendpanga Oswald ZONGO (1978)	Des ténèbres à la lumière (2013)	Poetry	From Darkness into Light
Emmanuel ZOUNGRANA	L'As de pique en débandade (2012) Marwèllé l'enfant aigri (2014) Enfants chéris (2014) Sentinelles (2014)	Novel Novel Short story Novel	The Ace of Spades in Dissarray Marwèllé the Angry Child Cherished Children Sentinels
Paul Pingdwindé ZOUNGRANA	Et si les armes devenaient des fleurs (2015) To Be or Not To Be (2016)	Poetry Drama	And if Weapons Turn into Flowers

Chapter 5

For further reading on Burkinabe Literature: "Littérature du Burkina Faso," Numéro spécial de Notre Librairie 101 (1990).

Alain Rouch and Gérard Clavreuil, "Burkina Faso," *Littératures nationales d'écriture française: Histoire et anthologie.* pp. 27–33. Paris: Bordas, 1986.

Bissiri, Amadou, Sanou, Salaka, and Willemse Hein, editors. *Burkina Faso: Emerging Literature and Artistic Creation in Burkina Faso (Littérature émergente et creation artistique* in *TydskrifLetterkunde),* vol. 44, no. 1 (2007).

Boyd-Buggs, Debra and Scott, Joyce Hope, editors. *Camel Tracks: Critical Perspectives on Sahelian Literature.* Trenton, NJ: Africa World Press, 2003.

Dakouo, Yves. *Emergence des pratiques littéraires modernes en Afrique francophone: la construction de l'espace littéraire au Burkina Faso.* Ouagadougou: Harmattan Burkina, 2011.

Gikandi, Simon, editor. *The Routledge Encyclopedia of African Literature.* London and New York: Routledge, 2009.

Kariye, Badal W. *A Book of African Writers: Let's Know, Learn, and Read the Names of the Best African Authors, A-Z by Country.* New York: Self-published, 2014.

Ndiaye, Christiane, editor. *Introduction aux littératures francophones: Afrique, Caraïbe, Maghreb.* Montréal: Les presses de l'Université de Montréal, 2004.

Sanou, Salaka. *La littérature burkinabè: l'histoire, les hommes, les œuvres.* Limoges: PULIM, 2000.

Somdah Marie-Ange, editor. *Écritures du Burkina Faso,* vol. 1. Paris, Budapest, Torino: L'Harmattan, 2003.

Introduction to Burkinabe Literature in English

Wise, Christopher, editor. *The Desert Shore: Literatures of the Sahel*. London: Lynne Rienner Publishers, 2001.

CONCLUSION
Perspectives

Burkinabe Literature in English is immensely rich in Burkinabe cultures and traditions, and is stylistically well-written. The reasons are twofold. First of all, the writers are born and brought up in Burkina Faso, though most of them are living abroad to such an extent that this literature could be called that of Burkinabe diaspora. Second, all writers, except for one, are university graduates. Half of them have master's degrees, and the other, doctorate degrees. The high graduation rate is a testimony that these writers have mastered the language of Shakespeare. Most of them are familiar with literature written in English, and the love and mastery of this language and literature is what led them to the adventure of writing. They have become ambassadors of Burkinabe culture, to the broader readership that uses the English language.

Most of the writers under consideration lived for a while or are still living in an English-speaking country. For example, Raissa Batieno completed a Master of Business Administration in Operations and Systems Management at Cleveland State University in Ohio, and is still living there. Pierre Claver Ilboudo obtained his Bachelor of Arts degree from the University of Lagos in Nigeria, and later, a Conference Interpreter's diploma from the Polytechnic of Central London (PCL). He also spent two years at

Introduction to Burkinabe Literature in English

the OAU regional office in Lagos, and then thirteen years at its headquarters in Addis Ababa, Ethiopia.

As for Cécile Kaboré, after her university studies at CESUP, she went to France for further studies. Mamadou Kousse learned English mainly through the American Cultural Centre in Abidjan (Ivory Coast), and through his artistic performances in many West African English-speaking countries. He is the only less qualified writer, and his works bear the marks and weaknesses of an amateur.

As for the late Rakissouiligri Mathieu Ouédraogo, after earning his PhD in Paris III, Sorbonne Nouvelle, in France, he did his post-graduate studies in curriculum development at the University of Nairobi in Kenya, before flying to the University of Chicago for studies in comparative education.

Mamadou Sawadogo also, after earning his master's degree in English, in 1988, went to Birmingham (UK) as a French language assistant. Marie-Ange Somdah, after obtaining his PhD in French, African, and Comparative Literatures at the University de Franche-Comté, went to Boston University and Harvard University Extension School (USA) for further studies. He later lectured at many universities in the USA and in Africa.

Malidoma Patrice Somé earned a Master of Arts from Brandéis University in 1987, and a PhD in literature in 1990. He taught Literature and French at the University of Michigan from 1990 to 1993, and was a visiting lecturer at Stanford University from 1992 to 1993. The late Sobonfu E. Somé lived with her husband in London, and later in the United States.

Prince Lamourd Thiobiany served as a Burkinabe diplomat, which enabled him to travel around the world and visit many countries. Michel Tinguiri, with a PhD in cultural anthropology from American University, lectures at Montgomery College in Maryland, USA. Noëlie Yaogo holds a master's degree in English, and was a secondary school English teacher for thirty-eight years, before going to Canada. Luc Zio is a scientist living abroad. Nathalia Zongo went to the USA for studies at twenty-one. She attended Brookhaven College in Dallas, Texas.

Thus, most of the writers are well acquainted with the English language, which accounts for the fineness of their creative styles

Conclusion

and expressions, and made them eligible for publication abroad. Though promising, the future of Burkinabe literature in the English language will depend on the fulfillment of a certain number of conditions: the development of local publishing houses and a local market, the inclusion of this literature within syllabi and teaching curricula, the creation of awards for literary productions.

The first condition for the development of Burkinabe Literature in English is the creation of publishing houses, or publication within the existing ones. Most works are published in foreign countries, mainly in the USA. For example, Patrice Somé and his wife, Sobonfu, Marie-Ange Somdah, Nathalia Zongo, Luc Zio, Raissa Batieno, and Michel Tinguiri are living in different States in the USA, and their works were published there. Except for one or two translated novels that used local publication houses (Harmattan Burkina), or are simply bound after being printed through printing houses like Imprimerie Presses Africaines and IPRESS Imprimérie, all the other works are not available to low- and middle-class readers and students. They are nowhere to be found in local bookshops.

Similar to Burkinabe literature in French of the 1960s up to 1982, Burkinabe literature in English has to be imported. This importation – which looks like returning to Burkina Faso its cultural objects – is costly, and many cannot afford it. This situation explains why Burkinabe Literature in English is not well-known. For the development of this literature, the authors should use their own funds to make their works available at local bookstores, and the Ministry of Culture may see to it that the National Library, and all libraries of secondary schools and universities, be provided with copies of Burkinabe literature written in English.

The second condition is the inclusion of this literature within syllabi and teaching curricula. It is actually one of the wishes of Noëlie Yaogo, who suggested to replace the study of Achebe's works with hers.

The third condition is the creation of awards for literary productions in English. Burkinabe literature in French increased exponentially with the creation of Semaine Nationale de la Culture (SNC) (National Cultural Week) which rewards talented novelists, playwrights, short story writers, and others. The creation of a similar body may encourage people to compete so that the best productions can be awarded. The result will be a contribution to making Burkinabe culture and traditions known all over the world in English, which is more widely spoken than French.